Photoshop® for Right-Brainers

Photoshop® for Right-Brainers

The Art of Photo Manipulation

Second Edition

Al Ward

Wiley Publishing, Inc.

Credits

Acquisitions Editors
Bonnie Bills
Pete Gaughan

Development Editor
Mariann Barsolo

Technical Editor
Colin Smith

Copy Editor
Sharon Wilkey

Production Manager
Tim Tate

Vice President and Executive Group Publisher
Richard Swadley

Vice President and Executive Publisher
Joseph B. Wikert

Vice President and Publisher
Dan Brodnitz

Media Project Supervisor
Shannon Walters

Media Development Specialists
Kevin Ly
Angie Denny

Media Quality Assurance
Kate Jenkins

Book Design and Composition
Side by Side Studios

Proofreader
Nancy Riddiough

Indexer
Ted Laux

Cover Design
Richard Miller, Calyx Design

Cover Art
Al Ward

Bottom Cover Photo
Photos.com

Acknowledgments

For some reason, the Acknowledgments page is always the hardest in the book to write. Someone who absolutely deserves to be mentioned is inevitably left out, so if you are one of those who wish to see your name here but do not, I apologize up front.

First off, I not only have to thank my wife and kids, but I really want to. Tonia, Noah, and Ali are the collective force that shares my life and more often than not is the reason I get out of bed every morning. They see (and tolerate) all sides of me, both bad and good; I can't think of any other three people I would rather share my life with.

Thanks to Bonnie, Mariann, and Dan at Sybex. They have made this project a joy to work on, put me back on track when I became hopelessly lost, and made sure my family did not starve in the process. I look forward to working with you all again.

The production team that Wiley put together for this book and its CD also deserves special thanks: production manager Tim Tate, copy editor Sharon Wilkey, compositors Mark Ong and Susan Riley, proofreader Nancy Riddiough, indexer Ted Laux, and director of Media Development Laura Carpenter VanWinkle.

Thanks to my good friend and occasional writing partner Colin Smith. No matter how often my wife tries to get him married off, he still keeps accepting our calls and coming to visit. Now that's friendship!

I can't thank Colin without also mentioning his website (**www.photoshopcafe.com**) and all the people who find solace in the forum there. The Photoshop Café has developed into a great source of inspiration and friendship where Photoshop users of all stripes can find acceptance. The coffee is always hot and fresh; I'll see you there.

I've got to thank my friends at the National Association of Photoshop Professionals (NAPP). Scott Kelby gave me my start in this business, and I'm forever in his debt. Jeff, Felix, Chris, Jim, Dave—without a doubt, you sincerely *rock*.

To the people who know my work and keep coming back anyway, those who both visit and join my website (**www.actionfx.com**).

To Mom, Dad, Ole, Linda, and my extended family (I'm from Montana, so there are thousands of people who qualify for this): I love you all, in spite of the restraining order. (Just kidding… I had it lifted so you can visit again.) Special thanks to everyone in the MLMBC (you know who you are). We share the same road, and I'm honored to be traveling it with you.

The greatest thanks and highest praise go to my God and Savior, without whom none of this would be possible or worthwhile. He saw fit to allow this Montana boy to realize his dream.

Again, if I forgot anyone who really needed to be here, please forgive me and consider yourself included. To all my readers and friends far and wide, my deepest regards and a hearty thank you from the bottom of my heart.

Contents

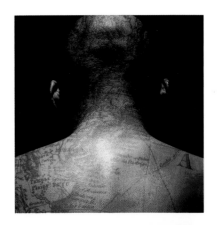

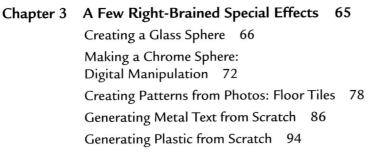

Introduction

Photoshop for Right-Brainers, Second Edition is a guide to using the software's toolkit to unlock your own creativity, as I've used it to unlock mine. The Pause button on my brain evidently ceased working from overuse during my Navy days, and now there is no stopping the cartoons, dramas, and horror movies broadcasting in my head. I'll wake on occasion with some incredible insight and be overcome with an urge to share this unrefined gem of intellectual acrobatics with my wife. She can barely contain her joy; you can see it in the way she smiles, nods, and says "Would you like bacon for breakfast?" or "Stop jumping around and talking nonsense or you'll scare the kids!"

For me, Photoshop has opened pathways for creativity that I had always known were in my head but had no way to translate to the real world. What originally attracted me to the program was not the capability to correct photographs but the power to warp photographs into something else. This journey started as an experiment in creating something from nothing (I think the first effect that I tried to master was creating fire from thin air) and developed into a career based on corrections, distortions, and manipulations. Photoshop gives me the ability to take the critters in my head and make them a visual reality. Teaching the program and writing about those discoveries was an unexpected, but extremely appreciated, bonus. It's sort of like writing a great (or even mediocre) novel; the novelist doesn't simply shelve the reams of paper to read to himself from time to time but rather tries to put the book into print so others can appreciate the story. Photoshop is my typewriter, and the entities and scenes that form on my screen are the novel. I share it in hopes that someone out there in the big old world will appreciate it. More often than not people do; occasionally I'll get an e-mail asking me if I want bacon for breakfast. Some folks are just odd.

Why I Wrote This Book

When I approached *Photoshop for Right-Brainers*, I wanted to do something a bit different from what I've written in the past. I certainly did not want to write another "These are the basics of Adobe Photoshop" book; there are many authors out there who have done an excellent job tackling that subject. I also did not want to simply create a recipe book of canned effects. I've done that before, and while recipe books have their place, I wanted this book to be a bit more personal. Don't get me wrong—this book is full of effects that you can follow along with and implement. What I want the reader to see, aside from the step-by-step process, is how I develop ideas for projects. Where do the concepts for the various effects come from? When an idea is pieced together in the imagination, what does it look like? And last, what tools in Adobe Photoshop CS2 can be used to make those scenes or creatures take on new life on the computer?

Right Brain? Left Brain?

About 30 years ago, the artist and educator Betty Edwards wrote a book that has become a classic and that is indirectly an inspiration for this one: *Drawing on the Right Side of the Brain*. At that time, it wasn't widely understood by the general public that the right and left hemispheres of the brain function differently and control different kinds of intelligence, so Edwards devoted a chapter to explaining her premise: The left side is logical, analytical, sequential, and verbal, and it tends to break things down into parts rather than look at wholes. The right side is intuitive, synthesizing, spatial, and holistic. It is, in short, the source of visual imagination and creativity. Today, that understanding is much more widespread, to the point where *right-brained* and *left-brained* have become a kind of shorthand for different ways of looking at the world.

This book, although targeted at right-brained designers and photographers, is not simply for them. I suspect that more than a few left-brained people (affectionately referred to as *lefties* in the text) are really closet right-brained people, waiting for someone to lead the way past their math, science, and politics and into the realm of artistic expression. My aim is not that this book appeal to only the right-brained crowd. Rather, I hope that the book may also serve in some small way as a beacon that guides lefties through the dismal smog of facts and figures and into the Technicolor world that righties have lived in and appreciated for generations. Even a lefty can be a right-brainer; the world could use a few creative politicians, after all.

What Should You Know Already?

Photoshop users are generally lumped into three main categories (not my doing): Beginner, Intermediate, and Advanced. This tends to paint Photoshop users with an extremely broad brush, not taking into account how many genres of digital manipulation for which Photoshop is used. For instance, a person can be exceptional at special effects but not have the slightest clue about how images are prepared for print.

In general terms, a person hoping to get the most from this book should at least be intermediate in his understanding of and experience with the software. By *intermediate*, I simply mean you should have used the tools, be familiar with the interface, have a concept of how layers work, and so forth. You should also be familiar with following tutorial-style instructions. If you have just purchased the software and have absolutely no clue what a pixel is, then you should probably pass on this book for now and come back to it after trying something a bit more introductory. If you have some experience with the program and have a keen desire to try things in new and interesting ways, then this is the book for you.

How the Book Is Organized

The book is organized in what I call a progressive format. That is to say, the chapters are complete unto themselves, but later chapters refer to and/or include techniques used in earlier chapters. As a result, the earlier chapters serve as building blocks for what you will see later. This helps avoid reviewing a series of commands multiple times, allowing space for more techniques.

> **Chapter 1, "Tools for Building Your Masterpiece,"** focuses on the most important tools and concepts underlying the techniques you'll explore throughout the book: blending modes, layer masks, adjustment layers, Blend If, extractions, and displacement maps.

Chapter 2, "Techniques for Embellishing Portraits," presents basic and advanced cosmetic corrections and enhancements that portrait subjects may often request, such as deepening (or completely changing) eye color, covering up old acne scars, and the like. Why stop there? This chapter also covers radical techniques for more dramatic changes, such as digital liposuction, face-lifts, and even swapping faces.

Chapter 3, "A Few Right-Brained Special Effects," ventures into the realm of special effects—that is to say, techniques for art creation that are not specifically photo related. This chapter looks at the creation of glass spheres, chrome objects, text effects—I even show you how to create floor tiles from photographs.

Chapter 4, "Texture, Color, and Layer Effects," explores a few tools and techniques that will enhance the art of any designer and help you achieve those tricky, elusive results you have been looking for. Apply Image is demonstrated, and you will also learn to add color to black-and-white images, apply textures by using displacement maps, turn photos into custom brushes, and even enhance old paintings by using common Photoshop tools.

Chapter 5, "Effects in the Real World," leads you through transforming natural and human-made forms. You'll mirror rock formations, create neon reflections on rainy streets, and turn sunny landscapes into nightmare scenes.

Chapter 6, "Animals," continues the theme of transformations as you add human features to animals and vice versa, create a Pegasus, and more.

Chapter 7, "Digital Alterations and Manipulations," ventures into the realm of graphic arts: digital manipulation for use in advertising, macro-enhancement, and other interesting areas.

Chapter 8, "Going Beyond Canned Filters," works with a Photoshop feature that is often misused. The projects here show that applying a filter should be a starting point, not a finished product. For example, you'll "age" a new photograph for a retro effect, turn photographs into line drawings, and turn a posed photograph into a "vector art" anime cartoon.

Chapter 9, "People as Art: Digital Manipulation," treats the human body as a canvas. You will color it, texture it, melt it, and mold it—painting a checkered flag onto a swimsuit model and turning flesh to stone.

Chapter 10, "Digital Intensive: Crash-Course Projects," takes bits of techniques learned throughout the book and utilizes them in three project-based tutorials: Contrast Woman, Portrait Collage, and Photo to Graffiti.

The appendix, **"Prepping and Displaying Your Work,"** gives you some quick pointers for creating web photo galleries, PDF presentations, and contact sheets. It also provides some helpful links and resources for you to explore more right-brained worlds.

Using the CD Files

The images used in this book are also provided for your use on the accompanying CD. Some were taken by the author, but the majority are provided by Photos.com. Please note that these photos are for your use with this book only; they are not in the public domain and may not be redistributed in any way, shape, or form.

At each point where you need to use a file from the CD in order to work through an exercise, you'll see a symbol in the margin like the one shown here, and the text will refer to the specific filename. That way, you'll use the same images as I did when completing an exercise. Also, some exercises use specific tools created by the author (gradient, layer style, or other saved preset). These are on the CD as well, and the text directs you to load them at the appropriate time.

I've also added 400 productivity-enhancing Photoshop actions to the CD for this edition. These actions automate such common tasks as resizing, changing resolution, sharpening and softening, creating photo templates, cropping, correcting color and tone, retouching, applying filters and effects, manipulating images, and more.

About the Author

Al Ward is a prominent figure in the Photoshop community. His website, **www.actionfx.com**, supplies Photoshop actions and information to users. He has written and contributed to numerous Photoshop books, including *Photoshop Most Wanted*, *Photoshop Elements 2 Special Effects*, and *Photoshop 7 Effects Magic*. He has written for Planet Photoshop, Photoshop Café, and *Photoshop User* magazine, and he is the official actions guru for the NAPP.

Feedback

Both the author and the publisher encourage you to offer feedback on this text. Was it useful to you? What did you learn that you did not know previously? You may leave your comments with the publisher at **www.sybex.com** or send the author a note through his website at **www.actionfx.com**.

Photoshop® for Right-Brainers

one

Tools for Building Your Masterpiece

Right-brainers *are typically artistic in some fashion, and this book is for people who, like me, enjoy the journey. Although right-brainers are constantly chiding left-brained people to think outside of the proverbial box, a right-brainer who works with a piece of software such as Adobe Photoshop CS2 needs to spend some time in the box, getting to know the tools and techniques that will lead to masterpieces at some future date.*

This chapter discusses a few of the most important techniques and tools that are used throughout the book, as well as some that are just plain good to know: blending modes, extractions, layer masks, those all-powerful adjustment layers, displacement maps, and the Blend If feature. I can't teach you to be an artist, but I certainly can show you some of the tools I use that you might find helpful in your own work, so let's take a look at some of these key techniques.

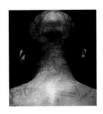

Using Blending Modes

For right-brainers, blending modes open entirely new doors that perhaps you haven't considered. For example, you can quickly collage two images by placing them in layers and experimenting with the blending modes for just the right mix.

Blending modes for layers simply tell Photoshop how the pixels in one layer will interact with the pixels in the layers beneath. You knew that already, though, right? Sure you did; at least, you probably already know if you have spent any time with Photoshop. As you work through the next few chapters, you'll use various blending modes. For each new mode that's introduced, you'll find a short definition.

Instead of rambling on about how you *should* use them, I'll show a few examples of how you *can* use them to your advantage.

From this book's CD, open the images **film.jpg** and **director.jpg** (see Figures 1.1 and 1.2). Here you have two images of similar tone and theme. You might consider what these two photos would look like merged. To check that out, one photo will serve as the foundation image, and the other photo will be pasted into a new layer in that document (see Figure 1.3).

Each blending mode, when applied to the Director layer, will give a different result. You might think that the Overlay mode would produce a good mix of the two images, so check it out! Figure 1.4 shows the image with the Director layer set to Overlay.

Although both images are visible, the result looks harsh, and the man is little more than a shadow—not really a good blend for this example. That is just a bit of personal taste. If you like the blend, then go with it!

Figure 1.1: Choose images to blend together. Here's the first image.

Figure 1.2: The second image

Try another test, this time selecting Darken for the blending mode of the Director layer (see Figure 1.5). This results in a very good melding of the two images. The outline of the man is clearly defined, and the reels provide a nice backdrop. The only thing that strikes me as being wrong with this version, other than being a couple of shades too dark, is the area where the filmstrip overlays the megaphone. Because that portion is darker in the Film layer than in the Director layer, the dark strip dominates. Think about it: the Director layer is in Darken mode, so those areas that are darker than the layer beneath will be darkened. Those lighter will not. The megaphone is slightly lighter, so it loses in the battle with the filmstrip.

There has to be a way to get these photos to work together, so I'll give it another shot. Follow along and see what you come up with. Change the blending mode for the Director layer to Pin Light (see Figure 1.6). That is actually a very good mix for definition between the two photos. The colors are still harsh, but the blending mode works.

Figure 1.3: Place both images into the same document for merging.

Figure 1.4: Director layer set to Overlay

Figure 1.5: Director layer in Darken blending mode

Figure 1.6: Another version using Pin Light blending mode

Figure 1.7: Find a blending mode that comes closest to what you envision; then perform the final corrections with other adjustments.

The Pin Light blending mode takes a look at the blend color and replaces colors in relation to that standard. If the light source, or blend color, is lighter than 50% gray, pixels darker than the blend color are replaced while those lighter do not change. If the blend color is darker than 50% gray, the inverse is true. This blending mode is useful for adding special effects to an image.

When you find a blending mode that does basically what you want it to accomplish, as I've done with this example, you may want to keep the blending mode and finish the corrections with other Photoshop features. No one tool or technique is a cure-all: it usually takes a combination of tools and commands working together to get what you are looking for.

Notice the red ring surrounding the yellow spotlight area. This can be reduced to help maintain the original mood and tone of the two images. One of the quickest ways to isolate

*Figure 1.8: Final
blended image
using original
colors*

and replace the red ring without altering the rest of the image is to use a Replace Color adjustment on the Director layer (see Figure 1.7). Use the Eyedropper to select the reddest pixel you can find (such as along the edge of the megaphone), and rather than change the color, just lower the Saturation until the red ring dissipates (see Figure 1.8). To add more color variations to the selection, hold down the Shift key while making your eyedropper selection.

As you work through the book, blending modes will become second nature. What I want you to take away from these brief examples, in particular for merging layers, is that your choice of blending mode will dictate whether a piece fails or succeeds. You have many to choose from, but usually one or two come close. You want to get to the point where you intuitively know what additional tools in conjunction with the blending mode will give you the results you are looking for. Photoshop isn't out to get you: it is only as smart and creative as you allow it to be. Photoshop is the tool; you are the craftsman.

Extracting an Image from a Background

I belong to several Photoshop-related forums and lists online (a favorite hangout of mine is PhotoshopCAFE at **www.photoshopcafe.com**), and it amazes me how many posts start with the heading "How do I extract an image from a background?" There is a perfect tool in Photoshop for just this situation.

If the background is a solid color, you can of course use the Background Eraser tool with fair results, but the Extract command is far more powerful. It is tricky to master, however. That may be the primary reason so many ask about it. In a lot of cases, a more complete and honest question might be "How do I extract without using the Extract command?" Certainly, if there ever was a tool in Photoshop that required patience on the part of the user, this is it. Nonetheless, with patience and care, it's possible to make excellent extractions with the Extract command.

Throughout this book, I'll be asking you to perform extractions at various stages, so I'll give you some practice with this tool right out of the chute. Open the image **moose.jpg** from this book's CD (see Figure 1.9).

Let's pull this guy off his background and give him a new home. Duplicate the Background layer. Create a new layer between the two moose layers and fill it with white. Rename the Background Copy layer **Extract** (see Figure 1.10).

Figure 1.9: Anyone seen a flying squirrel around these parts?

Choose Filter → Extract to open the Extract dialog box. It takes up the entire screen, but most of the space is devoted to the preview window. Along the upper left are the tools you will be using, and on the right are the options for those tools.

First, zoom way in with the Magnifying Glass, or press ⌘/Ctrl+(+). To get as clean an extraction as possible (in other words, to get the cleanest, most accurate edge), it is best to use the smallest Highlighter you can, while still picking up the fine hairs that may be present. Select the Highlighter tool.

Hold down the spacebar. Notice that the Move cursor appears. This is a cool shortcut that allows you to work without switching back and forth between tools while working close-up on the image. With the spacebar held down, position the image so that you can see where the moose enters the picture. Set the size of the Highlighter to 8 and begin tracing along the back of the animal. You want as little of the animal as possible beneath the pen, so cut it as close as you can, but ensure that the small hairs sticking up are completely covered by the pen (see Figure 1.11).

Work your way around the entire animal, antlers and all. When you get to tufts of hair (see Figure 1.12), increase the brush

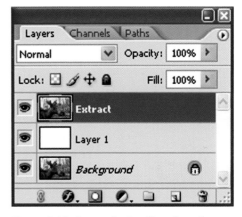

Figure 1.10: Set up the Layers palette for extracting.

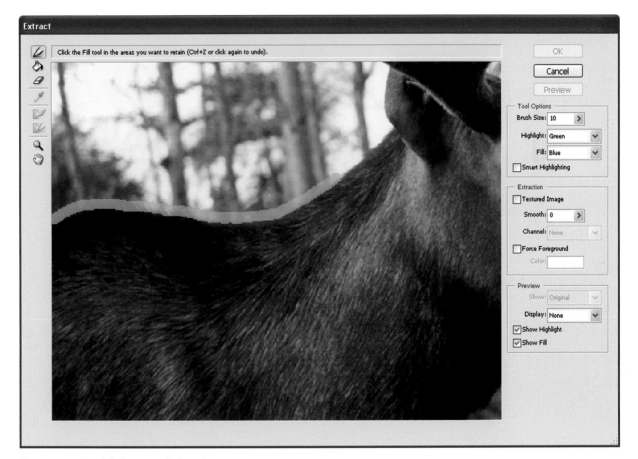

Figure 1.11: Highlight around the subject.

size to cover the strands but still maintain your close edge around the moose (see Figure 1.13).

After you have outlined the entire moose, go back in between the antlers and highlight those edges also. Every place where background can be seen needs to be removed if at all possible (see Figure 1.14).

After you think you have the entire creature outlined, select the Paint Bucket from the right and click within the selected area. This tells Photoshop what you want to remain; everything outside of this area (not colored) will be removed (see Figure 1.15).

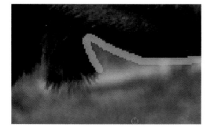
Figure 1.12: Working around hair is always tricky when extracting.

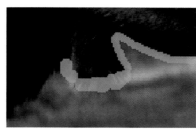
Figure 1.13: Increase the brush size to get the fine hairs.

Figure 1.14: Don't forget the spaces between the antlers.

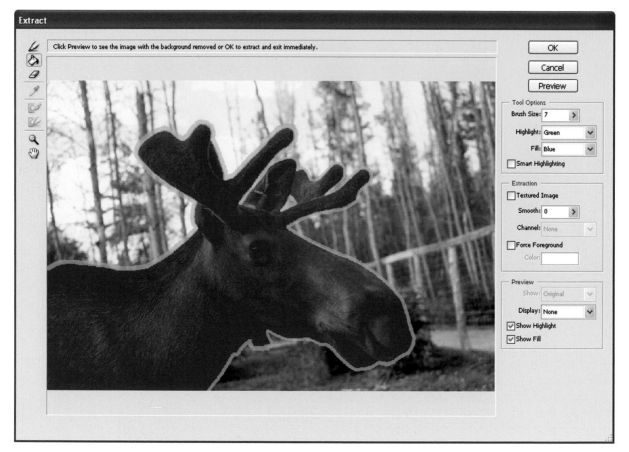
Figure 1.15: Fill the outlined area by using the Paint Bucket.

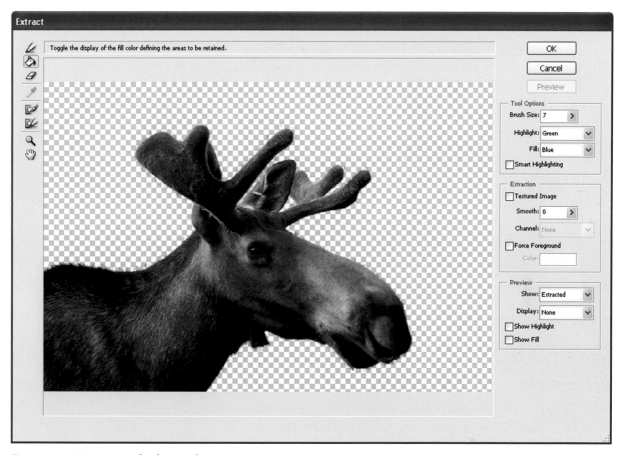

Figure 1.16: Moose, sans background

When you are ready, click the Preview button to view the extracted moose (see Figure 1.16). Don't click OK, because you are not finished yet. You need to check all the edges first and correct accordingly. Figure 1.17 shows areas where portions of the background made it through the extraction. The Extract dialog box has two tools that are made for cleaning up the edges: Cleanup and Edge Touchup.

Figure 1.17: Oops...still some background pixels remaining.

The Cleanup tool, found on the left-side toolbar, acts as an eraser when you are working in Normal mode. Again, keep the brush size small and run the Cleanup tool around the entire extraction. Some areas may not need it, but get the stuff that you can see. If you accidentally erase portions of the moose that you want to keep, hold down the Option/Alt key and pass over that area with the Cleanup tool. This will replace the pixels that were taken away (see Figure 1.18).

Figure 1.18: Clean up those edges.

The Edge Touchup tool, found just beneath the Cleanup tool, is a bit different. When you are using

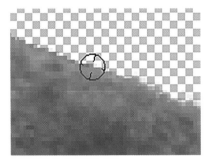

Figure 1.19: Edge Touchup helps define and sharpen the edge.

Figure 1.21: Preview the moose after the extraction.

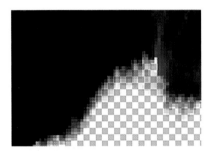

Figure 1.20: Some of the stray hairs should be retained.

this tool, the information, or pixels, that you want to keep need to remain under the crosshair, with the circle of the brush extending beyond the extraction (see Figure 1.19). Again, a small brush size will serve best. This tool helps darken and define the edge, wiping away anything that appears not to match what is beneath the crosshair.

Use special care when working around the hairs. Take away as much background as you can without deleting the fine hairs extending into that backdrop (see Figure 1.20).

When you think you have the extraction down perfectly, click OK to see a preview (see Figure 1.21).

Figure 1.22: Still some background left: clean up with the Eraser tool.

If you zoom in against the white layer that you created before, you'll notice pieces of the background that escaped the eye and were left behind (see Figure 1.22). What to do now? You guessed it: time to make yet one more pass around the moose, this time with the Eraser tool. Clean up all those stray pixels. Again, the key word with this process is *patience*.

After all that is done, you can find the moose a new home. Open the image **country road.jpg**, copy the moose, and paste him into the country road image. Position him with the Move tool so that he appears to be walking into the scene (see Figure 1.23).

That's it for extractions, but I can't leave this unfinished. The color of the moose doesn't really match the tone of the background that you have placed him in. Select the

Figure 1.23: The moose in a new home

Moose layer and, using the settings seen in Figure 1.24, give him a quick makeover with the Match Color feature. Click OK.

The next (and for this example, final) step in the process is to make an overall adjustment to the Levels in the image. Because you will be adjusting the entire end-photo, a Levels adjustment layer will work perfectly. I'll be discussing adjustment layers more later in this chapter, so please don't feel lost if you are not used to working with them. To add a Levels adjustment layer that affects the entire image, you need to select the top layer (in this case, the moose). At the bottom of the Layers palette, click the Create New Fill Or Adjustment Layer icon (fourth from the left) and select Levels from the list. Walk through each channel and do a standard Levels adjustment (Figure 1.25), finishing with the RGB channel. When you have inserted the Levels adjustment layer, your Layers palette will look like Figure 1.26.

Figure 1.27 shows the moose in his new home. Is that the ocean in the background? This must be a Maine moose.

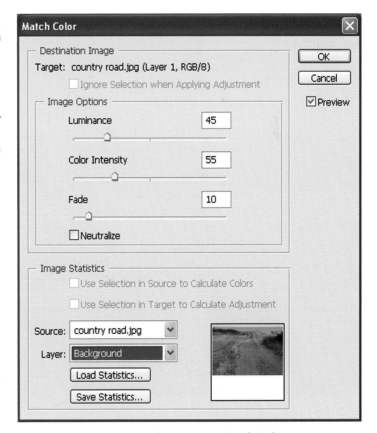

Figure 1.24: One more quick correction: Match Color

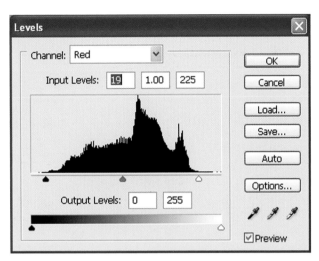

Figure 1.25: Finishing with a Levels adjustment

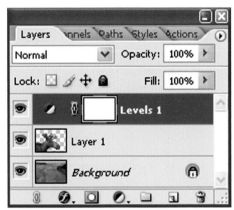

Figure 1.26: The Layers palette with the Levels adjustment layer in place

Figure 1.27: Our moose with an ocean view

Working with Layer Masks

As you delve into all the nifty things Photoshop allows you to do to your images, you may have already played a bit with layer masks. Layer masks, at their most basic, are simple bitmaps attached to a layer. The black in the bitmap, or mask, hides the pixels of the standard layer, and the white reveals those pixels.

I'll get to some examples of what I'm talking about in a moment. First, some possible uses. What benefit do you see from being able to hide portions of a layer? Here's one practical application using two layers with the same pixel information: you could correct the top layer or do some fancy special effect to it and then mask away portions of the layer so the correction or effect seems to occur only on certain portions of the image. Layer masks are also excellent for merging photos, either gradually or starkly, so collages are a breeze. Masks even go so far as to allow a savvy right-brainer to turn any photograph into a seamless pattern or even a floor tile.

Let me demonstrate what I'm talking about.

I'll begin with a practical example. If you have perused any medium to large electronics store online, in particular those that sell mid- to high-end televisions or computers, you may have noted that many display their products with an image on the screen. It is difficult to take a photograph of a television with the screen active and have it turn out with ad-quality resolution on the display. Often the retailers will, rather than leave the screen blank, use Photoshop to place an image on the screen to make the product shot more compelling. Layer masks can achieve this in quick order.

For this example, open **monitor.jpg** (Figure 1.28) and **tech.jpg** (Figure 1.29).

To see how masks can help when working with these two images, you first need to place them in the same document. To do this, simply copy the second photo and paste it into the first. They are different sizes, so choose Edit → Transform → Scale and resize the new layer to

Figure 1.28: A standard computer monitor product shot

Figure 1.29: A techno-collage to fill the screen

match the size of the first. In this instance, you need to be concerned only that the monitor screen is overlaid with the second image.

When working with a lot of layers, it is good policy to give your layers descriptive names. You're working with only two layers in this example, but it is still a good habit to establish, so rename the layers **Monitor** (base layer) and **Tech**. The top layer is where the masking will take place; you can create that mask now by selecting the Tech layer and clicking the Add Layer Mask icon at the bottom of the Layers palette (see Figure 1.30).

Figure 1.30: The layers have been named and a mask applied to the top layer.

As a demonstration of how masks help in this instance, you can quickly place the techno-collage on the monitor without overlapping beyond the screen's border. This is a piece of cake because the monitor face is roughly the same color across the object.

There are a few tools you can use to generate a selection of the screen. The Polygonal Lasso and Magnetic Lasso tools are safe bets, and even using the Select → Color Range dialog box would provide moderate success. Looking at the monitor, with its clear, concise edges on the border of the screen, you might see that the quickest and easiest way to generate the needed selection most likely resides in the Magic Wand tool and its default settings. Ensure that the Monitor layer is active in the Layers palette and use the Magic Wand to generate your selection by clicking directly on the screen (see Figure 1.31).

When the selection is generated, return to the Tech layer and select the mask. To reveal the monitor again and leave the tech image on-screen, simply choose Select → Inverse and fill the area outside of the screen with black, as seen in Figure 1.32.

If you have performed the masking technique properly, you will have a final product image with the tech image resident only on the monitor. Any additional corrections to the

Figure 1.31: Generating a selection of the area where the second image will be applied will help to quickly place the photo in the next step.

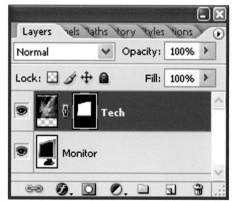

Figure 1.32: The only area in the mask that should be filled with white is the monitor screen.

Figure 1.33: Final product shot with screen image in place

Figure 1.34: I'm ready for my close-up.

mask that may be required can be performed by using the paint tools with either white or black to correct and clean up areas of the masked layer (see Figure 1.33).

For the digital artist, masks are frequently used to generate symmetry in a photo or working piece of art. Photographers may use masks for fine-tuning the appearance of a model; a wacky right-brainer may take things to the extreme and use one photo to create a perfect, albeit improbable, vision of beauty. Figure 1.34 (**ModelShot.jpg** on the CD) shows a young lady who has absolutely nothing wrong with her. Well, in the real world maybe. In the digital world, however…we can use Photoshop to give perfect symmetry. In other words, Photoshop Masks can be utilized in such a way as to make the right side of the face the exact, if mirror opposite, twin of the left.

Let's see what a mask can do to enhance this photo. With a photo open in Photoshop, duplicate the background layer. Name both layers accordingly: in this case I've named the layers Model-01 for the foundation and Model-02 for the layer to be manipulated with the mask. With the Model-02 layer selected, choose Edit → Transform → Flip Horizontal to rotate the image, and then click the Add Layer Mask icon at the bottom of the Layers palette (see Figure 1.35). By drawing a standard Black to White gradient across the mask and using

Figure 1.35: Model-02 layer flipped and mask firmly in place

Figure 1.36: A standard Black to White gradient in the mask gives the model a surreal appearance.

the default settings (that is, a gradual change from black to white), you'll see the photo take on characteristics of both layers (see Figure 1.36).

The result is interesting but not very realistic, as few people have ghostly hairs streaming down the sides of their semitransparent clothing. By manipulating the gradient used and decreasing the amount of blur or blending between the white and the black (Figure 1.37), much of that transparent effect can be taken away (see Figure 1.38). The model, however, appears pinched together. She has symmetry, granted, but it's the symmetry of an elf rather than a human.

This is quickly repaired by simply inverting the mask and moving the Model-02 layer until you get a more realistic marriage of the two layers (see Figure 1.39).

By working with the Paintbrush and using black or white in the mask, you can reveal aspects of the layer beneath to add characteristics taken away by the gradient. For instance, by painting in a black area of the gradient with white, the hair falling over her shoulder can be revealed once again (see Figures 1.40 and 1.41).

One final example demonstrates how shades of gray can be used in a mask to create character in your collages or backgrounds (see Figure 1.42). In this instance, I've taken

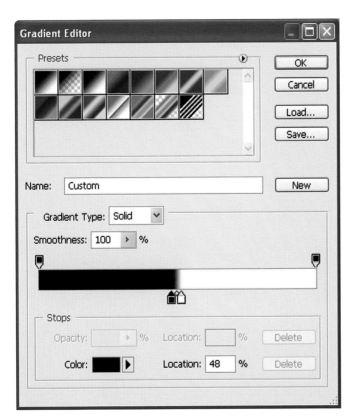

Figure 1.37: Narrowing the distance between Black and White color stops in the gradient eliminates much of the transparency effect, restricting it to a narrow area.

Figure 1.38: Has anyone seen a stray Hobbit pass through here?

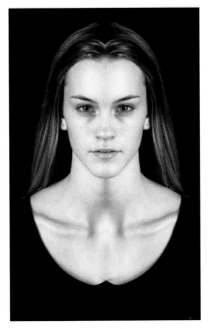

Figure 1.39: A more realistic marriage of layers

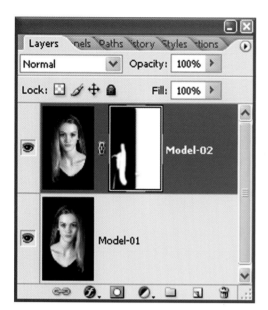

Figure 1.40: *The mask can be altered by using simple painting techniques.*

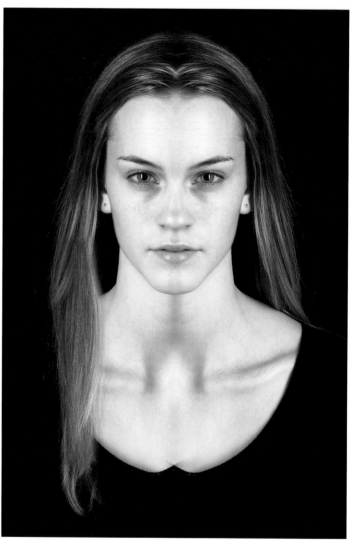

Figure 1.41: *With some further tweaking, this model could be ready for the cover of any magazine displaying perfectionist portraits of women.*

TechBG01.jpg and **TechBG02.jpg**, and placed them in the same document. The top layer has been duplicated, and the grayed mask applied to the top two layers.

When you look at the image with a mask applied, you'll see elements of both photos in the new document (see Figure 1.43). Basically this is the same effect as if you were reducing opacity or altering blending modes; however, you can use this effect in conjunction with opacity changes and blending mode changes for variations you may not expect. I have said that before, I will say this now, and I promise I will say it again: Experiment! You'll never know the effects you could have created unless you try subtly (or extremely, for that matter) altering settings in your images dreamt up by you. I can show you only a couple of variations in a few pages, but I really want you to explore your own creativity by using the tools at your disposal.

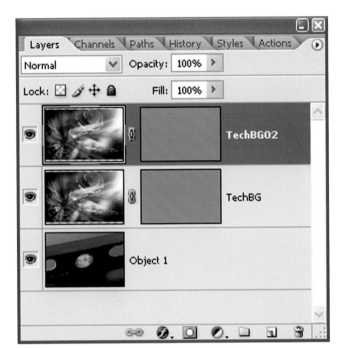

*Figure 1.42:
Using gray tones
in a mask is a
fast and easy way
to create collages
or to generate
backgrounds
with elements
from multiple
images.*

Figure 1.43: This techy background will fit in with any modern website.

Including Adjustment Layers

Something I have found to be incredibly useful for the past few versions of Photoshop was the inclusion of adjustment layers. Because of my interest in adding a personal touch to perfectly good photos, the final image often doesn't resemble the original except in passing. A long, long time ago, say three or four versions of Photoshop in the past, altering layer information was almost always "destructive." The actual pixels were altered, which could be troublesome if you forgot to save the original photo.

Adjustment layers have taken this concern, wrestled it to the floor, and given it a much needed wedgie. You can now make adjustments to an entire image or aspects of certain layers without worrying about destroying the original document. Of course you can always backtrack in the history, providing you remember to take snapshots along the way. Who has time for snapshots? Bah, humbug!

Adjustment layers work simply by creating a new layer separate from the other layers that will let you make your tweaks. Each adjustment layer has a mask attached so that you can "paint away" the adjustments from areas of the image where you don't want them to apply. You can alter the mask, and thereby the adjustment layer, by painting with black, white, or gray in the mask itself. Better yet, you can go back at any time, reopen the adjustment layer, and change the settings as you like. Adjustment layers each have the appropriate adjustment's dialog box attached. If you adjust Levels by using a Levels adjustment layer, you do so the same way you do a standard Levels adjustment. The only difference is that you are making the changes to a nondestructive layer as opposed to actual pixels.

To demonstrate this, I have chosen an image reflecting the theme of this book: a model of the human brain. Open the image **RightBrain.jpg** (see Figure 1.44).

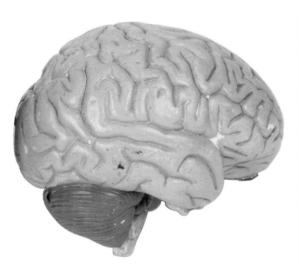

Figure 1.44: I just had to work a brain into this book somehow!

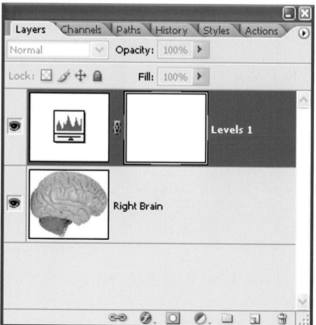

Figure 1.45: The Levels adjustment layer is in position and ready to go to work.

With the image open, click the Add Adjustment Layer icon at the bottom of the Layers palette. A menu will appear with a series of selections representing the types of adjustments you can make.

Choose Levels from the menu. A Levels adjustment layer will appear in the Layers palette (see Figure 1.45).

A Levels dialog box appears; you can make your Levels adjustment as you would if you were operating from the Image → Adjustments → Levels dialog box. Figure 1.46 shows a standard adjustment, moving the left slider to where the color information begins. Click OK to accept the adjustment.

I use this particular adjustment to darken the washed-out area of the brain, in particular the pink fleshy parts. I'm not sure that I want to adjust the gray area. By painting in the white mask with a black brush, you can wipe away the adjustment to that area, leaving the rest of the brain corrected (see Figure 1.47).

Let's say you would like to create a mock-up of this brain for a presentation of some sort. You have found the gray just doesn't cut it, and the brain seems flat on the projector. It's time for a color overhaul! By adding a Hue/Saturation adjustment layer that effectively colors the entire brain blue, but then hiding most of the image except those areas you want to have colored with the mask, you can dramatically alter the appearance of the piece (see Figures 1.48 and 1.49).

You can also add a couple of cartoonish, or "drawn" characteristics to the image. Selecting Posterize at the bottom of the adjustment layer menu lets you establish the number of levels that appear in the image. This basically separates the image into four levels of color, giving it a drawn or painted quality (see Figure 1.50).

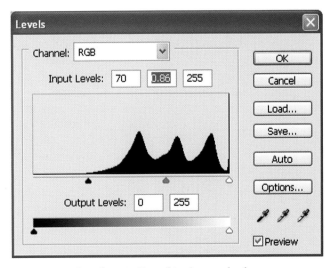

Figure 1.46: Levels are adjusted in the standard way.

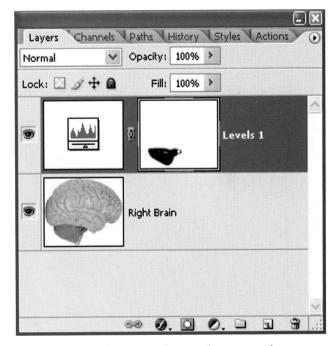

Figure 1.47: Use the paint tools to mask areas you do not want to be altered by the adjustment layer.

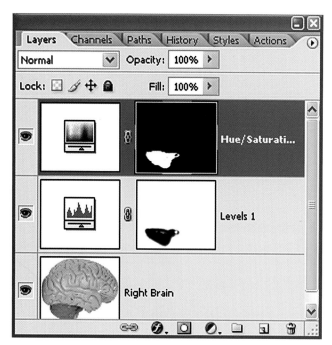

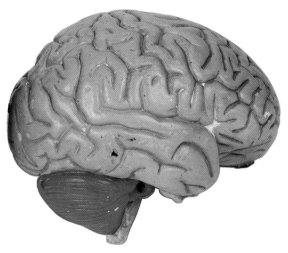

Figure 1.48: Painting may also reveal alterations to areas and leave others alone.

Figure 1.49: Break out the model paint! We need to give this gray matter an overhaul.

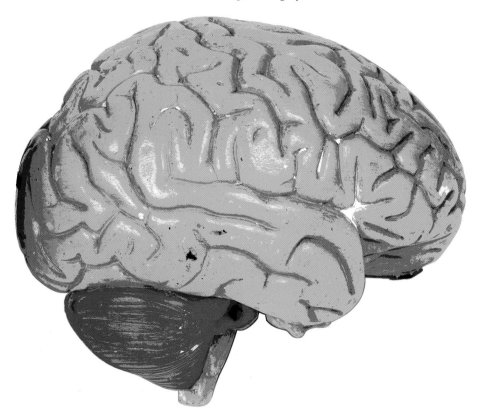

Figure 1.50: Model, photo, or painting?

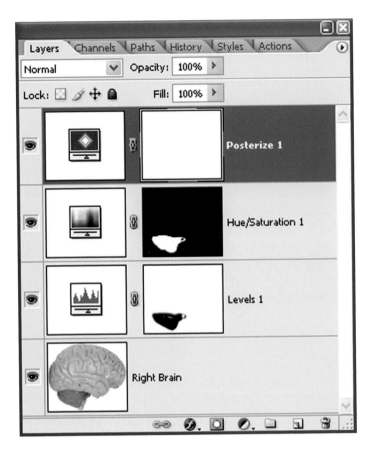

Figure 1.51: Four layers, three adjustments, and two altered masks give us the final "brain painting."

Keep in mind that all of these adjustments have in no way altered the original photo layer. Simply by adding three adjustment layers, you have been able to enhance the color, repaint an area of the image, and convert it to an artist's rendering. Figure 1.51 shows the Layers palette with all four layers in place.

As mentioned in the preceding section, "Working with Layer Masks," you can fade the effects of your adjustments with gray shades, rendering the adjustment semitransparent. Adjustment layers also have to heed the rules of blending modes, so play around a bit and have fun with them. Trust me, you have not seen the last of them in this book!

Displacement Mapping

Have you ever looked at an image created by someone else who seems quite proud of it, but it just doesn't look right to you? You hate to say anything that could be taken as a brutal kick to their ego, but you know deep inside that if they had just taken a few extra steps—a tweak here, an adjustment there—they could have a piece that really boggles the eye. This often occurs when people try to overlay an image on top of another. If the curves and contours of the two images match, the artist is well on the way to creating art that doesn't appear "thrown together."

Displacement maps can help. These are designed to help you conform one image to the shape of another, using the shades of gray in the image to create the distortions in the second. Displacement maps play a part in several of the techniques found later in this book, so a quick hands-on tutorial is in order to get up to speed.

Open the images **Back.jpg** and **Map.jpg** (see Figures 1.52 and 1.53).

The foundation image for this technique is the photo of a man's back. The thought here is to give him a map tattoo across his shoulders and the back of his head. The second image should work fine, but it first needs to be molded and stretched to match the highlights and shadows on the foundation image.

The best displacement maps tend to be those with the greatest variation in lights and darks. They are created from a channel that you select. I've chosen to duplicate the blue channel and use it as the base for my map because it gives the best white-to-black ratio across the image. The highlights are brighter, the shadows darker than the other channels. Of course these can be tweaked further by using Dodge and Burn, Brightness/Contrast, and so forth, but I prefer to choose the channel that will require a minimal amount of adjusting.

You can duplicate the blue channel by clicking and dragging it to the New Channel icon at the bottom of the Channels palette (second from the right, next to the Trash). A quick Contrast adjustment will help separate the whites and blacks further. I've chosen +25.

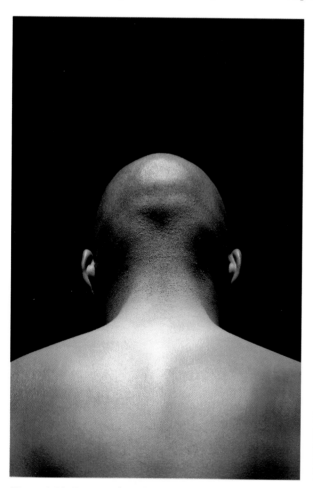

Figure 1.52: Deep in thought

Figure 1.53: A map of South America

Next apply a Gaussian blur to the map channel so that, when it is used to distort the second image, there are no sharp changes, and the alterations appear smoother and more transitional (see Figure 1.54).

The last link in the creation of the displacement map is to save it as a new .psd file. To do this, right-click the channel and select Duplicate Channel. In the dialog box that appears, name the new image and be sure to set the Destination of the Document to New. When the file opens as a new image in Photoshop, choose File → Save As and save the new .psd file to your hard disk. Remember where you placed it, because you will need it again shortly. When you have saved the new map, you can close it in Photoshop. Return to the **Back.jpg** photo and delete the extra channel, as it is no longer needed.

I'm going to take this opportunity to discuss Apply Image, something I'll cover in depth in Chapter 4, "Techniques for Artistic Effects." Apply Image has to be one of my all-time favorite adjustments in Photoshop. I'll reserve most of my praise until later, but because it works for this effect I'll dip into it just a bit here.

Apply Image allows you to blend two images together. Sounds simple enough, until you discover the number of ways you can blend those images! The effects can be rather astounding. For this example, however, all you need to know is that both images must have the exact same dimensions in pixels. I'll discuss why in Chapter 4, but for now simply adjust the size of the **Map.jpg** image to match the size in pixels of **Back.jpg** (see Figure 1.55).

You may now use the displacement map to warp the **Map.jpg** image. Select the map photo and choose Filter → Distort → Displace. The Displace dialog box will then ask you to what Horizontal and Vertical scale you would like the warp to take place. A setting of 10 for each should work fine in this instance, because the images are both 300ppi. If they were of lower resolution, then lower Scale settings would be in order.

The Displace filter uses a second image (displacement map) to determine how a layer or selection will be distorted.

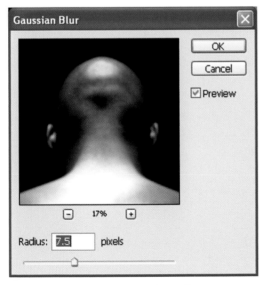

Figure 1.54: A blur helps conform the image to the map.

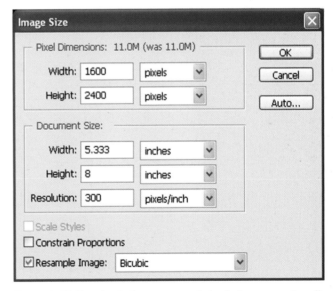

Figure 1.55: For Apply Image to work, both documents (or all that will be used in creating your final image) need to have the exact same dimensions in pixels.

Also in the Displace dialog box you are asked to choose either Stretch To Fit or Tile. Stretch To Fit works best here, because there is no need to have the edges repeat. Also, Wrap Around should be selected for the same reason under Undefined Areas (see Figure 1.56). After these settings are selected, click OK to apply the filter.

But wait, there's more! Now Photoshop will ask you what .psd image it should use as a map. By default it will take you to the location on your hard disk where you saved the displacement map: simply select it and click OK. The **Map.jpg** image will warp to conform to the contours of the **Back.jpg** photo.

Now on to my favorite Photoshop feature: Apply Image. After you choose Image → Apply Image, you use the Source drop-down list at the top of the dialog box to select the image you would like to apply to your photo. For instance, say you would like a darker, more color-rich version of your current image. You could use Apply Image with the same photo set as the Source, and the Blending mode set to Multiply (the default setting) to accomplish this (see Figure 1.57). I've applied the map to the photo of the back (see Figure 1.58).

To apply the distorted map photo to the man's back, you follow the same process of choosing Image → Apply Image, but then

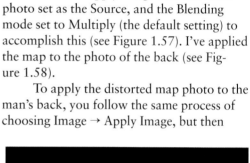

Figure 1.56: Setting up the Displace filter

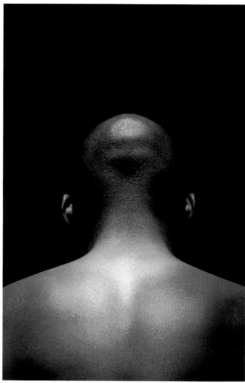

Figure 1.57: Apply Image can use the document you are working on as the Source image.

Figure 1.58: Applying an image to itself can have the effect of richer, more vibrant colors.

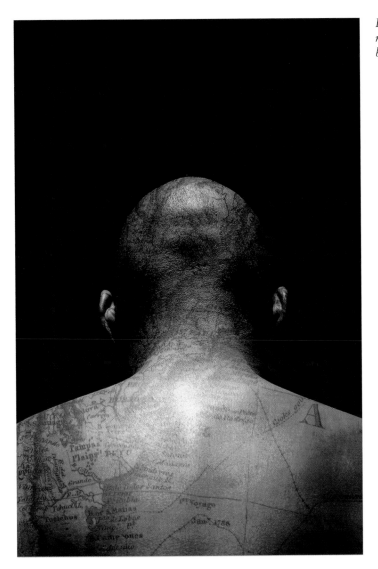

Figure 1.59: The map and the back combined

select **Map.jpg** as the Source. You may want to adjust the opacity of the merge and alter the blending mode to see what gives you the most visually satisfying mix. In this instance I've changed the Blending mode in the Apply Image dialog box to Overlay and reduced the Opacity to 70%. Apply Image has hundreds of variations; blending mode and opacity changes are integral to the effectiveness of the technique.

With these settings, the map conforms nicely to the original photo. After you add a mask to paint away the excess map from the background, the results are seen in Figure 1.59.

The combination of displacement maps and Apply Image are only the tip of the iceberg. I'd love to continue this topic now, but I'll force myself to wait until Chapter 4. In the meantime, I have one more cool item to demonstrate in this chapter.

Discovering the Power of Blend If

My good friend Richard Lynch, whom you may know from his *Hidden Power* books, also published by Sybex, started talking to me about Blend If a few years ago. A typical conversation may have sounded like a Laurel and Hardy routine:

> RL: Al, you've got to try Blend If.
>
> AW: Blend what?
>
> RL: Blend If.
>
> AW: Blend if what? What am I blending and why?
>
> RL: Blend If, man! It's the newest thing out there…you're nobody until you get on the Blend If bandwagon!
>
> AW: Dude, I don't know what you're selling, but get it outta here or I'll call the cops. If it's that cool, it can't be legal.

Well, maybe the conversation didn't go exactly like that. But it did pique my interest, especially because his books were the only ones I'd found that even broached the topic. So after much experimenting, head scratching, and throwing digital paper balls in the cyber-trash, I think (*think*, mind you) that I'm starting to grasp what he's been telling me all these years. At least from a right-brained point of view, I've found a few cool tricks that Blend If can be used for.

Blend If allows you to manipulate how certain colors will react to the color beneath them. Granted, this sounds

Figure 1.60: Wall photo with a rasterized type layer, pre-distorted with a displacement map

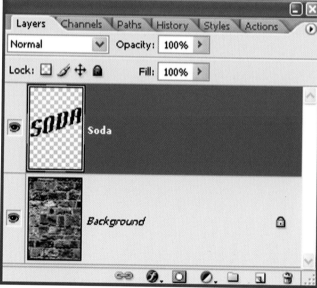

Figure 1.61: The type has already been conformed to the cracks and mortar in the wall image.

similar to Blending Modes, but Blend If is a bit more powerful in that it gives the user control over specific colors in the layer, and not the entire layer.

For this example, open the image **Wall.jpg**. I've already taken care of generating a displacement map of the wall and applied it to a rasterized type layer. The result is seen in Figure 1.60. Just to prove it to you, Figure 1.61 shows the Layers palette, complete with rasterized text.

Blend If is found in the Blending Options of the layer Styles, right at the top of the left-hand Layer Style dialog box. You can use this cool feature to make the text appear not only painted onto the wall, but with a little Photoshop magic you can make it appear as though it has aged with the wall, even wiping away those areas of text where the bricks have broken and worn away.

To follow along, create a displacement map as done in the previous tutorial. Generate a text layer, rasterize it, and displace it with the map. Now you are at the point I am with this project.

With the text layer selected, click the Add Layer Style icon at the bottom of the Layers palette. When the styles menu expands, select Blending Options from the top of the menu. The dialog box that appears is seen in Figure 1.62.

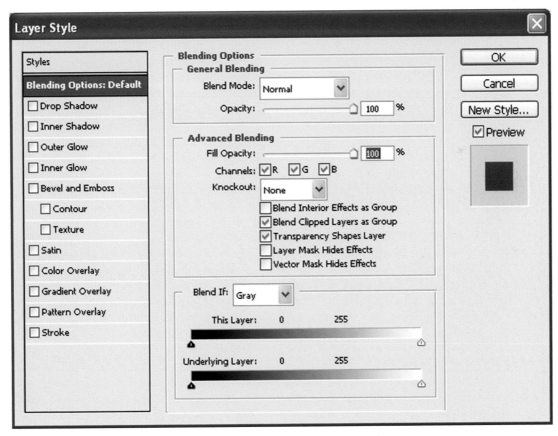

Figure 1.62: Default Layer Style dialog box with no style settings yet in place

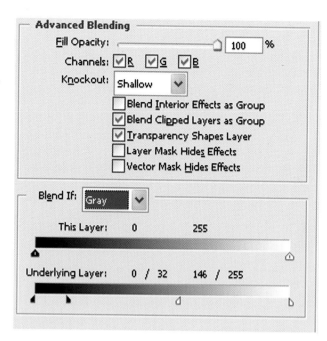

Figure 1.63: Blend If works on a series of sliders that can be divided to give you more control over the blend.

You need not worry about drop shadows or bevels for this technique. On the lower half of the current window is an area called Advanced Blending. This is where all of the cool Blend If things take place. For instance, I've set the Knockout to Shallow. Blend If defaults to gray, so that drop-down can be left alone for now; it is the highlights and shadows I'm concerned with.

At the very bottom is a slider area called Underlying Layer. What this means is that if the Wall layer is black, white, or a varying shade of gray, moving the sliders will render portions of the type visible, semitransparent, or invisible. Each slider (right and left) can be split in two by holding down the Option/Alt key and click-sliding it either left or right. This allows you to control the intensity and separation of the blend on your text as it attempts to match the luminosity of the wall. With the sliders in the positions seen in Figure 1.63, the type takes on the faded and aged characteristics seen in Figure 1.64.

You can also manipulate the color channels with Blend If. For instance, there is a hint of red in the bricks. You can further age the text by selecting Blend If: Red and adjusting the Underlying Layer sliders as seen in Figure 1.65. Figure 1.66 shows a close-up of the text after this adjustment. You could almost swear that the text was paint that has been around nearly as long as the building, and not simply a type layer altered by Photoshop!

I've in no way covered every cool tool you will explore in this book on your way to the perfect masterpiece, but I've covered a few of the more important ones, or at least those that will show up frequently. Again, please don't be content to simply use the images supplied with the book. I encourage you to try these techniques on your own photos, stimulating those right-brain cells and creating your own art. I assure you it will be far more gratifying to you, and for me as well. I can't turn you into an artist, but I suspect there is already one inside you, lurking just beneath the surface and ready to make itself known. If I can help you to realize at least that much by showing you these techniques, then I am indeed a happy man.

Figure 1.64: The text takes on the aged characteristics of the wall beneath.

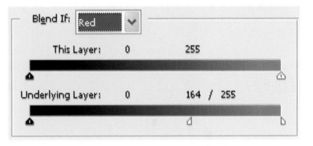

Figure 1.65: Blend If allows you to work with channels to get a more sincere meld between layers.

Figure 1.66: The text looks so real you could swear it has been there for a very long time.

two

Techniques for Embellishing Portraits

Very few people *like the way they look in photographs.
Here you're going to learn how to help with that.*

This chapter deals specifically with the alteration of people—from light portrait retouching to drastic alterations. However, the techniques demonstrated are in no way restricted to images of people; these few examples of corrections and alterations have thousands of possible applications that aren't exclusive to a specific photo type. What the techniques will do is help you work through a process (or at least demonstrate one way of doing things), and after you've learned a procedure, you can then find ideas for applying it to your own artistic renderings. Even better, after the right side of your head is tingling with ideas, you will soon find that you can subtly or drastically alter the steps in a technique to generate some pretty amazing results. Who knows, you could revolutionize a new artistic form—or at least generate some interesting pictures to e-mail to family members.

*The images referenced as source files for these techniques can be found in the Chapter 2 **Source Files** folder on this book's CD.*

Enhancing Eye Color

I love working with eyes. They've been called windows to the soul, and this is close to the truth. You can discern many things from a person's eyes, from emotional state to truthfulness (or lack thereof). I've known people who swear their eye color changes depending on their mood, and after experiencing a couple of foul tempers, I learned to discern those ill moods just by checking to see whether the eyes were a soothing hazel or a wicked shade of green. Green is rarely good—any fan of comics can tell you that.

Fortunately for me, my love for tweaking eyes works well here, as eye manipulation is a popular topic in the Photoshop community.

The most popular question about working with Photoshop, and therefore the most often answered, is how to solve the red-eye problem. Because that information can be found nearly everywhere, I'm not going to get into it directly; after you are done with this chapter, you will have figured it out, trust me.

What I'll show you first is one way to enhance the existing eye character in a photo. Take a look at Figure 2.1. This is the image **Stare.jpg** from this book's CD; it should be open in Photoshop as you begin. The enhancement you'll add here is to make this mixed color richer and brighter. To do that, you'll use duplicated layers, layer masks, and a couple of blending modes.

Duplicate the Background layer and change the blending mode of the new layer to Overlay. Note that the entire image becomes a bit darker as the new layer blends with the background. This does help enhance the color of the eye, but the skin around the eye becomes darker also. A mask will alleviate this problem quite nicely.

Overlay blending mode either screens or multiplies the pixel information, depending on the base color. Even when colors or patterns overlay pixel information, the highlights and shadows of the original pixels are maintained. The base color is not replaced; rather, it is blended into another form of the original color.

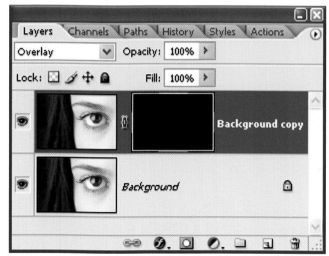

Figure 2.1: You will enhance the richness of the brown eye color.

Figure 2.2: New layer and mask in place

At the bottom of the Layers palette, click the Add Layer Mask icon. By default the mask is filled with white, allowing the contents of the entire layer to be seen. You do not want all of the pixels to be seen, however, just those of the iris and pupil. With the layer mask selected, choose Edit → Fill and fill the mask with black set to 100% opacity, blending mode set to Normal. Figure 2.2 shows the Layers palette at this point in the process.

Set white as the foreground color. Select the Paintbrush tool and, with a soft-edged round brush, paint over the iris and pupil. Adjust the brush size accordingly so that you are painting only within the diameter of the iris. Although it's not necessary if you have a steady hand, you may want to create a selection of the area. In this instance the Elliptical Marquee tool will work just fine, because the area being enhanced is round. As you paint, the pixels on this layer will be revealed. The layer is still set to Overlay, so the color of the blended layers comes through (see Figure 2.3).

To brighten the eye a bit (the goal is to brighten the colors without darkening the eye), create a new layer above the Background Copy layer and set the blending mode to Soft Light. With the foreground color still set to white, paint over the iris in this layer also. The change is subtle yet effective. Figures 2.4 and 2.5 show before and after shots. See the difference?

Figure 2.3: Painting in the mask

Figure 2.4: Before lightening occurs

Figure 2.5: After lightening

Variation: Enhancing Lip Color

In a manner similar to the eye technique just covered, lips can also be enhanced and given new life digitally. This technique is especially popular for women—they can now look as though they spent hours meticulously applying makeup without even cracking the seal on their lipstick.

One idea I want to work into your way of thinking (if it's not already there) is that techniques you've seen performed on eyes/hair/leaves/concrete or whatever can also be used to enhance other texture types, other subjects, and so forth. Although both eyes and lips reside in the same neighborhood on a body, the characteristics that make eyes recognizable as eyes and lips as lips are very different. But just because the color and texture are different does not mean that similar techniques to color or correct them cannot be used.

Open the image **smirk.tif** (see Figure 2.6). The woman in this photo doesn't really need a lot of makeup, but her lips could be a bit richer in tone. This technique will use the colors already resident in the image as the foundation palette.

Figure 2.6: What could she be thinking?

As before, create a duplicate of the Background layer and set the blending mode to Overlay. Because the lips are the target of this piece, notice how they take on a deeper shade of red.

To deepen the hue even further, select the Burn tool and set the Brush to 70, the Range to Midtones, and the Exposure to 50%. Before you darken things too much, keep in mind that not all people require multiple applications of makeup. You may wish to try the next step with a reduced exposure setting. Again, experimentation is encouraged.

Run the brush over the lips, being careful not to linger too long in the same place or burn the same area repeatedly. If you do linger or make multiple passes, the Burn tool will continue to saturate the pixels until they become extremely dark. In nice, easy strokes, run the brush over the lips until the richer reds emerge. If you overdo it with this tool, the lips will gradually turn black, so take it easy!

The Burn tool has its foundation in traditional photography. Burning is used in that medium to increase exposure to areas of a print, and the Burn tool in Photoshop works in the same manner. You can use it to increase saturation in a photo, darkening select areas.

Create a mask for this layer and fill it with black. In the mask, paint with white over the lips to reveal the richer tones (see Figure 2.7). Just for kicks, I'm going to use the mask to reveal the richer eye color also.

Figure 2.8 shows the final corrected image with just these simple adjustments. The new lips appear to have a light application of makeup, without being over-the-top. Sometimes it's cool to be subtle.

Figure 2.7: Black hides, white reveals.

Figure 2.8: Pale to deep red in a couple of quick steps

Altering Eye Color

Altering eye color is simpler than it has ever been, thanks to the Color Replacement Brush tool. This is grouped with the Brush tool and the Pencil tool in the Photoshop CS2 toolbar (Photoshop CS grouped it with the Healing Brush and Patch tools). This powerful and easy-to-use tool relieves a lot of the stress suffered by both amateurs and pros alike, who used to spend a lot of time wishing such a tool existed.

Before I get into the nuts and bolts of this cool feature, let me say that it still has a drawback: it is destructive to the layer (meaning that it alters the pixels), so it is not a miracle cure for every recoloring ailment. In the next variation I'll take you through another process that allows you to preserve the original layer. But first let's do some painting!

Open **blue_eye.jpg** (see Figure 2.9) and find the Color Replacement Brush in the toolbar.

As with other tools, this one has settings that can be changed in the options bar. For this technique, set the blending mode to Hue and ensure that Find Edges is selected for the Limits setting. The Brush size should be 20, the sampling mode should be Continuous, the Tolerance should be 30%, and Anti-aliased should be checked. With the Find Edges setting, Photoshop will look for boundaries to paint within while the new color is being applied, thus allowing only the hue of the iris and not the areas outside it to change.

Hue blending mode creates a color based on the luminance and saturation of the base color and hue/tone of the blend color.

Before you change the color of the eyes, you will want to choose a new color. Open the Color Picker (click the foreground color) and select a new color (see Figure 2.10). Click OK.

Duplicate the Background layer to keep the original image unaltered and start painting over the iris with an appropriately sized brush. I love the Hue setting, because the color change is subtle yet clearly evident (see Figure 2.11). The reflections are retained, the pupil remains black, and the eye color still looks natural.

Figure 2.9: Window to the mind

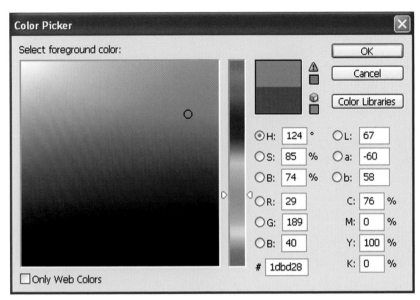

Figure 2.10: Choose the new eye color.

Figure 2.11: By using the Hue blending mode, the changed color in this example retains a natural appearance.

Figure 2.12: Replacing the color in Saturation mode gives this image a much more artificial appearance.

For colors that are richer, change the blending mode of the brush to Saturation. A richer blue is displayed, but the eye clearly looks manipulated and unnatural (see Figure 2.12).

Delete the previously retouched layer and duplicate the Background layer. Change the foreground color to a light blue hue and change the blending mode of the brush to Color. Those of you familiar with retouching may recognize this mode, because this was a primary mode for retouching in earlier versions of Photoshop.

Figure 2.13: Enhancing eye color with the Color blending mode

Figure 2.14: Creating an eye of deep blue

Paint over the iris again. When I'm working with eyes and lips, the Color blending mode is by far my favorite. The eye color teeters on the edge of natural and unnatural; it could be real, but it could be enhanced. At least that is what viewers will think, and I like to keep them guessing (see Figure 2.13).

If the brush didn't pay attention to your command telling it to stay within the borders of the iris, a layer mask can fix the problem. Just create a mask for the layer and paint with black over the color that extends beyond the iris. Another alternative to correcting spot areas is the History Brush.

To really make the eye glow with inner life, duplicate the colored layer and change the blending mode in the Layers palette to Overlay. This will also darken the skin, as seen earlier, so just create a mask, fill it with black, and then paint with white in the mask over the eye to reveal it again (see Figure 2.14).

Color blending mode creates a color based on the luminance of the base color and saturation of the blend color.

Altering Hair Color

To demonstrate that similar processes have multiple applications and that you shouldn't make things harder than they have to be, let's apply a similar coloring technique to altering hair color.

Open the image **punk.jpg** (see Figure 2.15). Note that this photo has already had some exposure and color manipulation applied to it. I've chosen this image to demonstrate that even manipulated photos can be altered to meet an artist's or photographer's requirements.

Duplicate the Background layer and select the Paintbrush tool. Set the blending mode for the brush to Color and set the other options as shown here:

Brush   90
Opacity   30%
Flow   50%

Figure 2.15: Red-haired model

Figure 2.16: Changing the red to purple

Select a color and place it in the foreground. Use the brush to paint over the hair sweeping off to the side and follow the hairline. Continue painting until all the red pixels have been swapped with the new color (see Figure 2.16).

I bet you guessed how to clean up the excess paint that has spilled over. If you said layer mask or History Brush, you are absolutely right! See how things work together for the common good?

For a little added splash, create a new layer above the painted layer and set the blending mode for the new layer to Color (see Figure 2.17). Select varying shades of color for the foreground (green, blue, mauve, stucco…) and paint over a few strands of hair. Use Figure 2.18 as a reference if you like.

Figure 2.17: New layer set to Color blending mode

Figure 2.18: Trying out a variety of colors

Variation: Subtly Enhancing Highlights and Natural Hair Color

The previous technique showed a pretty drastic alteration, but the majority of alterations that people attempt in Photoshop are subtle—simply enhancing color or changing it slightly. Here's one method for changing color that retains the natural look of the hair.

 Open the image **retouch.jpg** (see Figure 2.19).

You will start by adding highlights, so duplicate the Background layer. Select the Dodge tool and change the options to these:

Brush	80
Range	Midtones
Exposure	34%

Change the blending mode for the Background Copy layer to Overlay. Using the Dodge tool, brighten a few strands of hair similar to the painting of color done in the previous technique. Do not dodge the hair too much; a few highlighted strands will do (see Figure 2.20).

Figure 2.19: Our hair model

Figure 2.20: Highlights with Dodge

Figure 2.21: New layer in Color mode...again

Next you can add color as in the previous technique, but drastically toned down. Create a new layer and set the blending mode to Color. Select a color somewhere between red, orange, and brown as the foreground color and paint over the hair in the new layer (see Figure 2.21). The adjusted image is shown in Figure 2.22. If the color is too harsh for your taste or needs, simply lower the opacity of the painted layer.

Figure 2.22: The finished result

Whitening Teeth

As of this writing, I'm a smoker (I say that in the hopes of quitting the nasty habit someday). I've given up the cigarettes but not the pipe. I also drink more coffee than the average bear. That combination of vices makes for a pretty unsightly smile if stringent oral hygiene is not followed. Photoshop, on the other hand, can help you put a sparkle on those pearly whites in no time.

Open **fangs.jpg**. Figure 2.23 shows the teeth you will be working on for this technique. I chose this image because I hate having my real teeth cleaned and because the teeth themselves (the photo's teeth, not mine) are tinted yellow as the result of age.

Duplicate the Background layer and lighten the teeth with the Dodge tool. You need not take out all the yellow—just lighten the teeth a bit.

Next, create a new layer and change the blending mode to Saturation. Select a light gray foreground color and, with the Paintbrush tool, paint over the teeth in the new layer. You can also accomplish this by choosing white but reducing the opacity of the paint. You will notice the yellow hue disappear as if by magic (or at least a powerful toothpaste). See Figure 2.24.

Figure 2.23: Yellow smile?

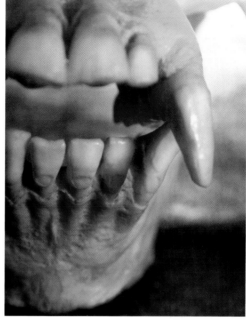

Figure 2.24: Some staining removed

Saturation blending mode creates a color based on the luminance and hue of the base color and saturation of the blend color. Gray produces no change, because there is no saturation associated with gray.

You can whiten the teeth by changing the blending mode of the brush to Hue, with these settings:

Brush   100
Opacity   45%
Flow   75%

If you want to make the teeth look like they have been overbleached, simply select the Background Copy layer again and apply the Dodge tool to all the canines, molars, and bicuspids you want until the smile meets with your satisfaction (see Figure 2.25).

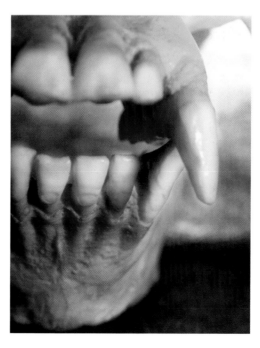

Figure 2.25: A smile made for the movies and politics

Removing Acne and Blemishes

Let's take a break from painting, dodging, and burning, and tackle another issue that appeals to retouchers everywhere. When I was going through those wonderful transition years from boy to grown-up, I suffered from a rather active case of acne. I absolutely hated it, and because Photoshop did not yet exist, I had to suffer through far too many photo sessions without any chance of the retouching that kids today have available. Having pictures taken for the yearbook was bad enough, but when you became a senior, the pictures were printed in…egad…full color!

That particular problem has thankfully faded into the distant past, but a couple of scars remain—both on my face and on my psyche. As with teeth and hair, Photoshop can act as a digital cosmetic surgeon with just a few quick tool applications.

Have the image **skin-rug.jpg** ready in Photoshop. As you can see in Figure 2.26, this lovely young woman has a few minor blemishes apparent on her cheeks, which don't look bad at normal resolution. When you zoom in (see Figure 2.27), blackheads and old acne scars become painfully apparent because of the high resolution of this image. If this shot were part of a model's portfolio, who knows what jobs she might lose?

Figure 2.27: Toooo much detail!

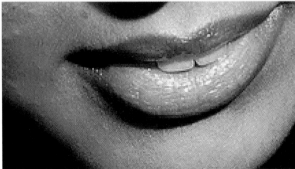

Figure 2.26: In a normal view, the model's old acne scars are barely visible. But zoom in, and…

Figure 2.28: New skin stamped into place

Figure 2.29: Acne and color replaced with new skin

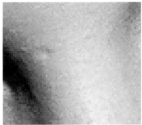
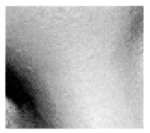

Figure 2.30: Acne scar   *Figure 2.31: Skin smooth once again*

Cleaning up the scars is simply a matter of covering them with samples taken from other areas of the face without blemishes. Select the Clone Stamp tool and enter these settings in the options bar:

Brush	70
Mode	Normal
Opacity	25%
Flow	35%
Aligned box	Checked
Use All Layers box	Unchecked

Hold down the Option/Alt key and take a sample from the woman's chin to apply to the blemished areas. Release the mouse and Option/Alt after the sample has been taken and stamp the skin pattern over the blemishes seen to the left side of her mouth (see Figure 2.28). There may be some discoloration; don't worry about that just yet.

Although they are separate tools, the Clone Stamp tool and the Healing Brush tool often work best in conjunction with each other. Select the Healing Brush tool and enter these settings in the options bar:

Brush	30
Mode	Normal
Source	Sampled

Figure 2.32: Lady of the islands

Again, sample a clear area of skin near where the blemishes were covered, and release the Option/Alt key. Apply the sample to the areas of discoloration (see Figure 2.29).

Figures 2.30 and 2.31 show an area of scarring between the model's eyebrows that is easily corrected by using the same technique.

As an added bonus now that the skin corrections are done, I applied a couple of the coloring techniques presented earlier to the final image, seen in Figure 2.32.

Erasing Wrinkles

This technique is also one close to my heart, and it gets cozier there with each passing day. Having officially reached that cumbersome middle-aged mark, I trust that I'll be looking for even more ways to imitate Dorian Gray (or at least in reverse, if that makes sense).

Take a look at Figure 2.33 (**laugh.jpg**). This lady looks as if she just heard my favorite "Waiter, there's a fly in my soup" joke, which has brought out a whole lifetime of laugh lines.

I'm sure you can help her out, though, and the process is very simple.

Duplicate the Background layer. By using the Clone Stamp tool or the Healing Brush tool (either works just fine) with the settings used in the previous technique, sample clear unwrinkled areas of the skin and then apply them to the wrinkles. Don't worry if she takes on an unnatural, baby-smooth appearance, as in Figure 2.34. To finish this correction, simply lower the opacity of the Background Copy layer until some of the wrinkles beneath show through (see Figure 2.35).

Figure 2.33: Laugh, and the laugh lines laugh with you.

Figure 2.34: Stamp the new skin over the wrinkles.

Figure 2.35: She looks 10 years younger!

Digital Liposuction

This technique uses the image **tummy-2.jpg**. Please open it now.

Notoriously, the camera adds 10 pounds. And even though most of us would not pay to see someone like Kate Moss belly dancing, the model for this technique (see Figure 2.36) has decided that her publicity stills should look a little skinnier than she actually is. In particular, she doesn't like the love handles in her photos. Whether she needs slimming or not, the Photoshop physician can help.

One way to trim down the love handles and still keep a natural curve is to generate a path and trim away the excess. Select the Pen tool and, in the options bar, click the Path button on the upper left. Select the standard Pen tool (as opposed to the Freeform Pen tool) Check out the options for the tool in Figure 2.37.

This tool can be tricky and is pretty daunting to those who don't use it on a regular basis. It isn't that difficult to work with after you play with it a bit, though.

Take a look at Figure 2.38. First, click the mouse just above where you want the correction to be made. Click another point along the seam of her pantaloons and, holding down the mouse button, drag to the left so that the adjustment handles appear. Then just manipulate the mouse until you get the curve you want.

Figure 2.36: I dream of Jeannie.

Figure 2.37: Pen tool options

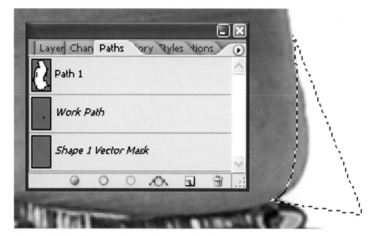

Figure 2.38: Create a path around the love handle.

Figure 2.39: Change the path to a selection.

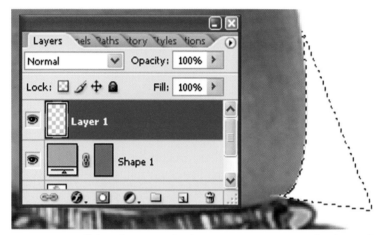

Figure 2.40: Fill the selection with white to wipe away a couple of pounds.

To help you generate perfect curves when using the Pen tool, practice dragging the first adjustment handle in the direction the bump of the curve is to go, and the second adjustment handle in the opposite direction. This formula will create an S curve. For more information on Curves, please consult "Drawing with the Pen Tool" in the Adobe Photoshop CS2 Help Files.

Click in the white area to create a new point, and then click on the first point to close the path. By closing the path, I mean that all the points of the path will be connected so that a "circle" is formed. At the bottom of the Paths palette, click the Load Path As Selection icon. This will create an active selection following the path (see Figure 2.39).

This edit is fairly simple, because the subject is already on a white background. To trim away the love handle, just create a new layer at the top of the layer stack and fill it with white (see Figure 2.40). If the subject were on a different background, you would need additional

Figure 2.41: Before (left) and after (right)

steps (extracting and deleting the excess pixels) to complete the retouching. Figure 2.41 shows the before and after images.

Variation: Using the Liquify Filter

Another way to tighten up those elusive curves is to use the Pucker tool in the Liquify Filter dialog box. Use the same image as before (**tummy-2.jpg**); either open a new instance of it or click the original state in the History palette to revert to the unaltered photo.

> The Pucker tool, found in the Liquify Filter dialog box, moves the pixels within the brush area toward the center of the brush while you either hold down the mouse button or drag. The longer this tool is applied, the more compressed the pixels in the brush area will appear.

Choose Filter → Liquify. Select the Pucker tool on the left, and then set up these options/settings for the tool on the right-hand side:

Brush Size	35
Brush Density	60
Brush Pressure	60
Brush Rate	80

You are reducing the brush size, density, and pressure from their default 100%, because the pinching of pixels that occurs when using this tool needs to be gradual. Reducing the brush density and pressure simply gives you better control and will help prevent harsh distortions. The Liquify tool likes to manhandle pixels, and overapplication will quickly stretch and pull the image to the point where the subject is no longer recognizable as a life form.

Now center the cursor over the inside edge of the skin of the love handle. As you click and hold the left mouse button, the pixels surrounding the cursor will be drawn toward its center. Slowly move the mouse up and down the edge, to the seam of the pantaloons, and watch how the pixels are drawn in. *Do not* linger in one spot for long, or the edge will become lumpy and distorted (see Figure 2.42).

Another place where women (and some men) want to look more like a fashion model than a belly dancer is the upper arms (see Figure 2.43). Using the same careful technique, pull the fat in on this area also.

After you have the hang of the process, reduce the exposed shoulder, forearm, and the other side of her waist to keep her body in proportion (see Figure 2.44). That is the main problem (and a major attraction for a lot of users) with overapplication of this filter: the loss of believable proportions. Using it delicately, however, can create some startlingly realistic results, as you will see later in the book.

Now that the model has been trimmed and tucked in her upper areas, we've left her with a rather prominent backside. You don't think so? Trust me, if she stood up right now she would be asking for—rather, *demanding*—her money back (see Figure 2.45).

To fix this, increase the size of the brush and run it over her derriere until the proportions look right to you. Figure 2.46 shows the before and after shots; another proud customer of the Photoshop Weight Loss Program.

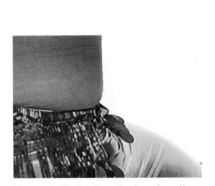

Figure 2.42: Reduce the love handles again—gently!

Figure 2.43: Shrink the fat forming on the upper arms in the same way.

Figure 2.44: Slimming

Figure 2.45: One more area to cover

Figure 2.46: Before (left) and after (right)

Face Swapping

This technique uses the image **face_swap.jpg**. Please open the photo now.

Have you ever wished you could swap lives with someone else for a day? In Photoshop you can. Swapping faces or body parts with another person is fairly simple in Photoshop. Figure 2.47 shows a pair of women in close proximity to one another, so the lighting on each is nearly the same. That will help achieve a decent face change.

> When changing faces, it is best to use images that have the same dimensions as well as lighting from the same direction. This will help the final image trick the eye of the viewer.

Before performing cosmetic surgery on one of this pair, you need their faces to be at the same angle. The woman on the right has a slight tilt to her head, whereas the woman on the left is on a level plane with the horizontal dimensions of the image. In Figure 2.48 I have brought down a guide and placed it just above the left woman's eyes so you can see what I mean.

The eyes of the woman on the right are not level, however. To fix this, first duplicate the Background layer. Select the Magnetic Lasso tool and create a selection around the woman on the right (see Figure 2.49). If you have a problem including all of her hair in the selection, switch to the Polygonal Lasso after the initial selection is made and click the Add To Selection button on the top left of the options bar. Then simply create selections around the hair and portions of the woman that did not make it in the first pass with the Magnetic Lasso.

Figure 2.47: I wanna be just like you...

Figure 2.48: A level gaze

Figure 2.49: Select the subject on the right.

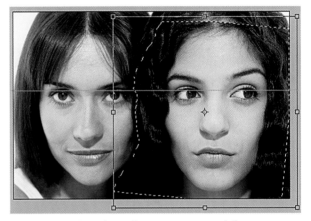

Figure 2.50: Rotate the woman so her eyes are level with the guide.

Figure 2.51: Transform the woman to match her eyes to those of the other subject.

The Magnetic Lasso tool is used for making selections around an image. The key to using the Magnetic Lasso is to snap the border of the selection to clearly defined edges. For the best results, use this tool to make selections around subjects in a high-contrast background, or in backgrounds that allow a clear border to be defined around the object being selected.

After the woman on the right is selected, she needs to be rotated so her eyes are on the same horizontal plane as the other subject. Quick application of the Transform tools will perform this nicely. Choose Edit → Transform → Rotate and move the selection around until the eyes are on the same plane, or level with the guide as seen in Figure 2.50. Accept the transformation after the eyes are level.

Choose Edit → Transform once again, only this time selecting Scale. Move the top of the Transform down so that the woman's eyes are level with those of her counterpart. You also may need to adjust the width of her face to prevent distortions (see Figure 2.51). Accept the transformation when you are ready.

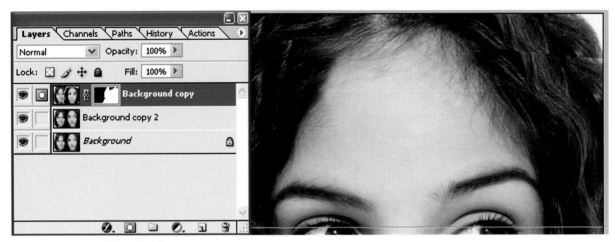

Figure 2.52: A mask for blending seams

Figure 2.53: Patch tool set to Source

While the selection is still active, create a layer mask for the layer. Ensure that the selected area is filled with white and the reverse with black, as seen in Figure 2.52. This sets the image up to wipe away the seams created at the top of the woman's head during the transformation process. Switch to the Paintbrush tool and paint over the seams (seen along the sides of the top of her forehead) where the hair no longer matches the layer below. Set the foreground color to black and paint over those seams in the mask until the seams disappear, blending the hair with that of the layer beneath.

It is now time to put the Patch tool into play. Select the tool from the toolbar and set the options as seen in Figure 2.53. Ensure that the Patch tool option is set to Source.

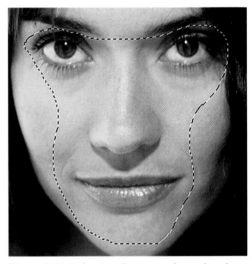

Figure 2.54: Selecting the area to be replaced

Initially the Patch tool acts just like the Marquee tool in that you draw a freeform selection around the area you want to edit. Use the tool to make a selection around the eyes, nose, and mouth of the woman on the left. Although the Patch tool is set to Source, this term can be a bit confusing because it indicates the area that will be replaced. Why the switch? Only the gurus at Adobe know, but I suspect an evil joke being played on the left-brainers (see Figure 2.54).

Figure 2.55: Not twins, but sisters certainly

After the selection is made, just click and drag the mouse to the right. Notice that the face goes away, and it appears that a new copy of the woman is being moved around within the selection. Continue moving the mouse until the facial features of the woman on the right appear within the selection in the same spots as the left woman's original features. When you have the new face in place, the Patch tool will automatically match the color, texture, lighting, and seams to the original face, blending it in to appear natural. If you find a few areas where the tool didn't quite do its job, simply load the Healing Brush tool and clean up the edges to merge the new face with the old head. Figure 2.55 shows the final alteration.

Digital Face-Lift

This technique uses the image **facelift.jpg**. Please open the photo now.

I've already touched on wrinkle reduction in this book, but the changes made there were fairly subtle, more to enhance the photograph rather than the subject of the photo. That was a studio technique a customer would find flattering. This technique takes the process of wrinkle reduction to the extreme, by physically altering the image of the subject to reduce age and give the appearance that she really isn't in her mid-60s but ceased aging years earlier.

When I first started playing with digital face-lifts, my subjects often ended up looking like some creature that could survive only in the imagination. After numerous failed attempts, I began looking at how real cosmetic surgeons approached their work and altered their clients. Most of the changes a person undergoes are subtle: a slight narrowing of the bridge of the nose, a removal of skin so that the remaining skin can be pulled back to remove wrinkles, and so forth. If the client elects for more trips to the surgeon, the alterations become increasingly apparent until the skin appears stretched, the lips cease moving in a natural way, and the eyes seem in a permanently open state. I won't name any names, but I'll bet you can pinpoint some examples of cosmetic surgery extremes.

Just because it can be done in Photoshop does not mean that a plastic surgeon could get the same results! Playing with pixels is one thing, but my publisher and I accept no liability for what might happen if you alter your picture and then ask a surgeon to duplicate the effect. You're beautiful just the way you are; having known you for two chapters now, I wouldn't change a thing.

Figure 2.56: Our subject, before digital cosmetic surgery

On to the technique. The woman in this photo (see Figure 2.56) has wonderful skin tone and bone structure, but the years have added a few creases and an age mark or two that can certainly be wiped away digitally. The primary correction in this photo will be wrinkle reduction as performed earlier in the book, but this will be combined with a few other adjustments to create a younger looking, albeit still mature, businesswoman.

Start by duplicating the Background layer. The woman has many fine wrinkles all over her face and neck, but her cheek (see Figure 2.57) has a smooth area that can be used to clean up the rest of her face. Select the Healing Brush tool and, with the following options, take a sample of the smooth skin:

Brush	50–80
Mode	Normal
Source	Sampled

Although similar to the Clone Stamp tool, the Healing Brush not only applies a sample (or pattern) to an area, but also attempts to match the texture, shading, lighting, and transparency of the pixels it is applied to (source pixels). The result gives far better seamless blending than the Clone Stamp in the case of facial reconstruction and other effects.

Apply the sample beneath the woman's eye and on her lid to clean up the minute folds and discoloration seen there. Overlay most of the wrinkles seen in this portion of the face, but leave a couple of tiny crow's-feet. Repeat the process around her other eye and also take out the more prominent wrinkles on her forehead (see Figure 2.58).

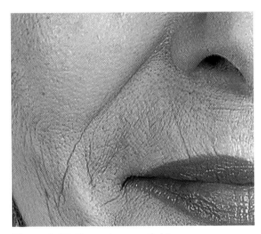

Figure 2.57: Smooth area of skin

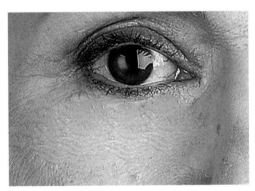

Figure 2.58: Age around the eyes reduced

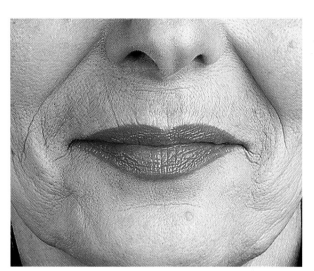

Figure 2.59: Chin and cheeks, pre-alteration

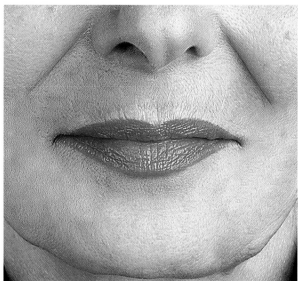

Figure 2.60: Chin and cheeks after new skin is applied

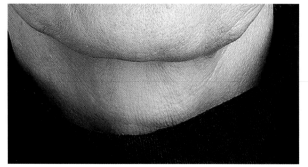

Figure 2.61: And now the neck…

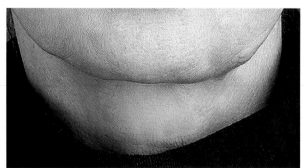

Figure 2.62: The years are melting away.

Move down to the lower portion of her face, as well as her neck (see Figure 2.59). To correct this area, take another sample from the smooth area on her chin to cover the mole that is being carefully, but not entirely successfully, concealed by makeup. If you recall the touch-up done on the young woman earlier in this chapter (removing acne and blemishes), the technique is the same, although the wrinkles here are more pronounced and frequent. A few wrinkles are needed for realism, but most can go away (see Figure 2.60).

Continue the same technique on her neck (see Figure 2.61). Again, take samples of the smooth areas on her neck and apply the Healing Brush tool in the same manner as before, covering the lines that years of head turning have produced (see Figure 2.62).

You will now get a bit more practice with Liquify. The Liquify tool is fantastic for digital face-lifting, as long as it isn't overdone. You will use it to tighten the areas of the face that have been pulled and stretched by gravity. This is going to help shave years off the woman.

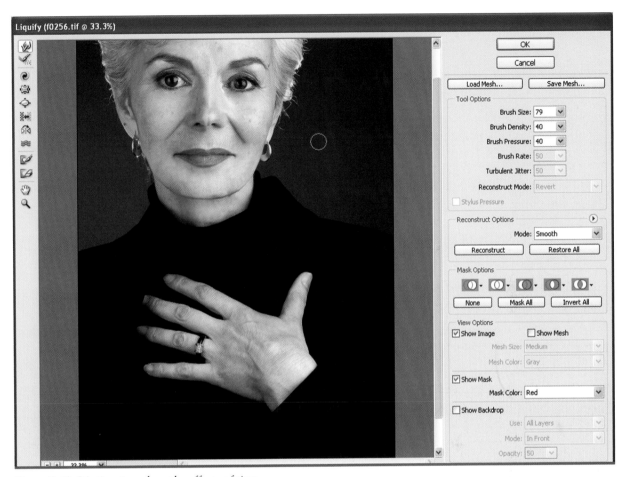

Figure 2.63: It's time to reduce the effects of time.

Choose Filter → Liquify. As in the previous technique, the size of the brush (no larger than needed to make small corrections), reduced density, and reduced pressure will help draw in the flabby skin. These are the settings that I've found work the best:

Brush Size	50–80
Brush Density	40–60
Brush Pressure	40–60
Brush Rate	50–80

Look at Figure 2.63, which shows the woman before any Liquify adjustments. What you want to do here is run the tool along the cheeks, much as you would if using the Highlighter during an extraction. Do not linger in one place for long; move the mouse as fluidly as possible (see Figure 2.64). Reduce the nose size, and pucker the areas above and below her eyes to open them a bit (see Figure 2.65). Also, move along the edges of her neck to slim it.

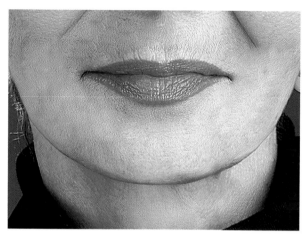

Figure 2.64: Rounding the chin has a staggering effect on the aging process.

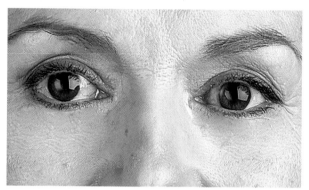

Figure 2.65: Lifting the eyes and narrowing the nose also helps restore some lost vigor.

After you have finished Liquifying, you can employ the hair-coloring techniques described earlier in this chapter. Note that proceeding with hair coloring will most likely make the image retouching look obvious, so if you want a natural feel to the end result, I'd forgo treating the hair. I'll proceed with hair treatments here, but thought you should be aware of the downside.

As a refresher, I'll step through the process quickly:

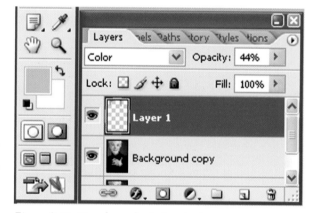

Figure 2.66: New layer for hair coloring

- Select a color for the woman's hair and place it in the foreground. Create a new layer.
- Change the blending mode of the new layer to Color and, with the Paintbrush tool set to Soft Light, paint over the woman's hair in the new layer. If the color is a bit stark for your tastes, try reducing the opacity of the paint layer or changing the blending mode to Soft Light (Figures 2.66 and 2.67).

Figure 2.67: Blending mode of the brush set to Soft Light for a more natural look

Figure 2.68: One more look at the model before her digital makeover

Figure 2.69: From mid-60s to later 40s, thanks to Photoshop

When finished, you will have a much younger looking version of the original woman. I hope that you have a greater appreciation for the Liquify filter than when you started. It is a great tool for massive distortions of features but is also powerful and masterful at slight alterations. Often the slightest changes can make all the difference in the world (see Figures 2.68 and 2.69). You may want to lower the layer opacity so you can better blend the effects with the original layer.

three

A Few Right-Brained Special Effects

One of the side benefits *of being an author of Photoshop books and articles is being asked to teach the software in a classroom. As I go through the course, eventually I get to the Liquify Filter. As soon as I mention we will be working with that dialog box, the mood of the class always changes from attentive study to giddy expectation: they know we are about to do something "cool." I bet I could create an entire month's worth of curricula and fill every seat in the room simply by warping faces. People like Practical, but people love Cool.*

This chapter is not about the Liquify Filter, but rather on using images to build ideas. I'll introduce a few special effects designed to expand your understanding of what the software is capable of and to add a few nifty tricks to your digital arsenal. Photographs will be used, but they serve as foundations for the end effect rather than the end product itself. Continue reading, and I'll demonstrate what I mean.

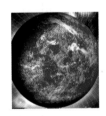

*The images referenced as source files for these techniques can be found in the Chapter 3 **Source Files** folder on this book's CD.*

Creating a Glass Sphere

An effect does not have to be difficult or the process exceptionally long to give it the *special* moniker. Case in point: glass sphere effects have been around since Photoshop's humble beginnings. This is one of those effects that can be created in a myriad of ways with multiple variations. The end result can be simplistic or complex, depending on how much time the artist puts into the project. The more time spent working on the sphere, the more realistic (one hopes) the glass is going to be.

Here, you're going to take an image and add a sphere effect to it.

 Open the image **Bee.jpg** (see Figure 3.1). I believe you'll find that the colors inherent in a photo add to the end effect in many cases, and the glass sphere technique definitely benefits from the colors in the photograph itself.

By now you should be in the habit of duplicating the Background layer at the beginning of these projects, so please duplicate the Background layer now. Rename the new layer **Sphere** (see Figure 3.2).

Before proceeding, stop and think about glass for a moment. We are all familiar with what a marble looks like, and in particular a semitransparent marble. What characteristics do you envision in your mind's eye that define this object as a marble? For one, a marble is round. That's a good starting point. In the case of a glass, semitransparent marble, you might note that objects behind the marble are distorted when seen through the glass; what you see will appear curved to match the shape of the glass. Another characteristic is how light plays

Figure 3.1: The colors in this photo will add character to the glass sphere in the end piece.

on the surface and in the interior of the sphere. You'll have reflections and assorted bright spots, as well as darker areas caused by the density of the glass around the curves.

With these points in mind, you can take your Photoshop knowledge and attempt to duplicate on the monitor what you see in your mind. Using the Sphere layer as a foundation, you will see in a few short steps the bee and the flower magnified through a reflective glass spherical object.

You'll start by making a spherical selection on the Sphere layer. To create a perfectly round selection, the Elliptical Marquee tool is the tool of choice. Certainly you could draw a selection freehand to try to create a perfect circle, but that's not necessary. In the options bar, you'll see several options available for the Elliptical Marquee tool when it is selected in the toolbar. One of these settings that can be changed is a drop-down menu labeled Style. The default setting is Normal, which will allow you to draw the selection yourself. Expanding this menu, you'll see a selection called Fixed Aspect Ratio. Selecting this allows you to draw a perfect circle every time. The tool's settings for this example are as follows:

Selection Type	New Selection
	(New Selection button depressed on the options bar)
Feather	0
Anti-alias	Checked
Style	Fixed Aspect Ratio
Width	1
Height	1

You can now draw your circle selection. Start in the upper-left corner, maybe an inch or two vertically and horizontally from the corner of the photo. Continue drawing your selection to the lower right so that the bee and the flower are mostly or entirely encompassed by the selection. Figure 3.3 shows what the selection should look like when you're done.

With the selection active, you're ready to start creating the sphere. The first step is to apply the Spherize filter to the selection. Choose Filter → Distort → Spherize. The Spherize

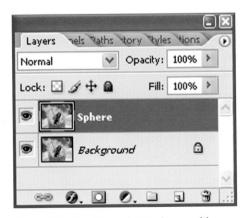

Figure 3.2: Duplicate the Background layer and rename the new layer **Sphere***.*

Figure 3.3: Make a circular selection around the flower and the bee.

Figure 3.4: The Distort filters help to alter the shape of the layer.

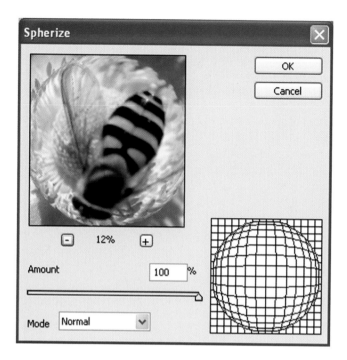

dialog box that appears allows you to tell Photoshop that you'd like to conform a selection or layer to a sphere. The setting of choice here is Normal mode, which comes up by default. Set the amount of the distortion to 100%. You can decrease the Zoom in the viewer window to better see how the filter will affect your selection. Click OK to accept the change (see Figure 3.4).

There are more filters you can use to get closer to a glass effect. The Lens Flare filter is perfect for generating reflections that appear on the glass and are refracted through it. With the selection still active, choose Filter → Render → Lens Flare. When the Lens Flare dialog box appears, you'll notice you have four Lens Type choices. Movie Prime is new to Photoshop CS2, and I can't wait to use it, so let's try it out. Select Movie Prime and set the Brightness level slider to 200%. You may click on the crosshairs in the example window and move it manually. The location of the crosshairs in the example window indicate where the light hits the surface of the sphere. Move it to the upper-left quadrant of the glass (see Figure 3.5).

Using some variety in reflection types sometimes helps with the realism of the final project, so apply the Lens Flare filter once more, only this time select 35mm Prime as the Lens Type. Move the Brightness slider to about 130%. This will reduce the amount of glare. Also reposition the crosshairs to the lower-right corner of the glass (see Figure 3.6). This will be the exit point of the light through the semitransparent sphere.

After you have the second Lens Flare in position, click OK to accept the settings. Now you can move on and manually add to the reflections in the glass, as well as darken areas that will help add to the realism. Dodge and Burn will perform these functions to perfection.

Click the Dodge tool in the toolbar. Note that the options bar changes to reflect the settings you can apply to this tool. First choose a 200-pixel Soft Round brush. Set the

Figure 3.5: *Lens Flare allows you to select a lens type and position angle. How light plays on this image will determine how realistic the final sphere appears.*

Figure 3.6: *An additional Lens Flare application lets you determine an exit point of the light passing through the glass object.*

Figure 3.7: *The Dodge tool options*

Range of the brush to Highlights. When you apply the tool to light areas in the layer, they will gradually increase in brightness. If you continue to use the Dodge tool in an area, it will gradually become stark white. Set the Exposure to 70% (see Figure 3.7).

You apply the Dodge tool just as if you were painting with the Paintbrush. Run the Dodge tool over the bright area where light hits the glass in the upper-left corner. The more you apply the tool, the brighter this area will become. Also work the tool in the lower-right area, although not as much as you did in the upper left. If you look at Figure 3.8, you'll see that I've also applied the Dodge tool to a spot in the center of the selection and to a few light areas around the perimeter of the selection. Again, think of how light plays on and through that imaginary marble.

Figure 3.8: Applying Dodge to lit points on the sphere enhances the effects applied with the Lens Flare filter.

Figure 3.9: The Burn tool options

The Burn tool is applied in the same manner as Dodge. Select the Burn tool and, in the options bar, set the Range to Midtones (see Figure 3.9). This will help darken the colored areas of the selection, especially along the edges of the sphere. Why is this important? Primarily it helps to distinguish the edge along the curve of the surface from the background (the unaltered portions of the layer). Figure 3.10 demonstrates the effect.

After the Burn tool has been applied, the glass is basically complete. You can add additional glasslike imperfections to the sphere if you like. One such blemish occurs when the glass is blown improperly and bubbles form in the interior. If you were to look at these imperfections closely, you would most likely see a smaller version of the scenery behind the sphere.

By copying the sphere you just created, placing it on a new layer, and shrinking it with the Transform tools, you can come close to duplicating this effect. Play with the blending modes of the layer for added flavor. In Figure 3.11 I've made a copy of the sphere, transformed the size and aspect, and changed the Blending Mode for the new mini-sphere to Overlay.

Let's see what has been achieved. Figure 3.12 is the final glass sphere, complete with distortions, reflections, shadows, and refractions.

The technique I've demonstrated is not simply restricted to glass. You could use these same steps (or variations thereof) to create bubbles, electrified crystal balls, and other semi-transparent globes. What you hope to see in the depths of the sphere is up to you.

Figure 3.10: Darkening the edges helps to define where the glass begins, separating it from the background.

Figure 3.11: Adding imperfections to the glass is a stylish touch.

Figure 3.12: The final image. The bee is magnified through a sphere of glass.

Making a Chrome Sphere: Digital Manipulation

If you are familiar with any of my online work or previous books, then you already know my attraction to metallic effects. I just love working with metal, and I'm not the only person out there with a metal addiction. Chrome effects especially draw a lot of interest, and Photoshop is an excellent tool for working in the medium without ever stepping into a forge or spending time with a welder.

First things first: you will need a highly reflective metallic image to create this effect. Because the end effect is a chrome sphere, the image will need a lot of chrome and the stark highlights produced by the metallic reflections. For this technique, open **WheelChrome.jpg** (see Figure 3.13).

To set up the Layers palette, convert the Background layer to a standard layer by double-clicking it in the Layers palette and renaming it **Wheel Chrome**. Duplicate the Wheel Chrome layer and create a new layer filled with a color at the bottom. I'm using a tan hue in this case. Make the original Wheel Chrome layer invisible, because you will be working with the Wheel Chrome Copy layer (see Figure 3.14).

Spherize is an excellent tool for generating spheres, but this tutorial is a bit different: instead of creating a sphere from nothing, you want this photo to become a sphere. Photoshop allows for that process as well, and the trick resides in the Polar Coordinates filter.

Choose Filter → Distort → Polar Coordinates. You will run this filter more than once to generate the sphere. For this first pass, select Polar To Rectangular in the Polar Coordinates dialog box and click OK (see Figure 3.15).

That makes for a pretty strange-looking warp, but at this point you are nearly halfway to the sphere shape. The image requires a little perspective change before the sphere can be

Figure 3.13: Reflections of chrome

Figure 3.14: Set up the Layers palette.

Figure 3.15: *Manipulating polar coordinates*

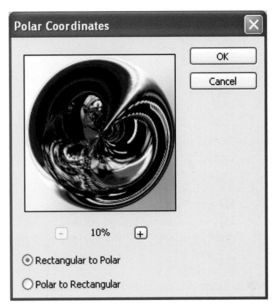

Figure 3.16: *Sphere in progress*

completed, so choose Edit → Transform → Flip Horizontal. Then flip the same image vertically (Edit → Transform → Flip Vertical).

Return to the Polar Coordinates filter, this time selecting Rectangular To Polar in the Polar Coordinates dialog box. In the preview window, you need to reduce the image size in order to see the whole sphere (see Figure 3.16). Click OK.

The edges of the sphere are a bit messy, so select the Elliptical Marquee tool and create a selection around the sphere, leaving out the rough edges (see Figure 3.17). Select Inverse and then press the Delete key. Remember, if you need to move the layer while using the Marquee, hold down the spacebar as a quick way to bring up the Move cursor.

Figure 3.17: *Erase the edge pixels from the sphere.*

The reflections are coming together, but by using a quick masking technique they can be maximized even further to enhance the chrome effect. Duplicate the Wheel Chrome Copy layer, and flip the new layer vertically with the Transform tools. Create a layer mask for the new layer and with a black-to-white gradual gradient, fill the mask from the lower-left corner to the upper right (see Figure 3.18).

Now look at Figure 3.19. Your reflections may not match mine exactly, but that's fine. It is extremely tricky to duplicate another person's masking effect. The point is that you

Figure 3.18: Add a mask.   *Figure 3.19: Reflective sphere*

should have a sphere with a highly reflective surface, with nearly identical duplication of the reflection across the face.

As it stands, the sphere is pretty straightforward, but it could use some depth of color, shadows, and additional reflections. For one thing, there is no apparent light source from any given direction. ⌘/Ctrl+click one of the sphere layers to generate a selection and create a new layer. Using a white-to-black/dark blue gradient set to Radial in the options bar, fill the selection with the gradient starting in the upper-left quadrant of the sphere and moving down to the lower right. Set the blending mode for the layer to Soft Light (see Figure 3.20).

To enhance the impression that this is a metal object, a touch of gray added to the point closest to the viewer will help. Set the foreground color to gray, and in a new layer, draw a foreground-to-transparent radial gradient out from the center of the sphere. Reduce the opacity of this layer to 80%.

Now you can use the Dodge and Burn tools to add highlights and shadows. Select the Dodge tool and, in the options bar, set the following attributes:

Brush	250, Round, Feathered
Range	Highlights
Exposure	50%

The Dodge and Burn tools find their roots in photographers' need to regulate exposure in specific areas of their images in the darkroom. Either light is held back (Dodge) to lighten areas of a print, or exposure is increased (Burn) to darken areas of a print.

Merge the two sphere layers containing the actual reflections. Select the newly merged layer and dodge in highlights in opposing quadrants. Start with the upper left, add a few to

Figure 3.20: Blending mode change

Figure 3.21: Dodging reflections

the lower right, and so forth. Keep in mind that the reflections will get narrower toward the center of the sphere (see Figure 3.21).

Steel and chrome have a subtle blue-gray quality that the eye may not realize initially but that is present in most metallic reflections. Rather than add more blue (that was accomplished with the radial gradient layer), you can simply remove some of the color to help the effect along a more natural path. To emulate this and assist in the realistic quality of the sphere, create a Hue/Saturation adjustment layer at the top of the layer stack with the following attributes:

Figure 3.22:
Layer
rearrangement

Hue	0 (no adjustment)
Saturation	−40
Lightness	0 (no adjustment)
Colorize	Unchecked

Click OK to accept the change to the saturation of color in the overall image. You still want to retain the blue from the gradient layer, so simply drag the gradient layer to the top of the layer stack, above the Hue/Saturation adjustment layer (see Figure 3.22).

Now you just need to add the reflection of the photographer. Open **photographer.jpg** (see Figure 3.23).

Figure 3.23: Caught on film

Figure 3.24: Layer for the cameraman

Extract the cameraman from his background and copy and paste him into the sphere document (see Figure 3.24). If you need a refresher on extractions, please take another look at the "Extracting an Image from a Background" section in Chapter 1, "Tools for Building Your Masterpiece." Now the man needs to conform to the curve of the sphere. Choose Filter → Distort → Spherize (see Figure 3.25), setting the Mode to Normal and the Amount to 100%.

Place the man's layer beneath the Hue/Saturation adjustment layer in the layer stack so that the blue will overlay his reflection and the saturation will be reduced for this layer as well (see Figure 3.26). Create a mask for the layer and, using a white-to-black radial gradient, fill the mask so that the area where the man resides is visible, gradually fading over the face of the sphere. ⌘/Ctrl+click one of the sphere layers to generate a selection, select the inverse on the man's layer, and press Delete. Be sure you are deleting the actual layer pixels and not the mask.

Finally, try filling the background layer with a gradient. I'm going to do away with the tan background and opt for a gray to gray-blue variation. Figure 3.27 shows the final result.

Unlike the glass sphere effect, which gives the impression that an object behind the sphere is being seen through the lens, this effect demonstrates reflections on a solid, nontransparent but reflective surface. Either way, now you have spheres for at least two occasions!

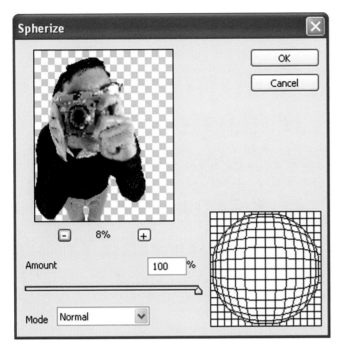

Figure 3.25: Rounding out the reflection

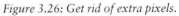

Figure 3.26: Get rid of extra pixels.

Figure 3.27:
Chrome sphere

Creating Patterns from Photos: Floor Tiles

As I teach, I'm often asked questions about Photoshop's capabilities that have little or nothing to do with photography. I've been asked whether Photoshop can be used for creating quilting patterns, digital stained glass that could then be used to create real stained glass artwork, or even floor tile patterns.

These are not questions one might expect concerning a program that has its roots in photo correction. The short answer I give these people is simply "Yes, it can." The process may require a bit of work and forethought, but generally if there are color elements involved, then Photoshop can handle the geometry. It is up to the designer or Photoshop pro to work out the details, often with some fairly astounding results.

Frequently techniques used to create a certain type of effect, such as those mentioned in this chapter, are simply variations and combinations of techniques you already know and have applied in other ways. One of the primary differentiating factors between "lefties" and right-brainers is the approach. A technical-minded person will approach Photoshop with a "What can it do?" attitude. Those with an artistic bent tend toward "What if I did this?" Both are solid approaches, but I'd venture to say the latter offers the more gratifying result.

For this experiment, let's delve into the world of geometric masking. Layer masks can expand the creativity of even the most die-hard left-brainer. By applying strict gradients to layer masks, you can turn *any* photo into a geometric pattern, simulating floor tiles or creating seamless backgrounds in just a few steps.

To begin this excursion, open the image **WoodFamily.jpg** (see Figure 3.28).

At its present size, this photo could be turned into a seamless background without any alteration to dimensions. Because the premise of this tutorial is to create a floor tile, and most floor tiles are square, this will be as well. Choose Image → Image Size (Alt+⌘/Ctrl+I) and uncheck the Constrain Proportions checkbox toward the bottom of the dialog box. Enter equal Width and Height values in either the Pixel Dimensions section or the Document Size section to turn the photo into a perfect square. Don't worry about Resolution just yet. See Figure 3.29.

In Chapter 5, "Effects in the Real World," we will be discussing symmetrical landscaping and patterns in the sky, both of which are variations on the technique about to be performed here. Those techniques use masking as well, so the placement of this tutorial is intentional because of the drastic nature of the masking that takes place. Chapter 5 will offer more refined examples; this technique is a bit radical.

It's time to set up the Layers palette for the technique. First duplicate the Background layer twice, so that you have three layers in the Layers palette. Select the topmost layer and flip it horizontally (Edit → Transform → Flip Horizontal). Stay with that top layer and add a layer mask by clicking the "Add layer mask" icon at the bottom of the Layers palette. Figure 3.30 shows the Layers palette at this point in the process.

Knowing that black in a mask hides and white reveals layer information, you may have already deduced a bit of what the next step might be. Drawing a stark black-to-white gradient across the mask would basically make the photo appear folded over onto itself. I men-

Figure 3.28: Wood family statuette

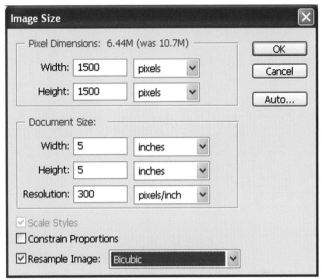

Figure 3.29: Resize the image to perfectly square dimensions.

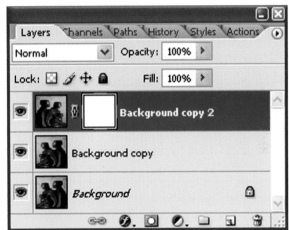

Figure 3.30: The Layers palette as you prepare to work with the first mask

tioned, however, that this technique is a bit radical, so the gradient for this layer needs to reflect that.

Click on the mask in the Layers palette to ensure it is active. The foreground and background colors have changed in the toolbar to Black/White or White/Black, as Photoshop realizes masks can work with only white, black, and shades of gray. After the mask is selected, select the Gradient tool in the toolbar and click directly in the gradient field in the options bar to open the Gradient Editor.

Take a look at Figure 3.31. By adding black and white color stops along the bottom of the Gradient Editor, you can create a gradient of stark black/white changes. The gradient seen in this example is going to help divide the image so it will no longer resemble a wooden statue—actually it won't look very pretty on the first pass at all. However, to generate the floor tile effect, this gradient will work wonders, setting up the geometry of the image as previously discussed.

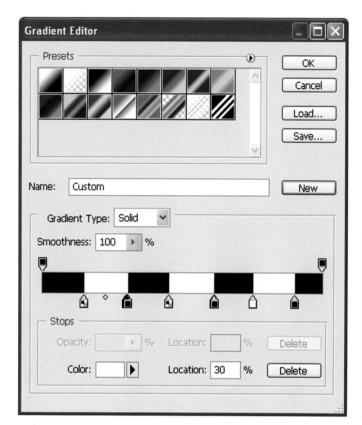

Figure 3.31: Radical gradient for a radical technique

Figure 3.32: Photo after one pass with the gradient

After you have created your gradient, click New to add it to your loaded gradients; then click OK.

It's time to get wild. Ensure that the layer mask is still active in the Layers palette and draw the gradient across the mask, left to right. Hold down the Shift key to ensure you draw it in a straight line. Start at the left edge, move to the right edge, and release. Instead of a folding effect on the photo, this instead divides the image into vertical strips, as seen in Figure 3.32.

The multistriped gradient served us well, but you need to use that one only a single time. The photo is divided into vertical strips, and now a standard stark black-to-white gradient can be used for the rest of the masking that will take place to turn this photo into a floor tile.

The next few steps will come in rapid succession as they are nearly identical. Select the top layer if it is not already, and merge it with the layer beneath (⌘/Ctrl+E). Duplicate the merged layer, and again flip it horizontally as before by using Transform → Flip Horizontal. Create a mask for the new layer.

Back to the gradient. At this point in the process you are ready to apply the gradient to the mask again, only this time a simple stark white/stark black gradient will work. Create a new gradient with half white/half black, with color stops that meet at the 50% mark. Save the gradient and click OK. Now draw the gradient horizontally from left to right across the mask again, as seen in Figure 3.33.

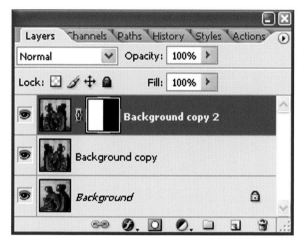

Figure 3.33: Another mask gradient, albeit simpler this time

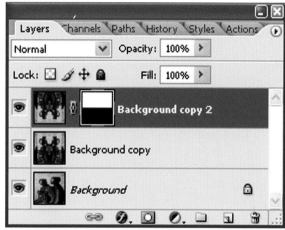

Figure 3.34: Working vertically with the mask

Once again, merge the top two layers. Duplicate the merged layer and transform it, only this time choose Transform → Flip Vertical. This process will allow you to make the pattern seamless on the top and bottom edges. Create a mask again for the top layer and, using the white-to-black gradient in the previous step, draw the gradient from the top edge to the bottom edge of the photo (see Figure 3.34). After the gradient is applied, the photo will, or should, look fairly close to the example in Figure 3.35.

Granted, the photo isn't looking much like a floor tile yet. Bear with me, as you are well on your way and will be there in a few short steps.

Merge the top two layers again, and again duplicate the merged layer. With the Transform tools, rotate the top layer 90° either clockwise or counterclockwise. Create a mask, click on the Gradient tool, and this time draw the gradient from the upper-left corner to the lower right or from the lower-right corner to the upper left. Figure 3.36 shows the Layers palette at this point, and Figure 3.37 shows the result. If for some reason your gradient is reversed, simply

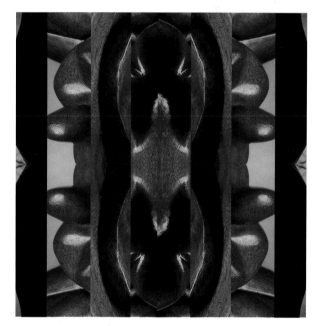

Figure 3.35: Geometry taking shape

select the mask and choose Image → Adjustments → Invert. White will change to black and vice versa.

By now you are probably getting the hang of the process, and action-savvy people may have already realized that this process is easily recorded and duplicated time and time again with an action. If you record the process, you can quickly turn any photo into a geometric pattern with a click of the mouse. This and many other pattern generating actions are included on the CD. My website, **Actionfx.com,** has many of these actions as does my book/CD combo, *Al Ward's Photoshop Productivity Toolkit,* published by Sybex.

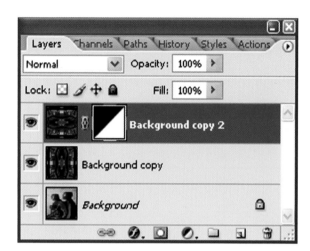

Figure 3.36: Working diagonally

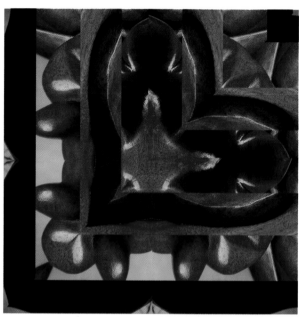

Figure 3.37: The pattern is starting to reveal itself.

Okay, let's finish this up. Merge the top two layers again and then duplicate the merged layer. Flip the top layer horizontally with the Transform tools, create the mask, and draw the gradient across the mask horizontally. See Figure 3.38.

Again, merge the top two layers, duplicate the merged layer, flip the top layer vertically, create the mask, and for the last pass draw the gradient from top to bottom (or bottom to top) in the layer mask (see Figure 3.39). The end result should look like the photo in Figure 3.40. If not that exactly, you should at least have a wooden geometric pattern. If

Figure 3.38: Once more with the horizontal gradient

you would like this exact image, please go back through the tutorial and keep a close eye on the black/white layout in the masks after you apply the gradients.

So is it a floor tile yet? Not really. A geometric pattern made of wood certainly, but not necessarily a tile. Fortunately, Photoshop has filters that will allow you to alter this image in such a way that it takes on the characteristics of a floor tile. In this instance, you can change the pattern from wood to wood-patterned linoleum by simply applying a Plastic Wrap filter.

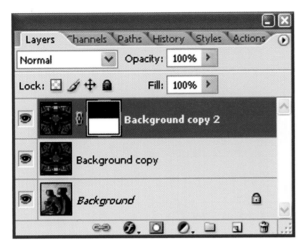

Figure 3.39: The last gradient/mask application—I promise!

Figure 3.40: Geometric wooden pattern from a statue photo—who thinks this stuff up?

Figure 3.41: Plastic Wrap and other artistic filters help add the tile-like realism.

Merge the top two layers one last time. Choose Filter → Artistic → Plastic Wrap (see Figure 3.41). The filter dialog box appears. Simply click Plastic Wrap, or you may choose one of the other filters available in the dialog box to see what your tile will look like when it is applied. Plastic Wrap in this instance provides that linoleum feel that I sought to duplicate, so I will just go with it. Keep an eye on the example viewer while moving the sliders attached to the filter until you get the effect you want and then click OK. My final tile is seen in Figure 3.42.

Okay, we're down to the wire. The photo has been turned into a floor tile, and the floor tile has been turned into a linoleum floor tile. The question is: is it seamless? A quick test will tell us in short order whether the tile effect has worked.

*Figure 3.42: Ta-
da! Linoleum
floor tile in just a
few quick mask-
ing steps.*

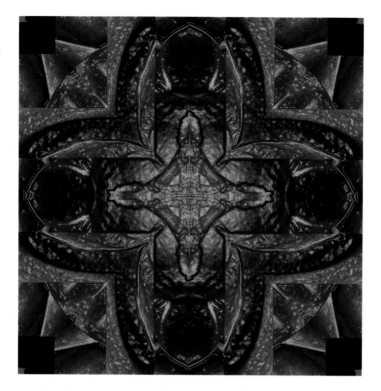

*Figure 3.43:
Define and save
the new pattern.*

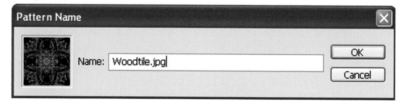

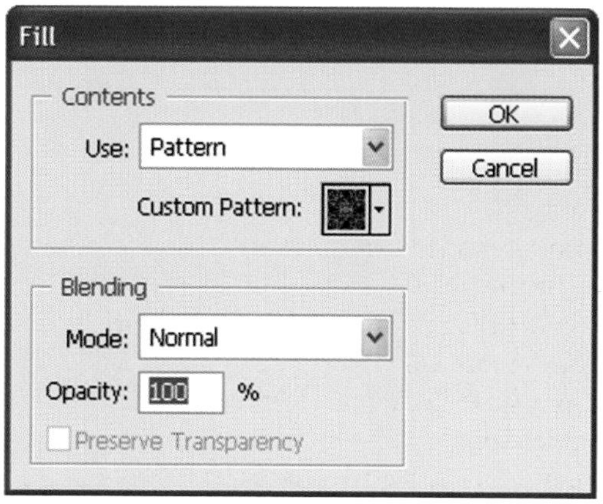

First, define the pattern by choosing Edit → Define Pattern. Name the new pattern something catchy (for example, **Woodtile.jpg**) in the dialog box that appears and click OK. The pattern is now saved to the set of loaded patterns already resident in Photoshop (see Figure 3.43).

Next, create a blank document about four times larger than the tile. With the document open, choose Edit → Fill and change the Contents: Use setting to Pattern. Open the window of loaded patterns and find the new one at the bottom of the list (see Figure 3.44). Select it and click OK. This will fill the blank document with the pattern. Take a look at the filled document

*Figure 3.44: To test whether the pattern is seam-
less, fill a larger document with the tile.*

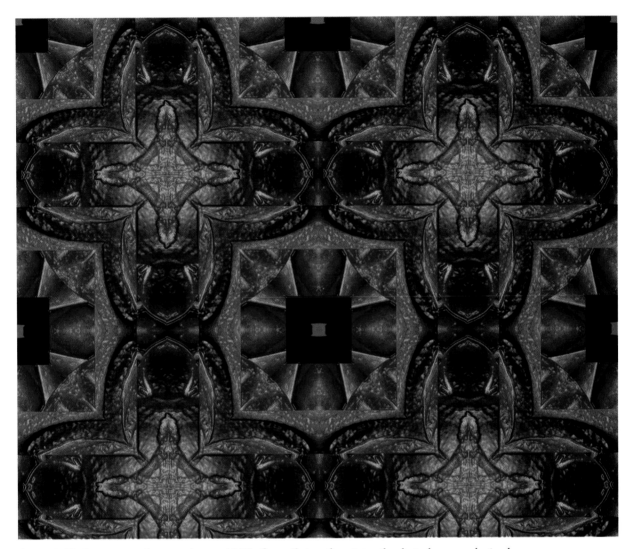

Figure 3.45: From artsy photo to cheap mid-70s floor tile in a few steps, thanks to layer masks (and some help from a filter)

(see Figure 3.45). The tile has come to life, with no resemblance to the original photo other than a few colors. Better yet, there are no seams, which was the reason for this final test.

Granted, you may never have a reason for generating floor tiles out of anything, let alone photos. However, this process can be useful to those who make patterns for backgrounds, layer styles, and so forth. This process may have been a bit tedious, but the exercise will help those not well versed in mask use in later chapters. You should have your masking muscle warmed up and ready to go for the techniques in Chapter 5. Masks are powerful, and as you can see when a little imagination is applied to their use, they can be a bit fun as well.

Generating Metal Text from Scratch

My roots in Photoshop began years ago with type special effects. Text special effects piqued my interest in the software and started me on this journey. Therefore, I would be remiss if I did not include at least a couple of instances of type effects in this book. The next two sections are devoted to text; I hope you enjoy them.

A long time ago, way back in Photoshop 4 (the version I started with), a process for creating stunning type special effects was a bit more tedious than it is today. To generate metal was a drawn-out process that took a long time to achieve and usually had mediocre results. Five versions of Photoshop have arrived on the scene since those early days, and fortunately tools have been added to Photoshop over the course of those years and versions that make text effects such as metal much easier to create in a shorter amount of time.

The technique I am about to demonstrate is simply one way to create metal from scratch starting with a blank document in Photoshop, and then use it for adding a metallic look to your text. As with many Photoshop techniques, this is only one of the processes that will allow you to create metal. Which technique works best is relative to the artist you ask. It seems in this industry we all have our own way of creating metal or glass or plastic. Often the techniques used will depend on the type of metal you are trying to create or the amount of realism you're trying to generate. Again, it's all relative, but this is one way you can use a combination of Photoshop tools to generate metallic type.

Start by creating a blank document 9 inches wide by 5 inches high, at a resolution of 300 pixels per inch. Set the Background Contents to White and click OK (see Figure 3.46).

For some added flair, draw a gradual black-to-white gradient through the image, from the top left to the bottom right. Set black as the foreground color and, with a large thick font, type some text. In this example, I've set my font size to 250px. Later I will be placing this on a space-themed background, so the word *space* will play well to the end effect (see Figure 3.47). Click on the type layer so that the name appears in the layer (see Figure 3.48).

Layer styles are excellent for getting started on the path toward metal. The problem a lot of people have when they create or try to create metal effects with type is that they

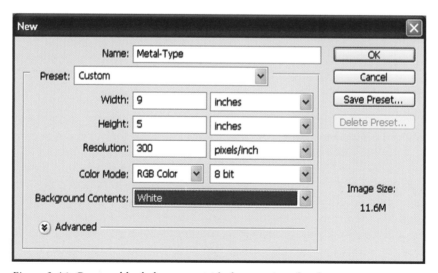

Figure 3.46: Create a blank document with these settings for the text.

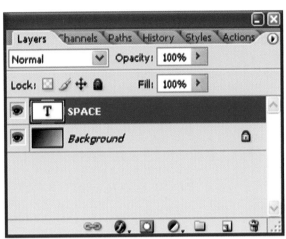

Figure 3.47: Large black text over a gradual black-to-white gradient background

Figure 3.48: Space—the final frontier

rely wholly on styles to get their results. True, styles will take you a long way toward creating realistic metal, allowing you to apply bevels, shadings, contours and so forth. Styles serve as a good foundation, but the following technique will take things a bit further than mere styles.

With the text layer selected, click the "Add layer style" icon at the bottom of the Layers palette. When the Layer Style dialog box pops up, select Bevel And Emboss from the left-hand selections.

When I work with styles, as a general rule I'll start with the Bevel And Emboss settings even before I apply color or anything else. In a sense it works like creating a foundation of the building before construction of the walls and interior begins. The bevel allows you to establish how lighting and shadows will affect the face and borders of the text at a foundational level.

Figure 3.49 shows a complete shot of the Bevel And Emboss settings portion of the Layer Style dialog box. This capture no longer has the default settings resident, as they have been changed to reflect the foundation for the metal text effect.

This is in no way set in stone and may need to be altered later, but right now represents a good start. The settings to change at this point are as follows:

Depth	460%
Size	18px
Use Global Light	Unchecked
Altitude	25°
Anti-aliased	Checked

With these settings, the type begins its journey to metal. Figure 3.50 shows the effect of altering the bevel on the text, particularly on the edges. They begin to acquire a reflective quality.

In the Bevel And Emboss area, there is an icon labeled Gloss Countour that appears as a small version of the Curves dialog box. This setting allows you to apply a contour to the text, which affects how light plays on the surface and edges. Clicking the small arrow next to

Figure 3.49: Initial Bevel And Emboss settings of the Layer Style dialog box

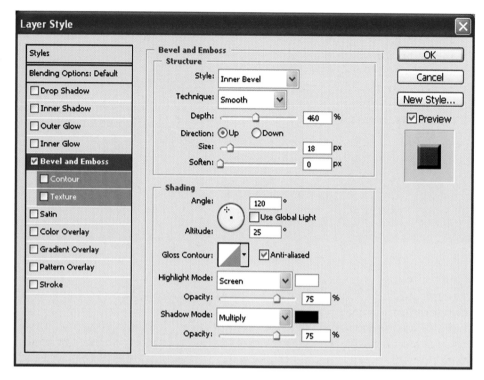

Figure 3.50: The type is beginning to take on the characteristics of operating in three-dimensional space.

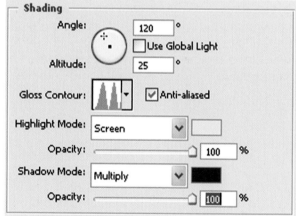

Figure 3.51: Additional adjustments to the Bevel And Emboss settings

the Gloss Contour window opens a small icon-view menu where you may select additional contours. To help with the metal effect, select the Ring-Double contour in this window.

To further aid the metal effect, change the Highlight color to a very light gray, and the Shadow color to a dark gray, not quite black. Set the opacity for both the Highlight and Shadow to 100%. See Figure 3.51.

You will now quickly step through a series of Layer Style adjustment settings. It would take pages to explain each in detail, so I ask that you make the adjustments without the long

explanations, instead looking to the effect each setting has on the text and seeing how they play
together to generate the metallic shine.

Select Satin from the left-hand Styles menu list.
Change the Blend Mode color to light blue. Open the
Contour and choose the Gaussian preset (see
Figure 3.52), and then enter the following settings:

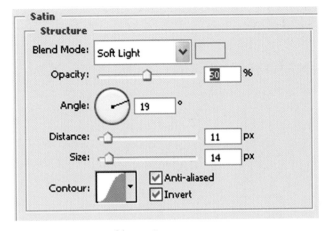

Blend Mode	Soft Light
Opacity	50%
Angle	19–20%
Distance	11px
Size	14px
Anti-aliased	Checked
Invert	Checked

Figure 3.52: Text in blue satin

Another setting that will help change the text
to metal is the Gradient Overlay. This operates like a standard gradient application to a
degree, but simply affects the text. Generally a gray-to-white variant gradient works best for
metal, and Photoshop has one that works well.

Select the Gradient Overlay setting from the left-hand Styles list. Click the small arrow
to the right of the gradient, and then the small arrow in the upper-right corner of the Gradient Picker that appears. From here you can choose to load additional gradient sets by selecting Load Gradients. Find the gradients that shipped with Photoshop in the Photoshop folder
(it should come up by default if you have not changed these settings previously) and choose
Metals.grd. Click Load, and the gradients in that gradient set will be available in the Gradient Picker. Open the gradients again and click the gradient labeled Silver when you place the
mouse over it. It will be a gray-to-white-to-gray-to-white-to-gray variation. Set up the rest of
the Gradient Overlay settings as follows:

Blend Mode	Normal
Opacity	60%
Style	Linear
Align With Layer	Checked
Angle	90°
Scale	100%

How is your text looking so far? It should be gradually becoming more metallic. The
Layer Style dialog box also allows you to add a Stroke to the text, but you are not restricted
to simply using a color: you may also stroke an outline around the text by using a pattern or
gradient. Select the Stroke settings from the left side of the dialog box. Change the gradient
to the Silver one used in the previous step, and alter the rest of the settings as follows:

Size	6px
Position	Outside
Blend Mode	Normal
Fill Type	Gradient
Gradient	Silver
Style	Linear
Angle	90°
Scale	100%

At this point, the type has taken on a decidedly metallic quality, thanks to a few adjustments to the Layer Style settings. Keep in mind that the actual pixels of the layer have not been altered (*yet!*). While the Layer Style dialog box is still open, click New Style to save these settings for later use. You will be able to apply these with a click of the mouse to any text, photo frame, button, or what have you. Try altering the settings a bit (not now, but later), and save additional variations on this metallic theme. After you have a few, save the Layer Style set to your hard disk, and you will be able to load and use them at any time.

After you have the style saved, click OK to apply the style to the text and close the Layer Style dialog box. Your type will closely resemble that seen in Figure 3.53.

You can further enhance the metallic effect with a series of nondestructive adjustment layers. *Nondestructive* simply means the adjustments are applied to a mask rather than altering the pixels in a layer.

For instance, let's apply a simple Levels adjustment. First, make a selection in the shape of the text by ⌘/Ctrl+clicking the type layer. On the bottom of the Layers palette, click the Add Adjustment Layer icon and select Levels from the menu. To get a more enriched color variation in the metal, it needs to be darkened a bit. Click on the left slider and move it toward the center, as seen in Figure 3.54, and click OK.

Figure 3.53: Type is well on its way to metal, simply by adding Layer Style settings.

Figure 3.54: Adjust the Levels with an adjustment layer to darken the text.

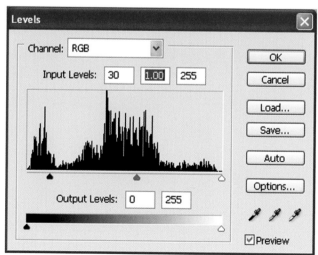

Remember when you changed the Gloss Contour in the Layer Style dialog box? A curve with a similar pattern will help enhance the reflections on the metal. ⌘/Ctrl+click the type layer again to generate the type selection, and again click the "Add Adjustment Layer" icon at the bottom of the Layers palette. This time select Curves and add/manipulate points on the curve to resemble Figure 3.55. Keep an eye on your type and watch as the metal becomes more enhanced. Click OK to close the Curves dialog box. Your type should closely resemble that seen in Figure 3.56.

To remove a bit of the color across the image, you can use a Hue/Saturation adjustment layer. Add one to the image, reducing the Saturation to −33 or so, leaving Hue and Lightness unchanged.

The last adjustment layer to apply for this tutorial is Brightness/Contrast. Select your type again and create a Brightness/Contrast adjustment layer (see Figure 3.57). Watch the type as you move the sliders, until you are happy with the shine on your metal type. You may judge this setting for yourself.

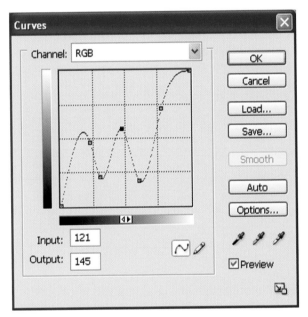

Figure 3.55: A Curves adjustment layer makes the metal shine.

Figure 3.56: Metal type with color reflections

Figure 3.57:
Brightness/
Contrast helps
the metal shine.

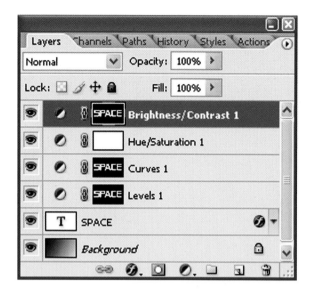

Figure 3.58:
Metallic oiled
type without
destroying or
altering the text
layer

Click OK when you are happy with the metal your text has become. Figure 3.58 shows the end result of the adjustments. The cool thing about this is you did not have to rasterize the text at any time: all of the settings used to go from plain black text to lustrous metal were nondestructive, whether as a layer style or an adjustment layer. What does that give you? Well, you have maintained the ability to select and change font characteristics (size, spacing) or select the text and change the font to something entirely different. You can even type new words, maintaining the metal effect all the while.

Let's apply this photo text by placing it on a somewhat more vibrant background. Open the image **Space.jpg**. Return to the type document and create a duplicate (Image → Duplicate). Render the background invisible on the duplicate and merge all the visible layers. Then copy the merged layer and paste it into the **Space.jpg** document. You can then move the type around the document with the Move tool or arrow keys, as I've done in Figure 3.59.

Figure 3.59: The metal type has a new home.

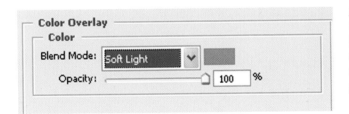

*Figure 3.60:
Color Overlay
helps match the
metal reflections
to the back-
ground colors.*

You can additionally tweak the text in this document, allowing it to take on the overall color of the purple/blue background primaries. To do this, simply select the pasted-in text layer and open the Layer Style dialog box again. Select Color Overlay; change the Blend Mode for the overlay to Soft Light; and change the color to a purple, pink, or blue (see Figure 3.60). Click OK.

The final image is seen in Figure 3.61.

Figure 3.61: Metal type in digital space

As I mentioned before, this is only one variation out of literally hundreds for creating metal type. If you find these sorts of effects of interest, then I encourage you to delve into the layer styles, using them with curves and even lighting effects. Often just a few slight variations in style settings render drastically different results.

Generating Plastic from Scratch

The same set of tools (layer styles) that started you on your way toward metal type are also extremely useful in generating glass and plastic effects. I've intentionally placed these two techniques together not simply for continuity, but also so you can see how strikingly similar the style settings are between metal and plastic.

For this effect, start with a new blank document filled with white as you did at the beginning of the preceding technique. Insert large black text in a new layer. For this plastic effect, I'm going to use a fat, rounded font to reflect the mood of rounded plastic I'm trying to convey (see Figure 3.62).

After the font is present and its layer selected, click the Add Layer Style icon at the bottom of the Layers palette and select Bevel And Emboss. As with the metal effect, the bevel and lighting/shadow attached to the settings in this area of the Layer Style dialog box will establish a solid foundation for the plastic effect. Figure 3.63 shows this dialog box with the Bevel And Emboss settings used to create foundational plastic.

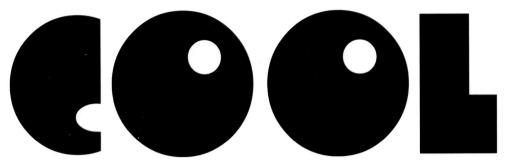

Figure 3.62: A large rounded font will add to the final plastic effect.

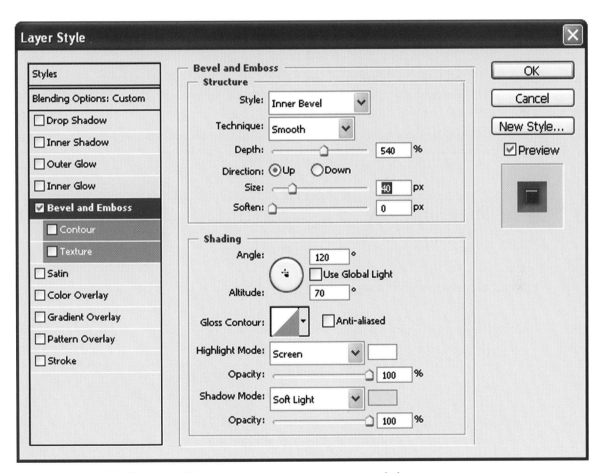

Figure 3.63: Bevel And Emboss will start you on your way to creating cool plastic type.

The default settings for Bevel And Emboss, as with the metal text, need to be altered in order to get a clear plastic shine:

Style	Inner Bevel
Technique	Smooth
Depth	500–550%
Direction	Up
Size	40px
Soften	0px
Angle	120°
Use Global Light	Unchecked
Altitude	70°
Gloss Contour	Linear
Anti-aliased	Unchecked
Highlight Mode	Screen
Highlight Color	White
Highlight Opacity	100%
Shadow Mode	Soft Light
Shadow Color	Light Blue
Shadow Opacity	100%

With these settings, particularly the altitude change to 65–70 degrees, the raised edges of the bevel become clearly reflective as seen in Figure 3.64.

Another setting available to get you on your way to plastic type is the Gradient Overlay. Color Overlay works well if you want your type to have a single primary color, but the gradient allows for multiple colors across the face of the type. Rather than creating a new gradient from scratch this time, select Gradient Overlay from the Styles settings and open the available gradients. Select Orange-Yellow-Orange, one of the default gradients already available to you (see Figure 3.65). Use the following settings.

Blend Mode	Normal
Opacity	100%
Gradient	Orange-Yellow-Orange
Reverse	Unchecked
Style	Linear
Align With Layer	Checked
Angle	125°
Scale	100%

One thing to consider when creating plastic is the transparency factor. If the type you want to create is going to have any transparency, the light will play a bit differently on and inside the object than it would if it were a solid, nontransparent piece. In other words, the inside edges of the text will be lighter than they would be if it were a piece of wood, metal, or even nontransparent plastic.

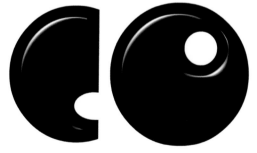

Figure 3.64: Altering the Bevel And Emboss settings can make the type highly reflective and take on plastic or glassy characteristics.

To further aid in tricking the eye, you can apply a subtle Inner Glow to softly radiate around the edges, furthering the plastic/semitransparent illusion. Select Inner Glow from the Styles list and enter the following settings:

Blend Mode	Soft Light
Opacity	75%
Noise	0
Solid Color	Checked, Light Yellow
Technique	Softer
Source	Edge
Choke	0
Size	70px
Contour	Linear
Anti-aliased	Checked or unchecked
Range	50%
Jitter	0

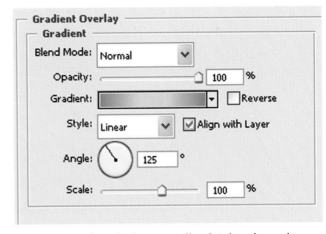

Figure 3.65: A bit of color, especially a bright color such as orange or yellow, adds to the effect.

How is that plastic looking thus far? Figure 3.66 shows the type at this stage in the process.

Now the opacity can be worked with to apply transparency to the type. To judge the amount of transparency being applied, you should have something in the background other than stark white. Open the image **blastoff.jpg**. With both the type image and **blastoff.jpg** open, you can select the text image and click on the type layer. Drag that layer over to the **blastoff.jpg** image. You can then select the Move tool or use the arrow keys to position the type on the new image.

To reduce transparency of the type layer, you may move the Opacity slider to 90% in the Layers palette, or open the Layer Style dialog box again and select Blending Options at the top of the list. Change the Blend Mode to Luminosity.

The plastic type at 90% opacity should still retain almost all of its reflective qualities but allow you to see the image faintly through the text, as seen in Figure 3.67.

At this point the plastic is effectively complete, although reducing the opacity has a tendency to make the type appear too light. This can be tackled with styles in a couple of ways.

Figure 3.66: Plastic type thus far

You can highlight the edges with an Outer Glow (see Figure 3.68), add a Stroke to outline the text (Figure 3.69), and darken the type a bit while maintaining the transparent quality with the Satin setting (Figure 3.70). The variables for enhancing the effect are limited only by your experience with layer styles themselves.

As with the metal text in the previous tutorial, the plastic type was achieved without altering the text layer itself. The type can be selected and changed, resized, warped, and so forth to fit your specific project. Remember to save the layer style when you are finished adjusting your settings by clicking New Style while the Layer Style dialog box is open, then apply the style to the text by clicking OK. The final plastic type image can be seen in Figure 3.71.

I hope you have enjoyed this little jaunt into the realm of special effects. As you move through the following chapters, you will find more project-based sections, somewhat in Chapter 4, "Techniques for Artistic Effects," and full throttle in Chapter 5. You may never have a need to generate chrome spheres or steel type, but the techniques you learned in this chapter will be seen again, albeit applied in other ways. Special effects are fun, but for a right-brainer they are mere stepping stones to greater creations.

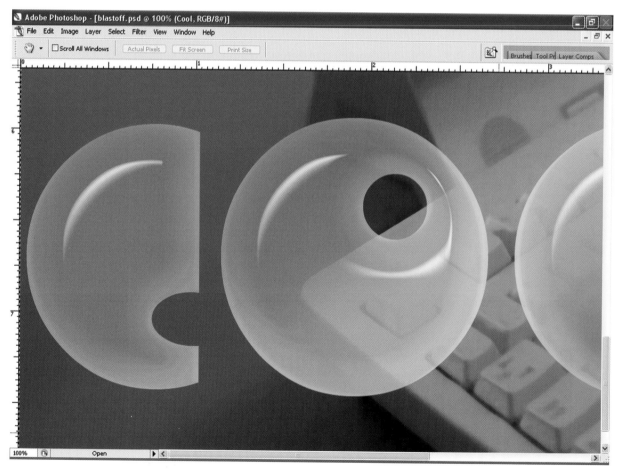

Figure 3.67: The image behind the text will be faintly visible, while the text retains the plastic reflections.

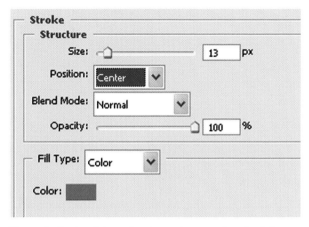

Outer Glow
Structure
Blend Mode: Screen
Opacity: 75 %
Noise: 0 %

Elements
Technique: Softer
Spread: 0 %
Size: 35 px

Quality
Contour: ☐ Anti-aliased
Range: 50 %
Jitter: 0 %

Figure 3.68: An Outer Glow helps to subtly define the edges of the text against the background.

Stroke
Structure
Size: 13 px
Position: Center
Blend Mode: Normal
Opacity: 100 %
Fill Type: Color
Color:

Figure 3.69: Applying a Stroke to the text sharply defines the edges.

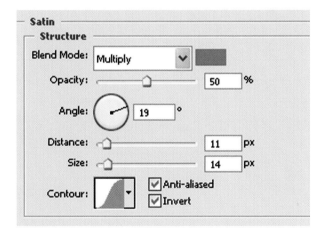

Satin
Structure
Blend Mode: Multiply
Opacity: 50 %
Angle: 19 °
Distance: 11 px
Size: 14 px
Contour: ☑ Anti-aliased ☑ Invert

Figure 3.70: Satin can be used to darken the text while retaining transparency.

Figure 3.71: Blastoff!

four

Texture, Color, and Layer Effects

My pocket dictionary *describes* artistry *as an ability attained by study, practice, and observation. I could add* imagination *to that; once the practice is there, the observations made, if there is no imagination, there is only duplication of what surrounds you or inspired you. A true right-brainer will get past this hurdle of imitation and begin creating new forms of art based on old ideas. Likewise, an artist working with Photoshop can create new genres by using tools intended for entirely different purposes. That's what you're going to accomplish in this chapter.*

Using Apply Image: Why I Love It

Nearly every person of an artistic bent has a favorite brush, palette, or tool set that they enjoy working with consistently. A woodworker may have a shop filled with all manner of power tools, yet he may prefer to take the edges off the cabinet he is working on with a trusty old handheld planer. Something about that tool *feels* right, and in his mind his work is enhanced by its implementation in the process of creation.

A while back I found that, as I would produce Photoshop-based tutorials for the National Association of Photoshop Professionals (NAPP, at **www.photoshopuser.com**) or other magazines/websites, I was consistently working with the Apply Image feature at some point in the project. My good friend in the industry, Colin Smith of PhotoshopCafe.com, still ribs me about it on occasion. He's even made the good-natured comment that someday I may actually realize what it is supposed to be used for. In truth, I really don't want to know.

Apply Image, in short, allows the user to blend the layer and channel of one image (called the source) with the layer and channel of the active image (called the target). In a way this works similarly to altering blending modes of layers in a single document, but in my mind Apply Image gives far more satisfying results and much more control over how the two images interact.

Let's get into this "coolest of the cool" feature and see what it can do. In this experiment, you'll use a background texture to bring out even more emotion in a photograph of a woman screaming.

Before you go any further, I have to point out the single most important aspect of Apply Image: both images must have identical pixel dimensions, or this feature will not work. Check the dimensions of your primary photo (pixel width, pixel height); then change the dimensions of the second image to those same settings.

In this demonstration, the woman image **tantrum.jpg** will be the primary, or target, document (see Figure 4.1). The image **texture330.jpg** will be the source (see Figure 4.2).

Ensure that Constrain Proportions is unchecked when you perform the resize operation on **texture330.jpg** (see Figure 4.3).

Figure 4.1:
I think she's having a bad day.

Figure 4.2:
Streaked and
stained with rust

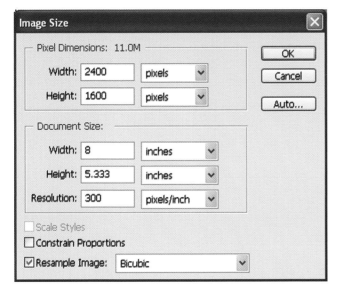

Figure 4.3: Both images must have the same pixel dimensions before Apply Image can be used.

Figure 4.4: Duplicate the Background layer in the primary, or target, document.

After both photos meet the pixel-dimension limitation, you can proceed with the experiment. Duplicate the Background layer in the woman document (see Figure 4.4).

Apply Image is found in the Image menu. Open the Image menu and select Apply Image from the list.

When the dialog box opens, you will see two primary areas: Source and Target. The target in this instance is the duplicate background layer just created in the **tantrum.jpg** document. But what you are concerned with here is the source. If the images do not have identical pixel dimensions, only the target document will appear in the Source menu in the Apply

Figure 4.5: Initial Apply Image settings

Apply Image

Source: texture330.jpg

Layer: Background

Channel: RGB   ☐ Invert

OK

Cancel

☑ Preview

Target: tantrum.jpg (Backgro..., RGB)

Blending: Color Burn

Opacity: 100 %

☐ Preserve Transparency

☐ Mask...

Figure 4.6: Scream, dream, and...

Image dialog box. When both documents have the same pixel dimensions, both will appear in this list. Because you've changed the size of the second document to match the first, open the Source menu and select **texture330.jpg** from the list. You are telling Photoshop to apply the selected layer and channel (in this case the Background layer and RGB channel by default) to the active layer in the woman document.

For this initial experiment, the only nondefault setting you will apply is changing the Blending setting to Color Burn. Apply Image, as you can see, allows you to manipulate blending modes just as you would in the Layers palette, only you are affecting far more than simply the layer (see Figure 4.5). After you click OK, the Apply Image settings are applied to the selected layer in the target document. Figure 4.6 shows the results of this first experiment.

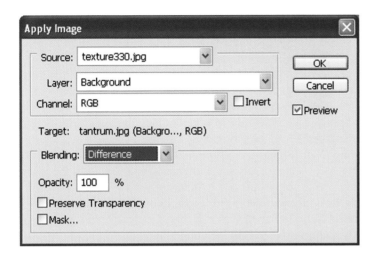

Figure 4.7: Difference mode in Apply Image

Figure 4.8: Changing the blending mode offers a starkly different result.

Granted, this example is a bit dark, and some may even say creepy. I can offer no excuse; much of the art that I create for myself is of a similar bent. Not because I enjoy horrific images, but rather the emotion of a well-done dark art piece. What I would like you to see is that you've achieved this stark, emotional piece of art with only two photos and only two changes to settings: an image resize and a blending mode change in the Apply Image dialog box.

This is just the tip of the iceberg! You could drastically alter an effect simply by changing the blending mode in the dialog box. For instance, if you step back in the history one step, open Apply Image again, and then change the Blending to Difference as seen in Figure 4.7, the resulting image is drastically different from the first rendering (see Figure 4.8).

Applying a Technical Background

Okay, everyone can relax now as we will move on and use Apply Image with an entirely different genre of digital art. Technical backgrounds and desktop images are popular, whether for websites, posters, or personal use. Apply Image is perfect for these types of photos as well.

Open the images **techWoman.jpg** and **techBG.jpg** (see Figures 4.9 and 4.10). Both of these images have already been stylized to a degree: the colors have been changed in the woman image and quite a bit of touch-up has already been performed. In the second photo someone has designed a tech background, probably for use as a splash page for a website.

Remember the rule for using Apply Image: the source document and target document must have the same pixel dimensions. I reiterate this simply because my e-mail tells me many miss this vital step and wonder why they cannot get Apply Image to work.

Ensure that the woman image is active in Photoshop, and choose Image → Apply Image to open the dialog box once again. Retain the settings used previously, with the exception of setting the Source to **techBG.jpg** and changing Blending to Add. You may also opt to play with Scale and Offset: in this instance I set the Scale to 2 and Offset to 1 (see Figure 4.11). Click OK. The resulting image is seen in Figure 4.12.

Figure 4.9: Windswept and purple

Figure 4.10: Digital art background

Figure 4.11: New Apply Image settings

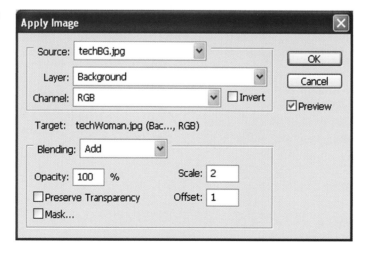

Figure 4.12: Apply Image for digital-themed desktop images

Something to point out at this stage is that you are in no way restricted to simply accepting what Apply Image gives you. For instance, much of the woman's facial features are dominated by the technical background, taking away from her eyes, which are my favorite features. Knowing what you know about Photoshop, you can simply use a layer mask to take some of the digital effect from that area of her face and leave it in the other areas. In Figure 4.13 I created a layer mask and applied a black-to-white radial gradient to the area of her face that I would like to leave untouched. This simply reveals more of the layer beneath and gives a much better mix for the final effect in my opinion. The alteration can be seen in Figure 4.14.

Figure 4.13: Layer masks help tone down Apply Image in specific areas of the photo.

Figure 4.14: The resulting image with the layer mask in place

Applying a Montage Effect

You have seen how Apply Image can be used for dark art and digital art pieces, but this is a powerful tool for standard photographers as well. In the following example I will demonstrate how you can merge two photos for a montage effect popular in all manner of portrait photography, from wedding photos to child photography to yearbooks. The premise is the same as before, but the application is different.

Open the photos **babycarousel.jpg** and **babystare.jpg** (see Figures 4.15 and 4.16). For this example of the astounding and incredible Apply Image feature, you will merge these two photos into a stylized collage.

The first photo shows a child of two or three trying to figure out if he really enjoys being on that wooden horse without Mom or Dad with him in the saddle. I went through this with my own children, so I absolutely love this shot. The second photo shows a younger version of the same lad, probably in his first year of life and wonder.

Before jumping into Apply Image, note that the color palette of these two images is quite a bit different. You can use Match Color to bring both images closer in the overall color scheme prior to the merge. Ensure that the second photo, **babystare.jpg**, is active and choose Image → Adjustments → Match Color. Take a look at Figure 4.17. By setting the Source to the first image, the overall hue or palette of the second photo can be altered to better match the

Figure 4.15: Junior's first carousel ride

Figure 4.16: A Precious Moments pose

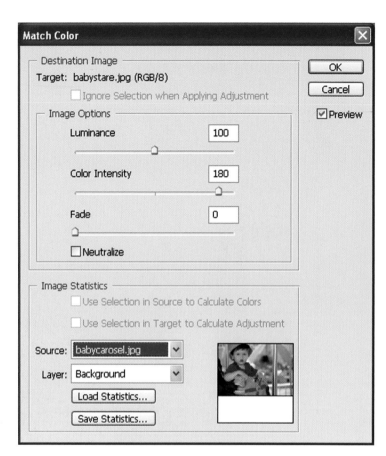

Figure 4.17:
Match Color in
action

Figure 4.18: Resize the second photo and
duplicate the Background layer.

tones of the first. All I've really adjusted is the color intensity after changing the Source to **babycarousel.jpg** and selecting Background for the Layer the change will be applied to.

After it is set up, click OK.

Click on the second photo and duplicate the Background layer (see Figure 4.18). Alter the size of this image to match the pixel dimensions of the first.

With the color changed and the image resized, Apply Image is ready to be applied. Keep the photo **babystare.jpg** active and choose Image → Apply Image. Ensure that the Source is set to the first image and that the Blending setting is Overlay (see Figure 4.19). Again, not a lot needs to be changed for this effect to take place.

The addition of a layer mask, as seen in the previous example, will finish the effect. Rather than use a gradient this time, simply select a black paintbrush and paint over areas of the baby's face where the carousel is showing through (see Figure 4.20).

When you are done with the touch-up in the mask, you will have a montage of the child that any parent or grandparent would be proud of (see Figure 4.21).

This technique has a myriad of applications for photographers, depending on the style of photography and subject matter. I've not even touched on using Apply Image on masks, but teaching the entirety of what Apply Image is capable of is not my intent. I hope that you have seen by my hand and experienced for yourself through these examples what a truly powerful tool this can be, especially in digital art. If you feel you need more practice, keep reading; you will see this powerful feature throughout this text applied in a number of ways.

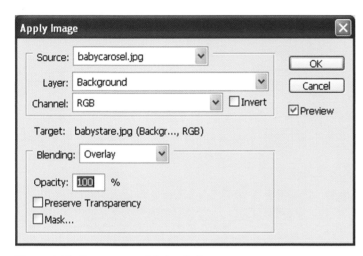

Figure 4.19: Once more with Apply Image

Figure 4.20: Use a layer mask to touch up the image.

Figure 4.21: The final montage

Adding Color to Black-and-White Images

In some circles, colorizing black-and-white images may be almost as controversial as retouching portraits. But we're not talking about Ted Turner and classic Hollywood movies; we're talking about you, the Photoshop artist working with images that might become more interesting when you add some color.

There are two simple ways of adding color to black-and-white: by adding a color cast or by tinting individual colors.

Method 1: Adding a Color Cast

At times, especially when dealing with black-and-white images, just a simple overall color cast can have a striking effect. For this first technique, you will learn how to create a quick tone change on a black-and-white photo.

This technique uses the image **Elderly.jpg** (see Figure 4.22). Please find and open it now.

I love the expression in this image. Even though you are given only a portion of the man's face, the eye carries a definite spark of some emotion or intense scrutiny.

Duplicate the Background layer in the Layers palette. Later you will work with nondestructive adjustment layers, but for this example you'll be working directly on the layer (actually editing the layer pixels) to ensure that both processes are covered. Rename the Background Copy layer **Aged,** as seen in Figure 4.23.

Choose Image → Adjustments → Hue/Saturation. When the Hue/Saturation dialog box opens, select the Colorize check box in the lower-right corner. Then adjust the sliders as seen in Figure 4.24 and click OK.

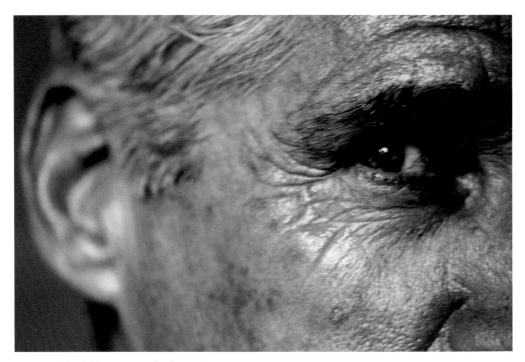

Figure 4.22: "What are you looking at?"

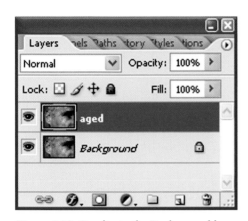

Figure 4.23: *Duplicate the Background layer and rename the duplicate.*

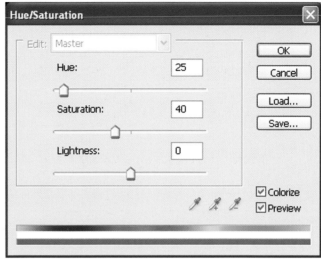

Figure 4.24: *Adjust the Hue/Saturation of the new layer.*

HSB, or Hue, Saturation, and Brightness, are the three fundamental characteristics of color. Hue is the color reflected from or transmitted through an object. Saturation is the strength of that color. Brightness is, of course, how light or dark the color appears. For more information on HSB, refer to the Photoshop Help file on *HSB model*.

This adjustment will give you a general tone resembling sepia (see Figure 4.25). I am not going for an exact sepia (browned) effect, but just want to give an earthier feel to the image.

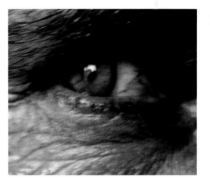

Figure 4.25: *Image resembling sepia (but not quite)*

Painting Selected Areas in a Color Cast

Sometimes one adjustment you make to an image will suggest another. In this case, after I had tinted the image, I decided that painting the eye in a contrasting color would add even more interest. To do that, you'll revisit a technique in Chapter 2, "Techniques for Embellishing Portraits": painting with the Paintbrush tool in Color blending mode. Double-click the foreground color on the toolbar to open the Color Picker dialog box. Find a light brown and click OK.

Select the Paintbrush tool and give it these settings:

Brush: 100
Mode: Color
Opacity: 70%
Flow: 65%

Notice that I'm using a Soft Round feathered brush. The important thing here is, again, to change the blending mode to Color.

In the Aged layer, paint directly over the iris. Painting over the reflections (white) or pupil (black portion) won't matter; in Color blending mode, whites and blacks are not affected. Only the color information in the painted area, other than black or white, will change.

Sometimes, depending on the color and the thickness of the application of the brush, the tone comes out a bit dark. By going over the colored area with the Dodge tool set to Midtones, you can lighten the color a bit. This adds extra life to the eyes; depending on how strongly you apply the tool, the eye can take on a mystical quality, burning with inner life. Select the Dodge tool and set these options:

Brush	44
Range	Midtones
Exposure	32%

Apply the Dodge tool to the irises, brightening the midtones. Don't linger too long in one spot, but just give the tool a general swipe around the perimeter of the pupil.

Occasionally you may desire a more vibrant or shocking color, and a simple reapplication of the Paintbrush tool with a different hue can have a striking effect.

For instance, change the foreground color again, this time using a yellowing green. Select the Paintbrush tool again and, using the same options set up previously, paint over the iris. This setting changes the hue of the eye, contrasting the eye with the overall tone of the rest of the image (see Figure 4.26).

Figure 4.26: Youthful spark in a wizened face

Method 2: Re-creating the Hand-Tinted Look

Not every black-and-white image can be colored by something as basic as a Hue/Saturation adjustment and some painting. Some images require a bit more to bring out natural tones.

I'm not certain this technique renders what you might call natural tones, however. This technique is more in the style of methods used years ago to color photographs of their time. Color film wasn't commonplace 60-plus years ago (yes, I realize that is the understatement of the year), so much of the color seen in old photos was added later. It gives the photo a retro feel, and I love retro.

Take a look at the image **BW-Portrait.jpg** (see Figure 4.27). Is that a cute kid or what? It is somehow hard to envision that this youngster would now most likely be in his seventies.

The first layer you will work on will correct the frame, giving it an aged paper feel. Create two copies of the Background layer and make the topmost copy invisible. Select the layer just above the original background.

I often switch back and forth between creating adjustment layers (which applies the adjustment to all the layers beneath it) and actually applying adjustments directly to a specific layer. If I don't want the adjustment to be destructive, then an adjustment layer works perfectly. If I don't care that the pixels on the layer are altered, or if I don't want the change to apply to the layers beneath, then I may apply the adjustment directly to the layer.

In this instance, you're going to use an adjustment layer. Create a new Hue/Saturation adjustment layer and move the sliders as seen in Figure 4.28. This will give the image a sepia appearance, implying age.

Select the topmost layer; this will be the second duplicate of the background created earlier. Create a mask for the layer. Using a black brush with the opacity for the brush set to 60%, paint around the frame edges in the mask. This will hide the black-and-white frame and reveal the colored frame beneath. The child will remain without color to this point (see Figure 4.29).

If you revealed a portion of the background also, don't worry about it in this case. The overall effect is to be one of age, so having the brown show through on the photo backdrop is permissible. The main goal is that the boy still be grayscale (see Figure 4.30).

You will be making another Hue/Saturation adjustment, but this time to the actual

Figure 4.27: Somebody's grandpa

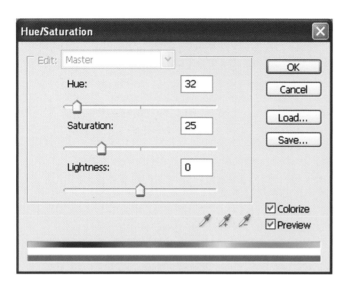

Figure 4.28: Hue/Saturation adjustment

Figure 4.29: Mask away the black-and-white frame.

Figure 4.30: Child in grayscale

layer. Choose Image → Adjustments → Hue/Saturation and enter the values seen in Figure 4.31. Click OK. This is going to give the child some color, albeit faint.

Create a new layer and change the blending mode to Color. As you should be well familiar with by now, select a foreground color for the hair and paint over the hair with the Paintbrush tool in that layer. If the hair appears too well colored, simply lower the opacity of the layer. After the hair has been tinted, change the foreground color again, this time to a tone that will likely match his skin color (see Figure 4.32). In the same layer as the hair color, paint over the skin areas of the child (see Figure 4.33).

Continue coloring in this layer, but change the foreground color to red to add some rose to the boy's cheeks. Switch to a light blue and paint over the irises—you should be well versed in this by now! Note that there may be some bleeding over of color beyond the borders of the hair and so forth. If you take a close look at this style of photograph, that was quite common and adds to the effect (so long as it isn't overdone).

For the final step, add some color to the table. Select a dark brown/red for the foreground color. Create a new layer at the top of the layer stack and set the blending mode to Overlay (see Figure 4.34). Now simply paint over the table surface. Figure 4.35 shows the final image, complete with a newly varnished table and the boy's reflection off the surface.

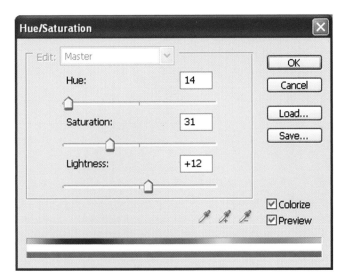

Figure 4.31: Hue/Saturation values—again

Figure 4.32: Coloring the hair and skin

Figure 4.33: Black-and-white slowly comes to life.

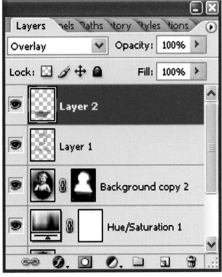

Figure 4.34: Painting the tabletop

*Figure 4.35:
Grandpa's baby
photo, fully
restored*

If you aren't sure what to do with a technique like this, I submit to you that photo restoration and coloring is becoming popular, especially among people of the older generations. You might be able to work a little digital magic and make an elder smile—that is reward in itself. Chances are, though, they will pay you for it as well.

Using Textures and Displacement Maps

Most of the work seen in this book consists of generating photo-realistic effects. Previously in this chapter you used Apply Image and colorizing to create photo-realistic effects. You are now going to add textures and displacement maps to your toolbox. Other areas of this book cover these subjects, to be sure; for this portion I'd like to give them a tighter focus and really show what can be done with each.

Texture photos are an excellent resource for digital art, as seen in the first Apply Image tutorial. They add character that didn't exist previously to photos, especially for dark or grunge effects. Let's say, however, you want an effect performed *on* a texture, rather than *with* a texture. An example of what I mean is the application of paint on a surface where none existed before. Applying color is no difficult task, but getting the paint to conform to the shapes and contours in the texture—well, that takes a little work. Not hard work, mind you, but a process nonetheless. Once again, Photoshop is ready, willing, and able to meet the need.

Open the image **bricks.jpg** (see Figure 4.36).

The filter of choice to get a color or pattern to conform to the contours of the wall is the Displace filter. Displace uses a displacement map consisting of white, black, and gray to produce positive and negative shifts in pixels to the image. For instance, a 0 (zero) value will produce the maximum negative shift, 255 the maximum positive shift, and a gray 128 value will offer no change. You have seen this filter in action once already when you applied the map to the man's skin in Chapter 1, "Tools for Building Your Masterpiece," but another look is warranted, especially for those unfamiliar or unpracticed with its operation. This is one powerful tool to have in your digital toolbox!

Figure 4.36: Another brick in the wall

Figure 4.37: The blue channel will be used as the foundation for the displacement map.

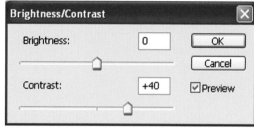

Figure 4.38: Brightness/Contrast is applied to further separate the lights and the darks.

Displacement maps for the type of application you will be using them for are created by using duplicates of channels, or rather a channel, with high contrast between the lights in the darks. In Figure 4.37, I duplicated the blue channel because it gives me the highest contrast. You can select each channel one at a time and judge this yourself visually, which is what I've done here. The channel will now be used to create a displacement map.

With the copy channel selected, a Brightness/Contrast adjustment can be performed on it to further increase the contrast between the lights in the darks. This will give you better displacement because you are moving the values away from the center (128) and toward zero and 255.

Figure 4.38 shows my setting; I have left the Brightness alone but increased the Contrast to +40. The Preview check box is selected to gauge the amount of contrast being applied visually.

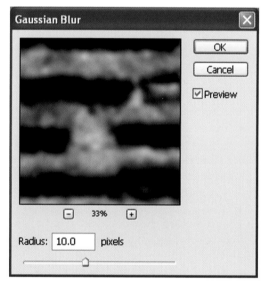

Figure 4.39: Apply a Gaussian blur to the duplicate channel.

The next step employs the Gaussian Blur filter. You will apply this filter to the copy channel to make the blend between whites, grays, and blacks more gradual. As in Figure 4.39, set the Radius of the blur to 10 pixels; the result can be seen in the viewer window when Preview is checked. Not looking for a total blur, you want some details and contours to still be present: they just need to be softened for when Displace is run.

Let's take a quick look at the original wall photo before you go any further (see Figure 4.40). Note the cracks in the wall, the separation of the bricks with the mortar in between, and the variation between the light and dark areas. For this experiment, I will demonstrate how to paint just the bricks without having to paint the mortar or the other lighter surfaces. Is

Figure 4.40: One more look at the wall

this even possible? You bet it is, and it's so simple you won't believe your eyes!

First let's finish the map. The map itself needs to be safe and secure as its own file. With the duplicate blue channel selected, right-click (or navigate via the channel's menu) and select Duplicate Channel. Names are not really important for this example, but if you do this for your own work you may want to name a new channel appropriately. The primary point here is to set the Destination for the Document to New (see Figure 4.41). Click OK. A copy of the channel will appear on the desktop as a new image. Save this image to your hard disk in a place where you can find it shortly, as it will come into use very soon. Also, delete the duplicate blue channel in the original wall photo.

It's time to apply color to this thing. Return to the original document and create a new layer, as shown in Figure 4.42. Fill the layer with a gradient created by using a yellow and gray pattern with no separation between the two colors. Fill the layer diagonally. I'm not going to explain the process of creating a gradient, simply because in this case color doesn't matter and I've demonstrated gradient creation elsewhere in the book. You could use a photo rather than color, so this is just an example.

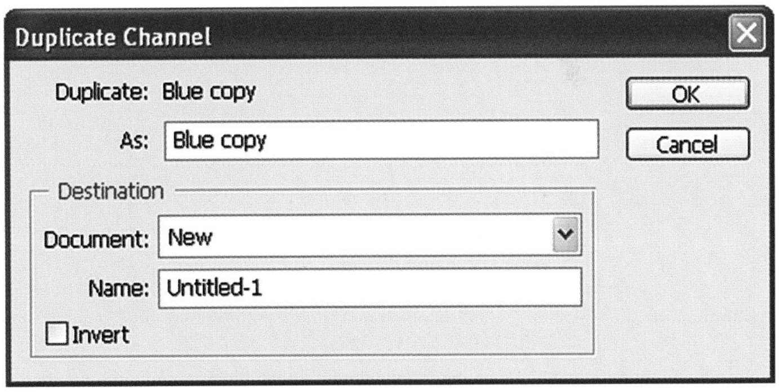

Figure 4.41: The map channel is saved as its own image.

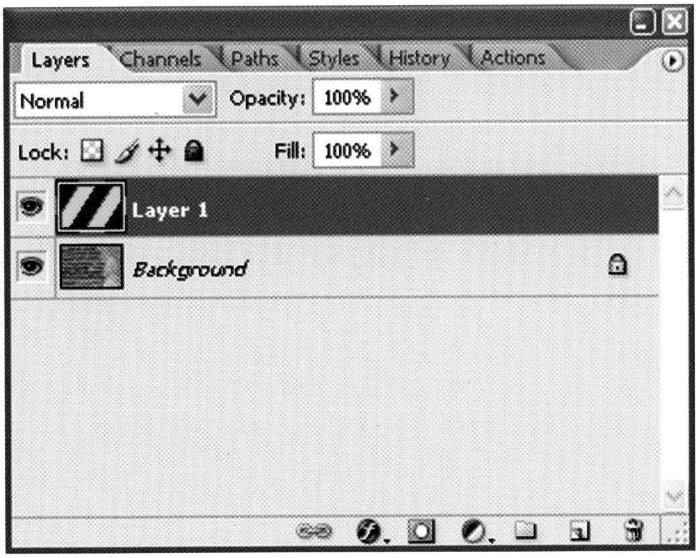

Figure 4.42: A gradient will serve as the paint on the bricks.

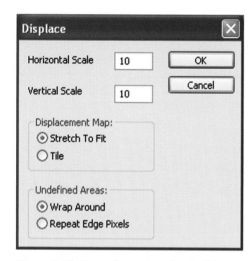

Figure 4.43: Enter the settings for the Displace filter.

Figure 4.44: After the map is applied to the layer, the layer will distort to match the contours and colors of the wall image.

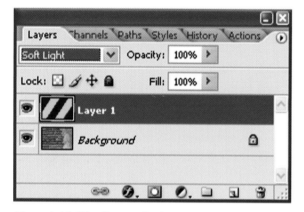

Figure 4.45: Blending mode change

With the layer selected that will be conformed to the shape of the wall (in this case Layer 1), you can go ahead and access the Displace filter. Choose Filter → Distort → Displace. In the dialog box that appears, set the Horizontal Scale to 10 and Vertical Scale to 10. In the Displacement Map section, select Stretch To Fit, and in the Undefined Areas section, select Wrap Around; then click OK (see Figure 4.43). Photoshop will ask you to find the displacement map to use; navigate to the map you just created, select it, and click OK. After you do this, the selected layer will distort based on the color values of the map, from zero to 255, making the pattern appear to conform to the contours of the wall.

After running the Displacement filter and using the map I created on the gradient layer, the straight lines separating my colors and distorted to conform with the lights in the darks in the wall, as seen in Figure 4.44.

Next you'll want to ensure that the wall can be seen beneath the paint. Change the blending mode of Layer 1 to Soft Light to make the bricks visible once again (see Figure 4.45).

The next step in the process concerns wiping away color, or paint, from specific areas of the wall and leaving it on others. For this example I want you to apply yellow paint only to the bricks, and leave the white and gray mortar untouched. I don't want the gray paint, or the gray areas of the gradient, to show up either. The effect I am looking for is of a wall that had yellow bars painted on at one time, but then was covered by the mortar. Over time, the mortar has chipped away, revealing the painted bricks once again.

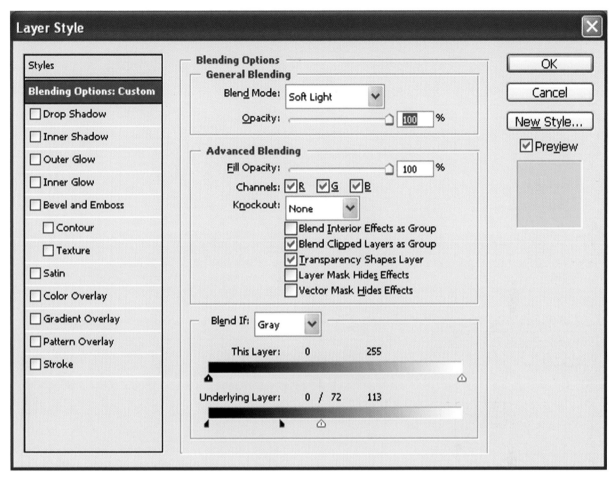

The simplest Photoshop feature that will render the most realistic result, at least in my experience, is Blend If. The Blend If settings are found for each layer in their Layer Styles. To change the Blend If settings for the gradient layer, click on the layer in the Layers palette (it should be active still) and open that layer's Layer Styles. When the Layer Style dialog box opens, select Blending Options at the top of the list on the left-hand side. The Blending Options section in the center of the dialog box will display the Blend Mode (in this case Soft Light, reflecting the setting you changed earlier), the Opacity of the layer, Advanced Blending settings (the Fill Opacity can be seen here also), and then Blend If settings at the bottom.

Whereas the displacement map allows you to distort the layer based on color information, Blend If allows you to manipulate the visibility of colors based on the color information of this layer and the layers beneath. Basically you will be telling Photoshop which colors can be visible and which invisible based on the colors in the layer beneath. Figure 4.46 shows the Layer Style dialog box with Blend If affecting the gray tones. By manipulating the sliders beneath the This Layer field and the Underlying Layer field, you can adjust the visibility of

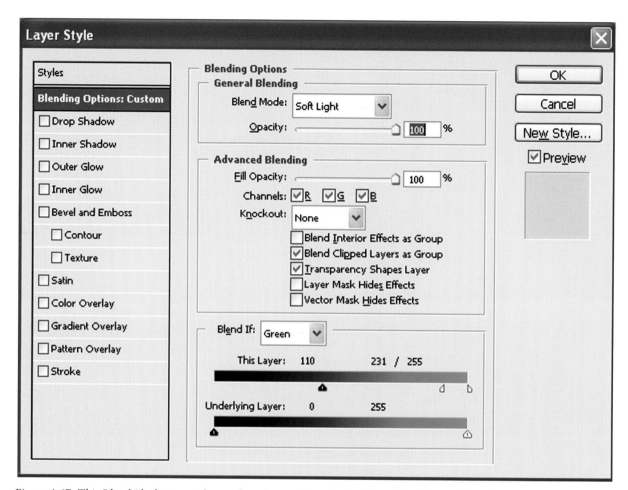

Figure 4.47: This Blend If adjustment leaves the yellow only on the bricks, wiping it away from the mortar.

the gray color in the gradient. To separate the paired sliders, hold down the Option/Alt key and move a single slider with the mouse. The combination you see in this figure effectively lights the gray away in all areas of the layer. The color information is still in the layer—it has simply been rendered invisible by this adjustment.

To retain the yellow but remove it from the mortar, the adjustment seen in Figure 4.47 effectively lights it from the mortar.

Figure 4.48 shows the final image. Note that the paint is primarily on the bricks, with a couple of spots on the mortar, and no trace of gray to be found. Because of the displacement map, the paint conforms to the contours of the break, and the Soft Light blending mode allows you to see the brick beneath the paint. When working for photo-realism, no one filter or technique is going to get satisfying results—99.9% of the time it will take combinations of techniques to get a realistic result. This combination allows you to fool the eye so the viewer will assume that it's natural rather than a fabrication. When you can do that, you'll know the satisfaction that digital artists, in particular photo-realistic artists, thrive on.

Figure 4.48: The mortar has fallen away, revealing an old paint job.

Adding Real-World Texture to Skin

You've seen the result of using displacement maps (and a couple of other tools) for applying paint to a wall in photo-realistic way. Right-brainers are rarely satisfied with simply generating photo-realism of realistic objects. Right-brainers are more prone to stretching the boundaries, creating photo-realism where none should exist. For example, the digital artists who visit websites such as deviantART (**www.deviantart.com**) use texturing on the human form to evoke emotion or shock value from their work.

In this example, I will demonstrate one way to apply real-world textures to human skin. For those of you with no interest in dark art, consider this exercise in the imagination. You might easily perform the same technique by applying steel textures to a glass bottle, aging a billboard, or what have you.

Open the images **calm.jpg** and **cracked.jpg** (see Figures 4.49 and 4.50).

On the first image, select the channel with the best separation/contrast between the lights and the darks as performed in the previous tutorial, and create a displacement map. Remember to apply the blur as you did before (see Figure 4.51), and save a duplicate of the new channel to the hard disk. Delete the extra channel from the woman image, and select the RGB channel to return it to normal (see Figure 4.52).

Figure 4.49: A serene close-up

Figure 4.50: Cracked earthen texture

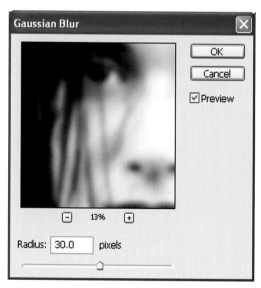

Figure 4.51: Gaussian blur for the displacement map

Copy and paste the texture photo into the woman's document. Apply the Displace filter by using the displacement map just created with the Displace settings seen in Figure 4.53.

Let's try something a bit different before you make the leap to the final image. With the textured layer displaced and ready to be affixed to the face, you have some room for experimentation. First, duplicate the texture layer and shut off the topmost version. Next, select Layer 1 and change the blending mode to Pin Light as seen in Figure 4.54. Select the top layer, turning it on, and change the blending mode to Difference. Reduce the opacity a bit to 65–70%, as seen in Figure 4.55. Watch the change the image makes when you apply these two settings.

You'll note that the hair looks a bit strange, so create a layer mask in the Difference layer and paint over the hair areas with black.

Now make a Curves adjustment layer and create a curve similar to the one seen in Figure 4.56. The result should look like Figure 4.57.

Figure 4.52: Return the woman's document to its original state.

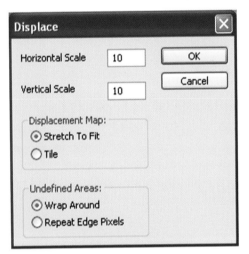

Figure 4.53: Displace filter settings

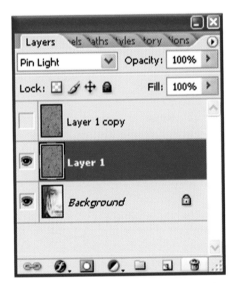

Figure 4.54: Set the blending mode for the first texture layer to Pin Light.

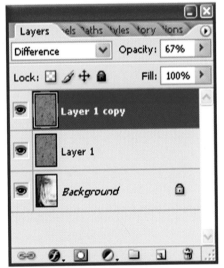

Figure 4.55: Turn on the second texture layer, change the blending mode to Difference, and reduce the opacity.

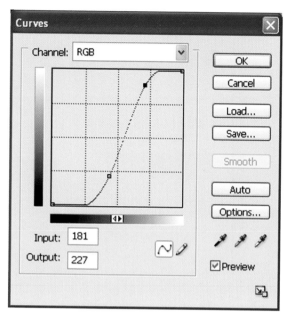

Figure 4.56: A quick Curves adjustment lightens the lights and darkens the darks.

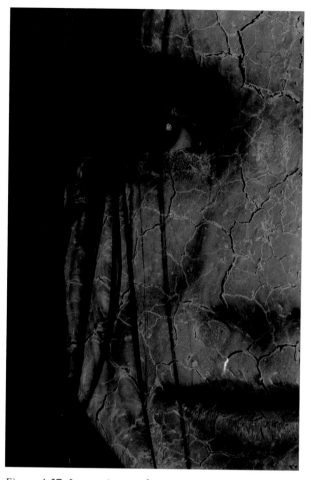

Figure 4.57: Interesting results

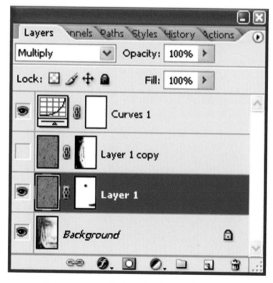

Figure 4.58: Manipulating the layers for an entirely different effect

As I've demonstrated before, a technique such as this is usually only a couple of quick steps away from something entirely different—but equally interesting as or even better than the first rendering. Because you started this adventure attempting to combine texture with skin semi-photo-realistically, the next step will get you to that destination.

Shut off the Difference layer, as it won't be required at this point in the process (see Figure 4.58). Select the first texture layer and change the blending mode to Multiply. This will affix the texture to the skin. When I'm working with this technique, I tend to stay away from texturing the "soft areas" of the face, such as the eyes and mouth. Again, a mask with black paint applied to these areas will wipe the texture away, revealing the unaltered lips and eye beneath. Figure 4.59 shows the resulting textured face.

You could also use the mask to remove the texture from the hair if you so choose; I will leave that up to you.

Figure 4.59: Texture mapped to the face

As I close this section on textures and displacement maps, I want to leave you with three quick variations that I created for personal enjoyment and that fit the same theme (see Figures 4.60, 4.61, and 4.62). All three images use the same techniques as seen in this section, with only slight variations in technique applied to fill out the final piece. If you have no desire to texture faces, I can understand. Simply keep in mind that these same processes can be used in any number of ways. The application is up to your imagination.

Figure 4.60 : The Face of Nature

Figure 4.61:
Marbled

Figure 4.62:
Tattered and torn

Creating Brush Effects by Using Photo Elements

One of the ways many Photoshop artists are dressing up or "grunging out" their art is with the use of brushes created by using photographs or specific color range selections from photographs. Creating and saving paintbrushes in Photoshop couldn't be easier: you need only an open image or a selection in an image to snag those textures, lines, or color ranges, and then simply save the selection or image as a custom brush preset.

To demonstrate this technique, please open the image **balance.jpg** (see Figure 4.63).

With this image you could create a brush of the entire photo, in which case the texture of the paper would be included in the brush. However, for this example you will simply make a brush of the text. You can do this in a number of ways, but the easiest is probably to select the color range of the text as is generally uniform across the entire document.

Choose Select → Color Range. When the Color Range dialog box appears, click on the first eyedropper in the lower-right corner of the dialog box and then take a sample directly on the photo of the dark text color. Just move the mouse to a letter and click with amounts. The area to be selected will appear in the dialog box as white, with the unselected areas remaining black. If you'd like to add to the selection, hold down the Shift key and take another sample. Rather than creating a new selection, more will be added to the existing selection (see Figure 4.64).

After you are happy with the selection seen in the dialog box, click OK. At this point, to get a clean looking brush and to see exactly what a brush will look like, invert the selection and fill that area with white. Next, deselect and you can see your future brush (see Figure 4.65).

Figure 4.63: Balance sheet

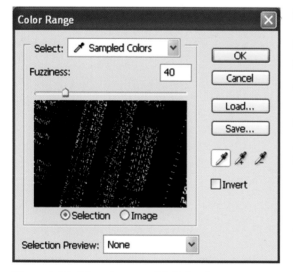

Figure 4.64: Select the text with Color Range.

Figure 4.65: Preview of the brush

To finalize the brush, you need only define it. Choose Edit → Define Brush Preset. A dialog box will appear and ask you to name the brush. You may either use the document name, which comes up by default in the Name field, or name it yourself and click OK (see Figure 4.66). The brush will now appear at the bottom of the Brushes palette.

Figure 4.66: Name and save the Custom brush.

Open the document **news.jpg**, seen in Figure 4.67. You may now click on the Paintbrush tool, and select your new brush from the options bar by opening the loaded brushes, scrolling to the bottom, and clicking on it. In Figure 4.68, I have used the brush just created and, with black paint and a brush opacity of 40%, painted the type from the first document over the newspaper in the second. It's that easy!

With ingenuity, imagination, and experimentation, digital artists

Figure 4.67: Newspaper photo

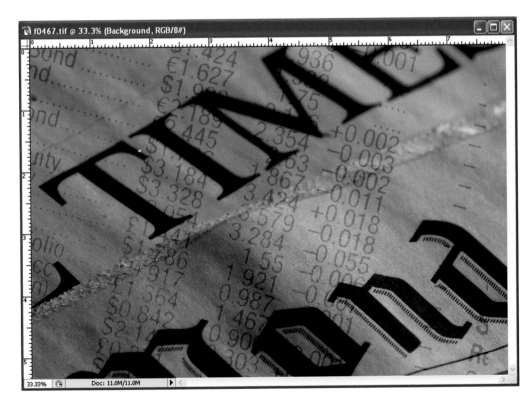

Figure 4.68: Paintbrush Overlay

Figure 4.69: Three dollars for a haircut???

Figure 4.70: Age and damage applied to an old photograph

have been utilizing brushes to age or otherwise add character to their photography for a variety of purposes. As mentioned, using a textured photo converted to a brush is a great way to add age lines to an otherwise unblemished photo. Grunge effects for posters or advertising is another great use for photo-brushes that has become popular.

As a parting demonstration, Figure 4.69 shows an old photograph that has stood the test of time rather well, being very well preserved from the ravages of age. With a simple texture brush is a variations in color when applying the paint. Figure 4.70 shows the same image after a couple of brush applications. Now the photo appears to have aged poorly, suffering from moisture stains and age as is the case with many old family photographs.

Lightening, Darkening, and Coloring

You can alter photographs of people, objects, animals, and scenery but that is certainly not the extent of what Photoshop is capable of correcting or, as in the previous tutorial, damaging. The art of the great masters can be corrected, cleaned, and enhanced also. Certainly you cannot use Photoshop to dress up the actual Mona Lisa, but you can definitely use it to dress up a copy with lightening, darkening, and coloring techniques that Photoshop has ready for you to use.

Open the image **chapel.jpg** (see Figure 4.71).

Figure 4.71: Painting from a master, with a nasty blue cast

Here is a small sample of one of the most famous paintings on the planet. Let's see if you can dress this up a tad. Not having visited the Vatican, I can't actually say whether the Sistine Chapel has a blue cast to its ceiling. However, this photograph of that ceiling clearly has a blue cast. The color in the hands, the color of the background—let's perform a correction that would hopefully make Michelangelo proud. Duplicate the Background layer (see Figure 4.72).

In this step you're going to do something a bit different. You are going to touch on something you haven't worked with in this book yet: the Channel Mixer. This will allow you to get better contrast by turning the layer that you're working on into a high-quality grayscale version of the original. You can physically set the percentage contribution for each color channel. With the Channel Mixer, you're not actually adding color information or altering color information in your image, but rather are adding and subtracting grayscale data from a source channel to a targeted channel. The result is a crisper grayscale version of the photo, which translates to lighter lights, darker darks, and more vibrant color.

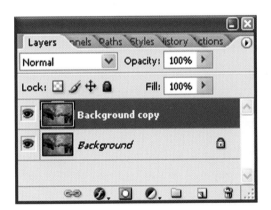

Figure 4.72: Duplicate the Background layer.

Okay, that may seem a bit vague; let's just walk through the process and see what happens. Choose Image → Adjustments → Channel Mixer and open the dialog box. Select the Monochrome check box in the lower-left corner and set the Output Channel to gray. Increase the amount of Red in the Source Channels section to 90%, Green to 30%, and Blue to 28%. Leave Contrast at zero and click OK (see Figure 4.73). You now have a monochrome, or grayscale, version of the painting in that Background Copy layer. Set the blending mode to Overlay.

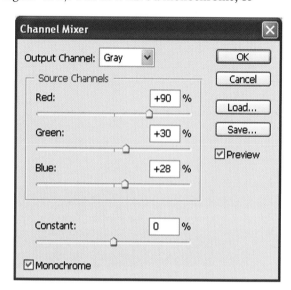

Take a look at Figure 4.74. This simple adjustment and blending mode change has increased intensity of the color and definition of lines tenfold. By adding a new layer with the blending mode set to Color, you can enhance the color of the skin as you did in Chapter 2 colorizing hair by selecting skin tone and applying it over the hands. Changing the blending mode of that Background Copy layer to Normal (see Figure 4.75) will wipe away the blue on the background and leave you with your own version of this famous painting, with just the hands in color and the backdrop in shades of black, white, and gray (see Figure 4.76).

Figure 4.73: Working with the Channel Mixer

Figure 4.74: Whites, darks, and color enhanced

I have demonstrated enhancing a painting in this example, but this technique most certainly works on photographs as well. Remember to focus not on what is being worked on, but on how you might use these techniques in other genres or in areas of correction specific to your interest or need. Photoshop is great that way. After you have a mastery of a technique, or even a rudimentary knowledge of a process of correction or alteration, Photoshop releases creative license to you. Digital art is not about the software, but about you realizing the vision in your mind.

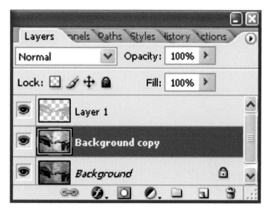

Figure 4.75: Skin colorization and background color removal

Figure 4.76: A new color palette for an old, famous classic

five

Effects in the Real World

As children, *we all looked up at the clouds and saw misty ships, crocodiles, or riders on horseback. It may seem fanciful, but to me these cloud shapes are examples of how patterns repeat in nature. Over the past few years, the emerging science of fractals—colorful patterns generated by mathematical formulae that repeat endlessly—has begun to show us the significance of these patterns. All things physical seem to be tied to similar mathematical formulae.*

Our world consists of similar (in many cases identical) patterns and formulae, whether calculating the rotation of solar systems around a central point or studying the arc of a single rotation of a strand of DNA. The universe is a wondrous combination of fractals built with a specific design in mind, using math as the foundation to tie all things together and dictate the boundaries that keep everything in operation. To those who stand too close to the canvas, it may seem chaotic and random. Stepping back, one can see the entire picture and begin to appreciate what the designer, as artist, envisioned when the first stroke of paint was lovingly applied.

Symmetrical Landscaping

I'm of the mind that patterns in nature are hardly random, but demonstrate incredible order rather than chaotic happenstance. The laws of thermodynamics tell us that the universe is gradually decaying to a more chaotic state, but Photoshop can assist digital artists in creating order in their landscapes. In Chapter 1, "Tools for Building Your Masterpiece," you experimented with masks applied to a human model to attain exaggerated symmetry. What happens when these same techniques (or strikingly similar techniques, at least) are applied to nature?

Before proceeding, let me make a personal aside. Although the technique you are about to perform is also seen elsewhere in this book (albeit applied differently), I'm including it here as well to reiterate a point: applying a process to varied scenes, models, and image types can produce entirely different artistic ends. The focus is not on the process, but rather on using Photoshop imaginatively and perhaps helping to get those creative juices flowing. Some people prefer working with a human canvas, and some nature. This technique is for the latter photographer.

 Please open the image **Horizon.tif**. Figure 5.1 shows the scene at the start: a beautiful sunset. The photo appears to have been taken shortly after a cloudburst. The storm has passed, and you can almost smell the damp grass and moist earth.

Figure 5.1: Sunset after rain

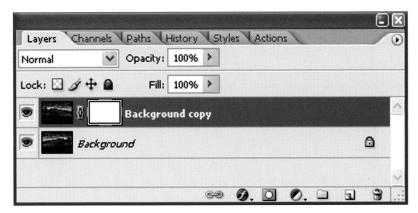

Figure 5.2: Add a layer mask to the flipped layer.

To add a bit of exaggerated symmetry, the picture can be folded over onto itself (as with the model in Chapter 1) with the help of a gradient applied to a layer mask.

Duplicate the Background layer. With the new layer selected, choose Edit → Transform → Flip Horizontal. After the layer has been flipped, click the Add Layer Mask icon at the bottom of the Layers palette (see Figure 5.2).

If you saved the gradient created during the process in Chapter 1, you may use it again here. If not, select the Gradient tool and create a black-to-white gradient with a 2% separation in the center, moving the Black color stop to 49% and the White color stop to 51%. This 2% separation allows for a narrow blended area between the colors. If both were set to 50%, the gradient would create a distinct line through the center of the photo when applied to the mask. The gradual transition from black to white, although narrow, will fool the eye just enough to suit our purposes here. To see the gradient settings, take a look at Figure 5.3. After the gradient is created, you may click New to add it to the loaded gradients and then click OK.

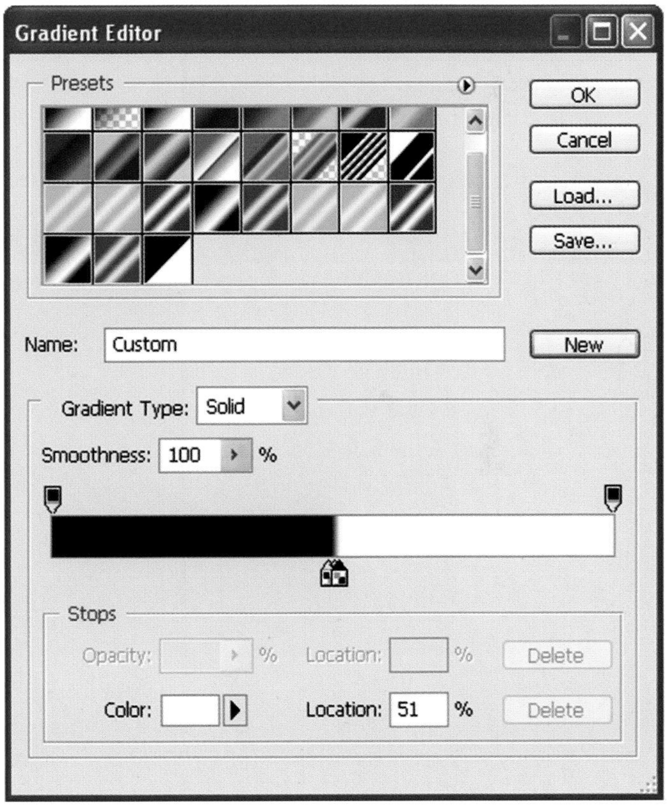

With the gradient created and selected, ensure that the mask is active and draw the gra-

Figure 5.3: Create and save the gradient.

dient across the mask, from the left edge of the photo to the right. Holding down the Shift key will allow you to keep a steady hand and maintain a straight gradient (see Figure 5.4).

Figure 5.4:
Apply the gradient to the mask.

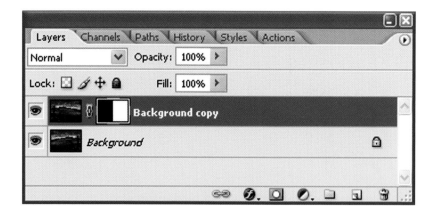

Figure 5.5:
A new scene revealed

Figure 5.5 shows the result of the gradient applied to the mask, revealing a landscape that is "absolute" in its symmetry. Everything from the clouds to the foreground grass is reflected perfectly. If you look closely and use a bit of imagination, you can almost see faces in the foreground grass!

The original photo had a crossroads-style sign in the foreground that would be an excellent addition to the scene. Also, there is another landscape alternative that you could use. To take a look at it, simply invert the colors in the mask (Image → Adjustments → Invert). By swapping the black and white in the mask (see Figure 5.6), a new scene is revealed. The sign is again present, and now a rough stone-bordered path appears to be leading to a cloven hill (see Figure 5.7).

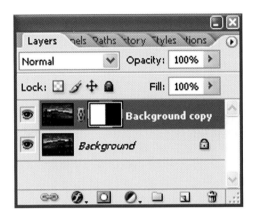

Figure 5.6: Invert the mask colors.

Figure 5.7: Path to a cloven hill

Figure 5.8: Set up a brush for additional painting in the mask.

   The effect thus far has basically generated a reflection, which is a bit too unnatural. Portions of the scene can be removed (or rather returned to their original state) while maintaining the odd mirroring over much of the photo. Simply painting with a black brush (see Figure 5.8) in the layer mask over select areas of the photo can have dramatic results.

Figure 5.9: Hide portions of the top layer by adding black to the mask.

In this example, you really need only a single sign to direct the way through this strange landscape. Working within the mask, you could paint black over the sign on the left side of the photo to reveal the original grass beneath. You could also opt to paint over the clouds and the hill's horizon to show the area where the sun is hitting the brightest. Another point in the mask you may wish to correct is the center of the cloven hill. Painting in the mask here will remove the gradual fade (see Figure 5.9).

The final scene maintains the unnatural symmetry while carrying on the illusion that this could happen in nature (see Figure 5.10). Hiding the sign and revealing a few original characteristics on the left side of the photo should give viewers pause: are they really seeing what they think they are seeing? What wonders Photoshop and a little imagination can accomplish.

Figure 5.10: Pathway revealed by Photoshop and the imagination

Patterns in the Sky

I have an affinity for performing the symmetrical masking technique on cloud formations. As a boy growing up in central Montana, I would watch distant puffs of white build and grow into towering thunderheads in the summer. Watching nature in action, weather in particular, is a fascination I will take to my grave—of this I'm certain.

In this example the technique will be much the same as before, but this time the foreground scene will remain unaltered and only the cloud formation will change. Open the image **clouds1.jpg** (see Figure 5.11).

As before, duplicate the Background layer. Create a mask and, with the gradient saved in the previous tutorial, draw the gradient across the mask from the left border to the right (see Figure 5.12).

Figure 5.13 shows the resulting mirror effect.

Returning to the original foreground scene is a simple matter; I would wager that you have already deduced how to accomplish this. That's right: fill in the lower portion of the mask with black. Because this photo has a relatively straight horizon, creating a selection with the Rectangular Marquee tool in the mask (see Figure 5.14) and filling the selection with black (see Figure 5.15) will effectively render a pattern in the clouds without altering the foreground. Figure 5.16 shows the final image.

Although I am not demonstrating it in this example, feel free to apply black or white paint to the mask in other spots among the clouds to reduce the amount of symmetry. If this were a recipe book, it would read "season to taste."

Figure 5.11: Plains country horizon

Figure 5.12:
Apply the same
gradient settings
as before to the
new layer mask.

Figure 5.13:
An interesting
intersection

Figure 5.14:
Select the lower
portion of the
mask to just
above the
horizon.

Figure 5.15: Fill the selection in the mask with black.

Figure 5.16: Patterns in the sky

Figure 5.17: An alternate view

Once again, this is only one version of the scene. There is another lurking here, and it can be discovered simply by selecting the mask and inverting the colors. When this is done, an entirely different cloud formation is revealed, and the road changes direction as well (see Figure 5.17).

Nature Patterns: Apply Image

As discussed in Chapter 4, "Techniques for Artistic Effects," Apply Image is one of my absolutely favorite tools in the realm of Photoshop. I will not go into yet another diatribe praising this incredible, life-changing feature (it has been known to reduce hair loss, enhance self-esteem, and reverse ozone depletion), although IMHO it is certainly warranted.

Apply Image can be used to generate patterned scenes as well. For this example, open the photo **clouds2.jpg** (see Figure 5.18). Here you have a tranquil sunset scene over the ocean, something I took for granted in my Navy days. Not to dismiss the beauty of sunsets in the Rockies, but there is something surreal about an ocean twilight. And in this case, you can create your own sunset with a symmetrical, surreal twist.

Figure 5.18: Sunset on the water

As before, duplicate the Background layer and flip it (see Figure 5.19). This time the effect will be created without a mask: you will use Apply Image on this layer to achieve the new scene. Choose Image → Apply Image. When the dialog box opens, set the Source to **clouds2.jpg**. You can use the original image (that is, the unflipped Background layer) and blend it with the flipped layer to get the scene-meld. Set the Layer to Background and change the Blending mode to Overlay (see Figure 5.20). Click OK.

The result gives you the mirrored scene again, this time with the colors enriched by the Overlay blending mode (see Figure 5.21). In this example, because Apply Image was the tool of choice rather than a mask, portions of the scene cannot be hidden. However, if you were to create a mask for this layer, then you could see what painting with black/white or gray would do to the final shot.

Figure 5.19: Duplicate the Background layer: no mask this time.

Figure 5.20:
Apply Image
settings

Figure 5.21: Apply Image settings

Creating a Neon Reflection on Water

When I first considered the following piece, I imagined a cobblestone street or walkway with a few stones removed, the recessed area serving as a puddle of water. But then I found this **access.jpg** image (see Figure 5.22) with the cover plate recessed into the surrounding walkway. The way my mind works, I thought, "Hey, that would be cool if it were turned into a reflective puddle." Don't ask me why I thought that, but it did enter my mind. You can use that recessed area to create a a half inch of semi-transparent water with a neon reflection inside.

Please open **access.jpg** and **neon.jpg** to start this exercise.

Duplicate the Background layer. Select the Polygonal Lasso and create a selection around the cover (see Figure 5.23). The area to the top left of the selection will be somewhat jagged, because the broken stones around the plate are more evident. You need not include the broken recesses in the selection, but don't simply create a straight-lined selection in this area either.

Move the selected plate to its own layer by choosing Layer → New → Layer Via Cut.

Next you will prepare the neon image to use as the puddle reflection. Go to the image **neon.jpg** (see Figure 5.24). Select the entire image, copy it, and paste it into its own layer in the sidewalk image. Flip the image (it will be a reflection so it needs to be reversed) by choosing Edit → Transform → Flip Horizontal.

Reduce the scale of the new layer to fit over the plate area. If the plate extends beyond the edges of the neon layer pixels, don't fret; that will be corrected in short order (see Figure 5.25).

Now use the Transform commands to adjust the size and shape of the neon image to fit within the boundaries of the plate (see Figure 5.26). After the transformation fits the correct dimensions, accept it.

Now you can start working to make the sidewalk match the neon, appear to be taken after dark, and look as though the stones are wet. How? Well, let's look at that. First, select the layer containing the sidewalk with the plate removed (see Figure 5.27). The neon image should still be open in the background of Photoshop. If not, you will need to reopen it and then return to this image and layer.

Figure 5.22: Recessed cover plate in a sidewalk

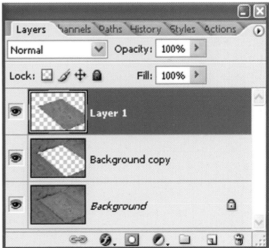

Figure 5.23: Selection of the cover plate

Figure 5.24: I love the blues.

Figure 5.25: Paste and flip the neon image into the side-walk image.

Figure 5.26: Transform the shape of the neon layer to fit in the cover plate area.

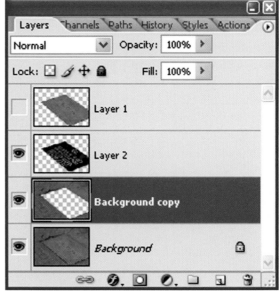

Figure 5.27: Select the sidewalk layer.

Choose Image → Adjustments → Match Color. This step will do two things for you: enable you to darken the image to make it appear as though the photo had been taken at night and enable you to create the illusion that the stone is wet. Before playing with the sliders, look at the bottom of the Match Color dialog box, at the Image Statistics section. Set the source to **neon.jpg**. The neon image will appear in the viewer to the right. Set the Layer to Background.

Now you can adjust the Luminance, Color Intensity, and Fade sliders. Use the settings seen in Figure 5.28 and keep an eye on the image itself.

You will see the image take on a blue hue with the lighter stones embedded in the brick becoming lighter, making it appear as though the sidewalk is wet. Click OK (see Figure 5.29).

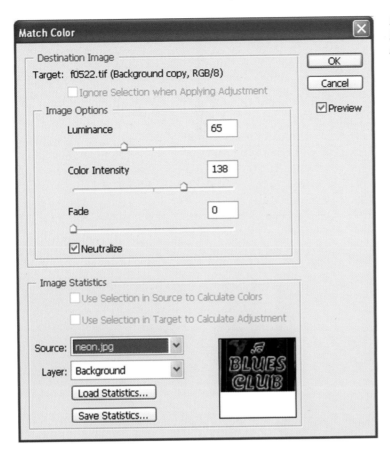

Figure 5.28:
Match Color
settings

Figure 5.29:
The sidewalk
at night

Select the Burn tool and set it to darken the Highlights:

Brush   125
Range   Highlights
Opacity   78%

First, darken the edges of the neon layer so that the light edges blend into the dark recesses of the sidewalk (see Figure 5.30).

Next, select the sidewalk layer and look at the cracks and seams where the bricks come together. By burning these areas, you can make it appear that the seams are wetter than the stone exposed more prominently to the air. Run the Burn tool over these cracks, and also around the edges where the plate recesses into the sidewalk (see Figure 5.31).

The stone looks wet, but more moisture can be added. The neon is reflecting off a pool of water, at least in my brain, so that effect can be simulated with a few ripples. Select the neon layer and make an oval selection with the Elliptical Marquee tool (see Figure 5.32). Click OK.

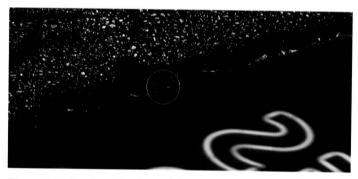

Figure 5.31: Use the Burn tool to add water to the cracks in the stone.

Figure 5.30: Darken the edges of the neon layer.

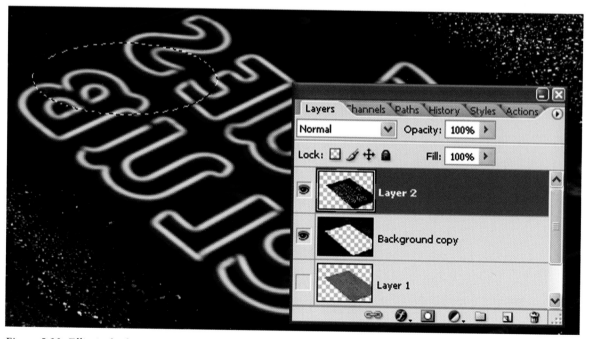

Figure 5.32: Elliptical selection

Open the Filters menu and choose Distort → ZigZag. Look at Figure 5.33 and enter the settings seen there to generate some ripples. Click OK.

Make four or more oval selections across the surface and repeat the rippling process each time. Alter the width of the selections to indicate variation in the size of the raindrops hitting the surface (see Figure 5.34).

Because the pool consists of water, some of the cover plate should be seen beneath the surface. To do this, make the cover layer visible once again and select the neon layer. Reduce the opacity of the neon layer to 80% (see Figure 5.35).

Reducing the opacity will wash out the color of the neon layer, but a quick adjustment of the Brightness/Contrast will fix that. Choose Image → Adjustments → Brightness/Contrast and change the Brightness setting to 50 and the Contrast setting to 52. Click OK.

The neon could be a bit brighter, as could the reflections on the ripples. Duplicate the neon layer and set the blending mode to Soft Light. Increase the opacity of this layer back to 100% (see Figure 5.36). Figure 5.37 shows the final image. Does it look like water to you? Did the vision stay true to that described in the beginning of this section?

This process has other possible applications. Transforming objects to conform to other molds is a good thing to know. You can conform labels to products, fit buildings to scenes where they do not belong, and so forth. Water and ripples can help you transform outdoor shots into pond reflections; you can add liquid to an image without a drop of fluid.

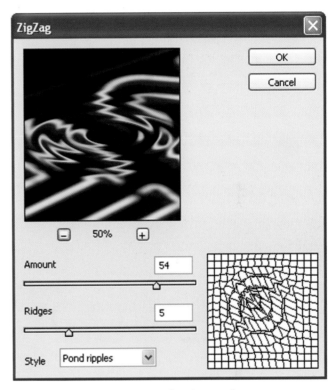

Figure 5.33: Use ZigZag to apply a few ripples.

Figure 5.34: Raindrops

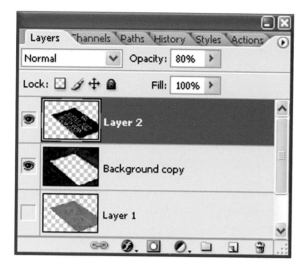

Figure 5.35: Add transparency to the water.

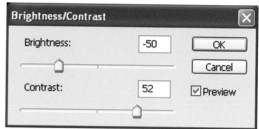

Figure 5.36: New Soft Light layer

Figure 5.37: Final water image

Changing the Mood

The idea behind the next two effects is to take a photo of an area and turn it into a more sinister version of itself. I've chosen two examples: a graveyard, which is already fairly dark by nature, and a serene wood at sunset.

Because two effects will be presented here, my brain has conjured two results. The first, to be centered on the graveyard photo, is to create a world of combined texture and line art that will render a stark, gloomy version of the original photograph. The second, centered on a calm woodland path, is to re-create my version of a forest in nightmares and horror movies—a place devoid of color, warmth, and hope, where ghostly images may appear at any moment on the path before you.

Both techniques will follow the same path to their fruition, although the effects will be quite different from one another. These effects will be realized by a combination of Difference layers, adjustment layers, and a liberal application of curves. Here we will dip into the realm of the night, letting the phantoms of our imaginations show us their world: stark and cold and…dark.

Start with the graveyard photo (see Figure 5.38); open **graveyard.jpg**. Although some daylight is evident in this photo, the scene still appears bleak, with the stone faces in shadow.

To start creating the effect that I have in mind, duplicate the Background layer. Choose Image → Adjustments → Invert (see Figure 5.39).

Figure 5.38: Graveyard at sunset

*Figure 5.39:
Graveyard
inverted*

Create another copy of the Background layer. Place this new layer at the top of the layer stack and change the blending mode to Difference (see Figure 5.40). This will draw out much of the color in the sky and clouds, as well as darken the edges of the tombstones and the chapel in the background. Why is that important? Because it will give the curve some darker areas to work on, as you will see (see Figure 5.41).

Before you get to the Curves adjustment layer, first create a Hue/Saturation adjustment layer and decrease the Saturation to –90. Click OK. I realize that this setting will take most of the color away that was cre-

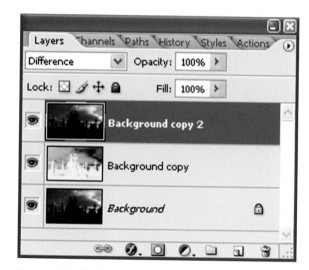

Figure 5.40: Difference blending mode

ated before, but what I mainly wanted there wasn't the color at all, but better definition to the lines in the image.

Now create a Curves adjustment layer, as seen in Figure 5.42.

Last, take away some of the effects that the curve had on the clouds by painting in the cloud area with black, directly in the mask for the Curves adjustment layer (see Figure 5.43).

Figure 5.41: Inverted scene, more color, better definition

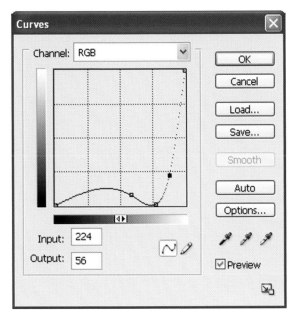

Figure 5.42: Curves adjustment

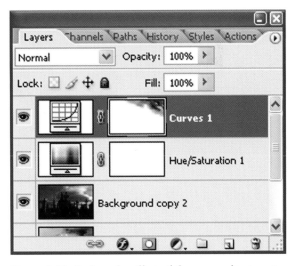

Figure 5.43: Reduce the effect of the curve adjustment on the cloud.

Figure 5.44: Gloomy surreal boneyard

Figure 5.44 shows the final image. Compare this to the original: this effect brought even the text on the stones out of the shadows, whereas in the original photo this side of the church and headstones was in darkness.

Now you'll apply a similar technique, turning a serene forest image into a scene out of *The Blair Witch Project*, *The Ring* movies, or any other popular horror movie of recent years. Actually, it reminds me of the woods in the *Evil Dead* movies. Long live Ash! (Something for my fellow Deadites out there…) To begin, open **forest.jpg** (see Figure 5.45).

As before, create two copies of the Background layer. Invert the first (Image → Adjustments → Invert), and set the blending mode for the second to Difference (see Figure 5.46). This time, reduce the fill opacity of the Difference layer to 40% (see Figure 5.47).

Figure 5.48 shows the new forest—very pretty in an odd sort of way.

Create a Hue/Saturation adjustment layer again, with nearly identical settings to those seen in the graveyard tutorial (see Figure 5.49). Next, create a Curves adjustment layer, this time using the curve seen in Figure 5.50.

The result is an image that almost appears to have been created with ink on a harsh negative (see Figure 5.51).

I can almost see a ghostly figure walking up the path toward me!

Figure 5.45: A pleasant walk in the woods

Figure 5.46: The Background Copy layer settings

Figure 5.47: Background Copy 2 layer settings

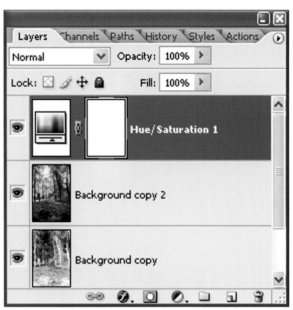

Figure 5.49: *Hue/Saturation adjustment*

Figure 5.48: *On our way to Happyland, via the '60s*

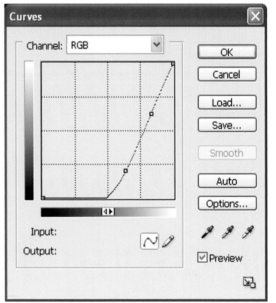

Figure 5.50: *Dark wood curve*

I hope you have enjoyed this little excursion into the alteration of scenic photos. This closes out the chapter on landscapes, although we are far from done working on natural images. Next you'll move on to animals—let's see what sort of right-brain mischief we can come up with in the animal kingdom. Let's see if we can make the Crocodile Hunter cringe!

Figure 5.51:
Haunted woods

Animals

At times, photos lend themselves *to the creative process simply by being what they are. Photographers are always trying to capture their subjects in the perfect light, the perfect pose, the perfect situation that conveys a mood or delivers a message. The photographer reaches out with their art to invoke a response in the viewer.*

The digital artist can work with Photoshop to reinforce the link between artist/photographer and viewer. Whether the artist is going for shock value, emotion, or comfort, Photoshop can be used to enhance the mood of a photo by using textures and pigments resident in the original, or to change the mood of the message that the image conveys by combining images. This chapter takes natural elements and creatures from the world around us to demonstrate these points.

Comical Critter Alteration

If you have ever purchased a greeting card or simply browsed the aisle at a gift shop, I'm sure you have seen cards with the humorous animal manipulations that have clearly been run through the Photoshop mill. Kittens and puppies in comical situations and poses can put a smile on the face of the most hardened, disgruntled card buyer. Are they cute? Most of them. Are they funny? Certainly they are. Do they sell cards for the company that distributes them? You bet they do. In turn this means a paycheck for the artist.

To open this chapter on creature manipulations, I am going to demonstrate one way in which these types of distorted, "warm-the-heart" effects can be generated. If you are already thinking about the Liquify tool, you are on the right track: that will certainly come into play for this technique. What I want to demonstrate primarily in this section is the Lens Correction filter. This is new to Photoshop CS2 and is powerful alone—and very powerful when combined with other Photoshop processes.

The work in this section will be performed on one of those images that are too cute in their own right. Please open **puppy.jpg** (see Figure 6.1).

If you take a quick peek at Figure 6.2, you will see I've skipped a couple of processes in my description to get to this point. These are covered elsewhere in this book, so they seemed a bit redundant to rehash here. All I've done is extract the puppy from its background (see Chapter 1, "Tools for Building Your Masterpiece") and used Liquify (Bloat tool) to increase the size of the eyes and nose. The extracted puppy is placed above a layer filled with white.

You will note that Figure 6.2 also has two grid lines, one vertical and one horizontal, meeting at a central point. I have created this grid by using the rulers to find the central point in the document. I then moved the puppy layer so that the center of the face, or at least the center of the area I would like to expand with the Lens Correction filter, is centered in the document. This is because the Lens Correction uses a center reference to apply corrections or, in this case, distortions. You will see what I mean momentarily.

After your puppy has been extracted, liquified, and centered, ensure that the puppy layer is selected and choose Filter → Distort → Lens Correction. The Lens Correction filter is designed to correct common lens flaws that photographers face, such as barrel and pincushion distortion, vignetting (darkening at the corners), and chromatic aberration (color fringe on an object's edge). It is also designed to rotate or fix perspective in a photo, a common problem when the photo was taken at a slight angle or above/below the scene. In a way this works like the familiar Transform tools, but Lens Correction is a bit easier to manipulate to dress up the photo.

A dialog box similar to the Liquify dialog box will appear with your puppy covered by a gray grid. The grid is simply to aid in correction, but this technique does not use the Lens Filter to correct, but to alter. For instance, if you move the Remove Distortion slider to the left (negative value), a barrel effect is applied rather than reduced. I am looking for a comical or cartoonish effect for the dog, and setting the Remove Distortion slider to a −45 value will increase the size of the face starting at the central point.

The second setting that I'm concerned with for this process is the Vertical Perspective slider in the Transform section. By moving this slider to the left, the top of the photo moves nearer the lens, and the bottom farther away. A slider setting of −100 will make the head/face appear larger, and the feet and body smaller.

Figure 6.1: A real-life pound puppy

Figure 6.2: The puppy has been extracted and distorted with Liquify.

Notice how the photo increases in size beyond the borders of the photo. This can be fixed as well to fit within the original frame by moving the Scale slider at the bottom of the Lens Correction dialog box to the left or by simply typing in the size percentage manually. A setting of 90% in this case reduces the size of the dog enough to bring it back within the frame. Figure 6.3 shows the Lens Correction dialog box with the settings adjusted. After you are satisfied, click OK to apply the changes to the puppy layer. Figure 6.4 shows the subject after Lens Correction has been applied.

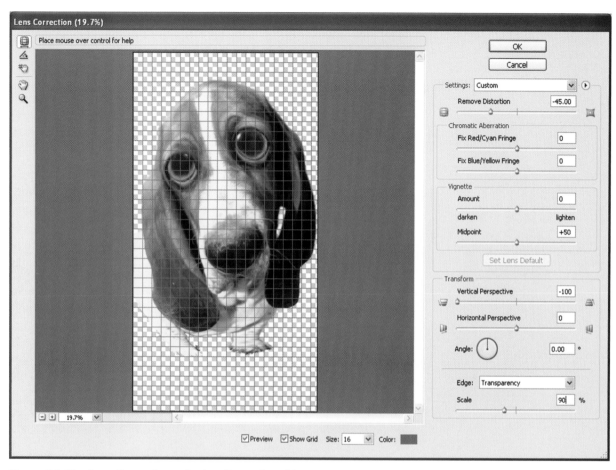

Figure 6.3: Use Lens Correction to further distort the subject.

Figure 6.4: Awww...

Figure 6.5: The Cutout filter gives a "paint-by-numbers" feel to the image.

This photo is cool in its own right and is certainly one you might expect to see on a "Get Well" card. You could stop when you reach this point, or continue on and create a hand-drawn version as I will do now. This is done using steps similar to those seen for the Anime Woman in Chapter 8, "Going Beyond Canned Filters."

To convert the image to a painting or hand-drawn image, choose Filter → Artistic → Cutout (see Figure 6.5). This separates the primary tones in the photo into levels, sort of like a paint-by-numbers kit. For this effect, simply set the Number Of Levels to 5, Edge Simplicity to 4, and Edge Fidelity to 1. Click OK.

Figure 6.6: Separate the colors further by using the Poster Edges filter.

Now that the colors have been separated, you can further enhance the hand-painted look by adding a border to the color separations. Filter → Artistic → Poster Edges works nicely here. Open the filter's dialog box and set the Edge Thickness to 2, Edge Intensity to 1, and Posterization to 2, as seen in Figure 6.6. Click OK.

Now you can duplicate the manipulated area and use blending modes (Overlay works well) or adjustment layers to enhance the color of the paint. Also, the technique used in Chapter 2 to alter the color of hair or eyes can give your pound puppy pretty blue peepers (say that three times fast!). My final image is seen in Figure 6.7.

Figure 6.7: We all just need a little love.

Attack of the Giant Bug—in 3D!

As a boy growing up in Montana in the late sixties to mid-seventies before the introduction of cable television or dynamic, computer-generated special effects, my Saturday afternoons were often spent watching the weekly fare offered by one of the local television stations. Winter in Montana, especially in those days, did not allow for many outdoor activities: the temperature and snowfall would keep my brother and me indoors climbing walls, much to my mother's dismay.

Every weekend the local television station would broadcast (at two o'clock precisely) some B-rated science-fiction movie or scary flick from the fifties or early sixties. My brother and I, as well as any friend that we had over at the house, would sit glued to the TV watching all manner of creatures, either diabolical or misunderstood, rampage through the streets or terrorize small communities such as we lived in. Occasionally one of these movies would be in 3D, which was always interesting to watch considering we did not have 3D glasses in central Montana at that time. When I finally did see my first 3D movie with the glasses, it was a revelation, and this genre would be a welcome comeback in the new millennium.

A few months ago a good friend of mine in the industry asked whether I knew how to generate in Photoshop 3D images similar to those seen in those old movies. At that time I did not, but he piqued my interest. This technique was born from that question. Keep in mind that, in order to see the effect properly, a pair of standard red/blue 3D glasses will need to be utilized. A simple Google search online will turn up many sites offering these items free or relatively inexpensively. I'm including this technique to show you a unique way that you might display your art. If you do not have a pair of 3D glasses at hand, you'll have to trust me: this works!

To begin, open the image **bigbug.jpg** (see Figure 6.8).

The trick to creating a 3D effect is to separate the photo into offset reds and blue/greens. Duplicate the background layer twice and rename the first copy **Blue-Green**, and the second copy **Red** (see Figure 6.9).

Because the layers need to be offset from one another, the canvas needs to be a bit larger to accommodate the offset so you don't lose the edges of the photo. Choose Image → Canvas Size and change both the Width and the Height to 125% of the original size. Click OK. (See Figure 6.10.)

Figure 6.8: Where does a bug like me find a little radioactivity these days?

Figure 6.9: Set up the Layers palette for 3D.

Select the Blue-Green layer; then choose Image → Adjustments → Levels. You are going to "get the red out" of this layer by selecting the red channel and moving the center slider in the histogram all the way to the right. You may also do this manually by typing 0.10 in the center Input Levels box in this dialog box (see Figure 6.11). Click OK to accept the adjustment.

You're almost done already. Select the Move tool and, with the arrow keys, move the Blue-Green layer 5–10 taps to the right. This provides part of the offset required for the effect. Now select the Red layer and change the blending mode to Screen. Go ahead and move this layer a few taps to the left—when the Move tool is selected, you can use the arrow keys to position the layer (see Figure 6.12).

Now you simply need to remove the blue and green. Open the Levels dialog box for this layer and select the blue channel. Move the center slider all the way to the left. Repeat this process with the green channel (see Figure 6.13). Click OK to accept the change.

The result is seen in Figure 6.14. If you have a pair of 3D glasses handy, the bug will appear to be residing on the glass of your monitor, giving it almost an aquarium affect. You can also use two photos of the same subject slightly offset from one another to try to further enhance the end result.

Because you are working with a single photo rather than an offset pair, the Transform tools can be used to alter perspective on each just a bit. The human eyes are offset by an inch or so; this allows us to judge distance and see things three-dimensionally. By transforming the perspective on each layer, you can create this quality. Select the Blue-Green

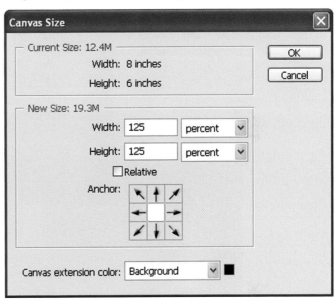

Figure 6.10: Increase the canvas size.

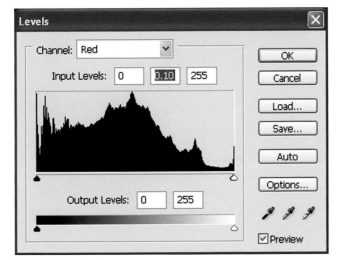

Figure 6.11: Use the Levels adjustment on the red channel to take the red out of the Blue-Green layer.

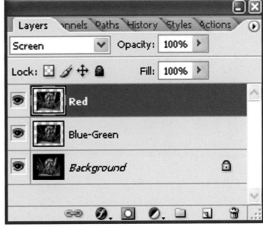

Figure 6.12: A blending mode change is required to make the Red layer opaque.

Figure 6.13:
Remove the blue
and green from
the Red layer
with Levels.

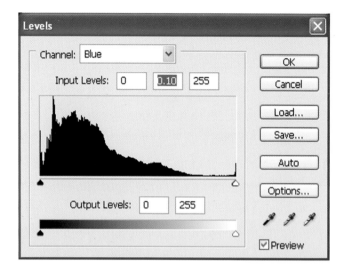

Figure 6.14: My
computer has a
bug!

layer and choose Edit → Transform → Perspective. Click on the upper-left corner of the bounding box and move it down slightly (see Figure 6.15). Repeat this process with the Red layer, but move the upper-right corner of the bounding box.

If the image is too dark, which it may well be after you put on a pair of 3D glasses, you can simply apply a standard Brightness/Contrast adjustment layer and edit accordingly. In this instance, increase the Brightness to 20 and the Contrast to 15 (see Figures 6.16 and 6.17).

Figure 6.15: Adjust perspective on each layer a bit to mimic how our eyes see the world.

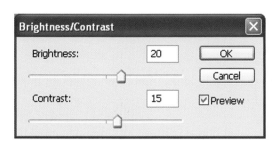

Figure 6.16: A slight Brightness/Contrast adjustment

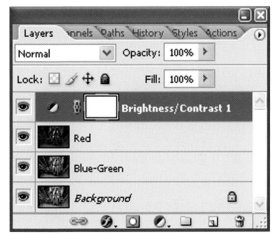

Figure 6.17: All layers in place

Figure 6.18: A science experiment gone horribly awry!

After the transformation is complete, furthering the offset to duplicate how our eyes see the world, you can crop the image as you like. The final shot is seen in Figure 6.18.

I expect to see 3D posters appearing for sale at the county fair in the near future!

Creature out of Place

Photographs themselves often inspire a digital artist to create. In the first edition of this book, I wrapped a snake around a woman to demonstrate how one can relatively easily take a subject from one photo and place them in a totally different environment. That environment need not be something desirable or comical, but can be quite undesirable for the subject in the photo. Dark artists manipulate photography in this manner frequently; others do this just for fun.

Either way, this technique demonstrates two processes: how to take a subject from one photo and put it in another (as you've seen with the moose in Chapter 1), and how to change the mood of a piece by using color and stark lighting/shadows. This will also demonstrate that, even though an image appears as though it is a little rough in the midst of the process, it can occasionally be salvaged and used anyway.

Figure 6.19: I'm telling ya, there's a huge spider here somewhere!

The two images used in this section are **yell.jpg** and **spider.jpg**. Please have them open and ready.

Select the image **yell.jpg** (see Figure 6.19). I envision the final image in my mind's eye on a dark or black background. For this reason, you should extract the subject from his surroundings. The edges are well-defined and there is no hair to deal with, so this extraction should go fairly smoothly. Go through the process seen in Chapter 1 and extract the man from the background, placing him in his own layer. See Figure 6.20.

Now create a new layer, fill it with black, and move it beneath the man layer (see Figure 6.21). Another point to consider is that the man's head is almost touching the top edge of the photo. I envision the spider resting on top of the man's head, so the canvas size will need to be increased. Choose Image → Canvas Size and increase the Height to 200% (see Figure 6.22).

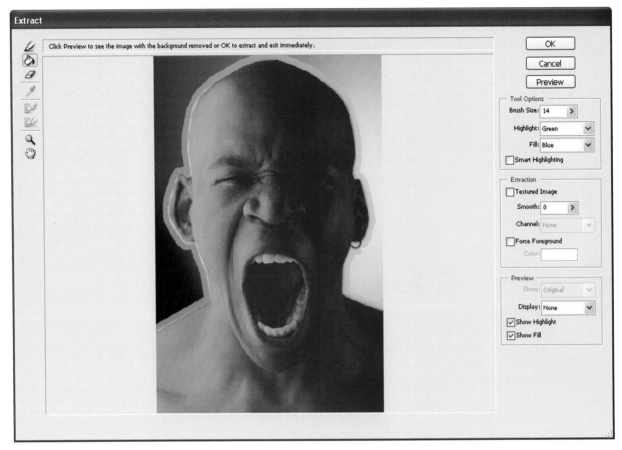

Figure 6.20: Extract the man from his natural habitat.

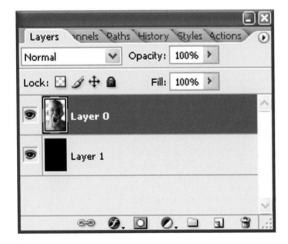

Figure 6.21: Extraction in action

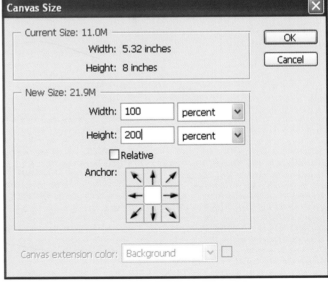

Figure 6.22: Layers palette pecking order thus far

Figure 6.24: Cousin to the 3D radioactive spider

The extracted man will be in the middle of the image, so select the Move tool and, holding down the Shift key, tap the Down arrow until the man is at the bottom of the canvas. If it isn't already, again fill the entire background image with black (see Figure 6.23).

Switch over to the image **spider.jpg** (see Figure 6.24). This guy (or gal; I've never been able to tell with spiders) is to be removed from its background also and pasted into the other image. Using the Extract dialog box and following the techniques used to remove the moose in Chapter 1, extract the spider from the background (see Figure 6.25).

Before closing the Extract dialog box, use the Edge Cleanup tools on the right to dress up the edges a bit. Because the spider has numerous hairs protruding from its legs, Photoshop may have a difficult time doing a clean extraction (see Figure 6.26). This need not be perfect: some pixels may be left

Figure 6.23: An expanded canvas

Figure 6.25: Spider searching for a new home with Extract

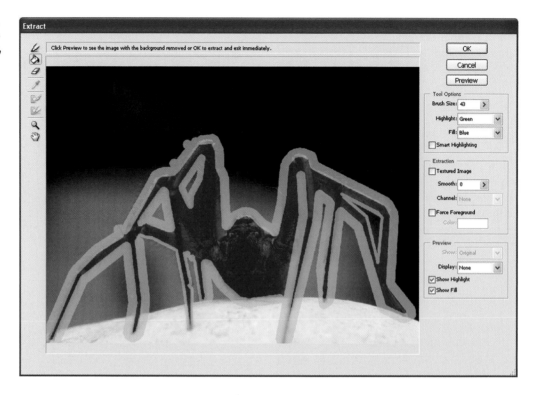

Figure 6.26: Use the Edge Cleanup tools to give this critter a shave and remove leftover background pixels.

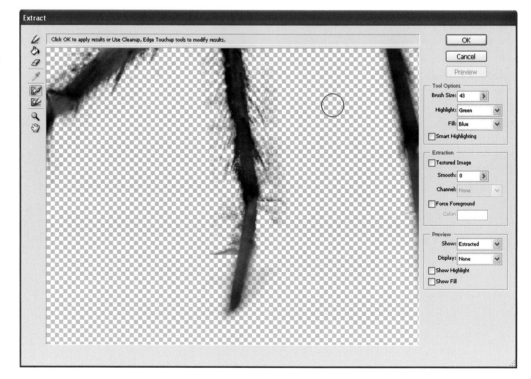

behind or left attached to the spider layer. No worries, as these will disappear shortly. After the spider has been removed from its background, copy and paste it into a new layer in the original image. Move the spider so that is just above the man's head (see Figure 6.27).

Now the spider needs to shed some weight. Use the Transform tools to manipulate it so that it appears to be standing on the man's head (see Figure 6.28).

I bet you are still worried about some of those extra pixels that remained after the extraction, aren't you? If they are really bothering you, click the Eraser and do some fine-tuning to the edges to your taste. Because of a step you will take shortly, it doesn't need to be perfect.

To make the spider appear at home in its new habitat, the light needs to hit the spider at the same angle as it is reflecting on the man's face. You can exemplify this illusion by using the Burn tool to create shadows beneath the spider legs on the man's head. Select the man's head layer. Click the Burn tool and using a semi-feathered brush with the Range set to Midtones and Exposure to 50% (see Figure 6.29), darken regions beneath the legs to make it appear as though shadows from the legs are on the scalp. Duplicate the spider layer and set the blending mode for the new layer to Overlay. This will add some color to the spider and help those edges a bit (see Figure 6.30).

This is turning into an emotional piece: I certainly would not want to be in this man's situation without a very large newspaper! You can now use color and stark contrasts to enhance the electric emotion this man must be feeling.

Figure 6.27: It's hard to find a good parking spot these days.

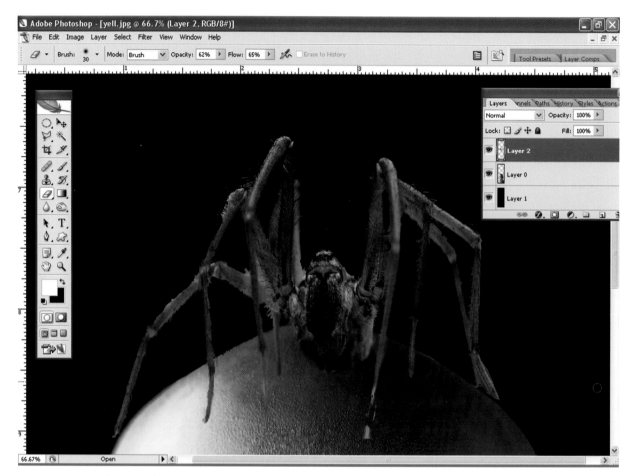

Figure 6.28: Use the Transform tools to conform the spider's size and shape to fit on top of the man's head.

Figure 6.29: Burning the shadows

First, merge all layers except the Background into a single layer, as seen in Figure 6.31. You're going to use our old friend Apply Image to enhance the contrasts in this image. Choose Image → Apply Image and set the source to **yell.jpg**. See Figure 6.32 for the exact settings: the main one to be concerned with is Blending. Ensure that this is changed to Hard Mix.

Figure 6.33 shows the end result. Just by that Apply Image adjustment, the emotion of this piece is changed dramatically as is the artistic style. To repeat myself once again, often just a simple change in blending mode or filter application or adjustment layer application can have a dramatic effect on your digital art. I encourage you to experiment with other blending modes and settings you've seen throughout the book to see how far you can take this!

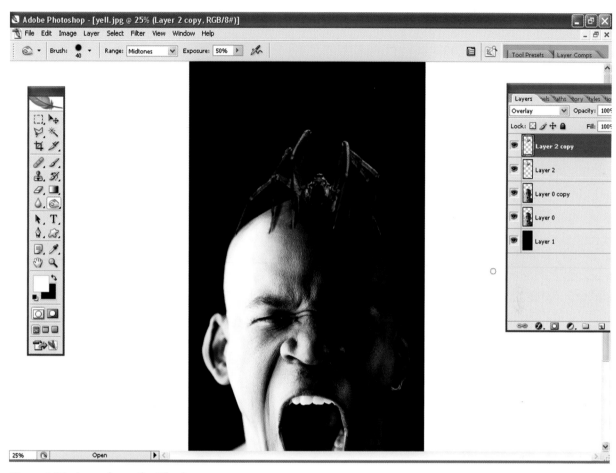

Figure 6.30: A new home for Charlotte

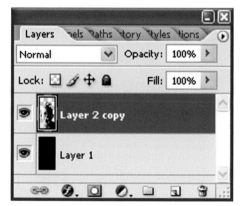

Figure 6.31: Merge them all together.

Figure 6.32: Apply Image revisited

Figure 6.33:
Honey, I found
your pet!

Crossbreeding Species

It is said that some people resemble their pets and vice versa. Often people choose pets that remind them of themselves both physically and in their nature. There seem to be factors differentiating "cat people" and "dog people." Most pet owners can be divided into one of these two categories.

In Photoshop, you can take this to the limit and beyond—not simply by creating a resemblance, but by actually merging the characteristics of two creatures into a single image, generating an entirely new species. For this piece I envision a combination of human and feline characteristics. Although it sounds as though this could be complicated to pull off, that isn't the case at all. Using some of the masking techniques already learned (you are probably pretty well versed in masks by now), combining a lion with a person will be a cakewalk.

Although I'm usually working until the wee hours of the morning, I try to watch *Late Night with Conan O'Brien* when I can. The humor is often rather base, but I'm a little off in my sense of humor. There is one bit they do on the show that combines photos of people to see what their children would look like. The following example is an offshoot of that.

Begin with two images from this book's CD: **leo.jpg** and **intense.jpg** (see Figures 6.34 and 6.35). Make a copy of the woman image and paste it into a new layer in the lion document. Reduce the opacity of the woman layer to 60%; this way you can see the lion beneath to line up the images in the next step (see Figure 6.36).

Choose Edit → Transform → Scale and increase the size of the woman's face so that her eyes overlay those of the lion. Also position the lips so that the woman's lower lip extends below the pleat in the lion's upper lip, below its nose (see Figure 6.37). When everything is in its proper place, accept the transformation.

Figure 6.34: King of the jungle

Figure 6.35: Queen of the business world

It's time to meld the two faces with a mask. Create a layer mask for the woman's face layer (see Figure 6.38). Select the Paintbrush tool and set black as the foreground color.

Using a fairly large, round, feathered brush, begin painting in the mask to hide portions of the woman's face, such as the nose, cheeks, and so forth. Leave her lower lip visible, as well as her eyes and strands of hair hanging down on the left side of the image (see Figure 6.39). Continue working on the mask with black paint until most of her face is hidden, leaving only the eyes, eyebrows, and the lower lip visible (see Figure 6.40).

For a few final touches, add some color to the irises as you did in the coloring tutorials in Chapter 2. I love emerald on cats, so I've applied green to the eyes here (see Figure 6.41). Also add some color to the lips.

Last, increase the richness of the color of the overall image. You can do this with Apply Image (Image → Apply Image). Use this image as the source and set the blending mode to Overlay. Adjust the opacity slider until you are happy with the tone.

Figure 6.42 shows the final lioness photo. I love the color of this piece, as well as the seamless melding of facial features from both photographs for a combined whole.

Figure 6.36: Preparing layers for the merge

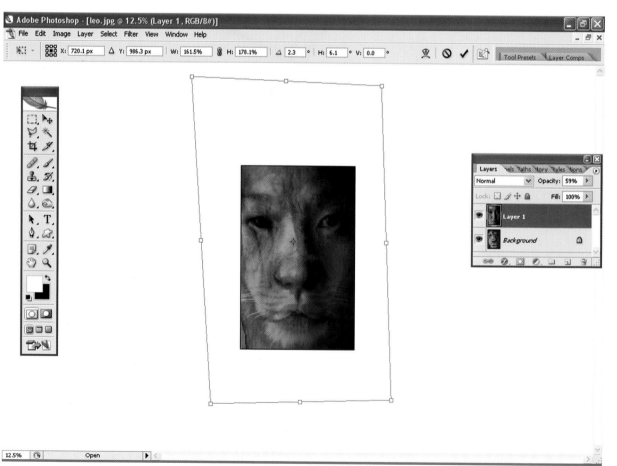

Figure 6.37: Match facial features between the two photos.

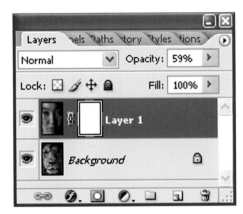

Figure 6.38: Create a mask for the woman's face.

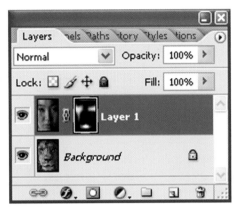

Figure 6.39: Hide portions of the woman, revealing the cat beneath.

Figure 6.40: The lioness revealed

Figure 6.41: Add color to the eyes.

Figure 6.42: The lioness realized

Crossbreeding Species 2: Pegasus

Following the theme of fanciful creature creation, let's delve into one more area of popularity: creatures of myth. I've long been a fan of the fantasy novel genre. If I feel the need to unwind and get away from the computer for a while, you will find me either working in my garden or yard, or simply sitting for hours with my nose buried in a sword-and-sorcery paperback. If you are into that sort of thing, I strongly suggest you check out the works of one of my favorite authors, R.A. Salvatore, creator of the dark elf hero Drizzt Do'Urden. Now there is time well spent!

Back to the technique. My thought for this piece is to create a Pegasus, one of the more noble and intelligent creatures from mythology, in a scene that could be in your neighbor's field on a cool January morning.

Open the images **horse2.jpg** and **swan.jpg** (see Figures 6.43 and 6.44).

Figure 6.43:
Grazing on a
summer's morn

Figure 6.44:
Hey, buddy...
tell me again.
Why didn't we
go south this
year?

Once again, masks will come into play to help realize the vision. First, copy the swan photo and paste it into a new layer in the horse document (see Figure 6.45). Reduce the opacity of the swan layer so the layer beneath can be used as a reference. Select the Move tool and position the swan photo so that the swan on the left is over the horse in such a way that the wings appear as if they could be protruding from either animal. Aim for the withers (top of the front shoulder) on the horse for the wing placement (see Figure 6.46).

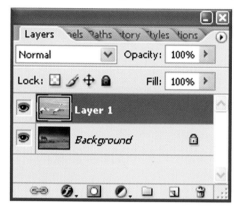

Figure 6.45: Place both images in the same document.

You may now create a mask for the swan layer and hide everything with the exception of the wings. Note that you will need to remove the neck of the swan from the photo as well, which will leave the gap in the wing (see Figure 6.47).

Paint with white in the mask over the neck again, revealing it. I'm having you reveal it again so you may use the Clone tool to replace the neck in this layer with wings instead. Otherwise, you will be left with a huge gap, and that just won't do.

Click the Clone tool. My settings are seen in Figure 6.48. All I'm doing is sampling portions of the swan's wing next to the neck

Figure 6.46: Position the trailing swan above the horse.

Figure 6.47: Mask away the swans, leaving only the wings.

Figure 6.48: Clone Tool Settings

and stamping it over the neck. Repeat the process until the neck disappears, leaving only feathers. Work as carefully as possible so that the feathers in this area match the direction and size of those in the rest of the wing. Figure 6.49 shows the Layers palette at this stage of the game.

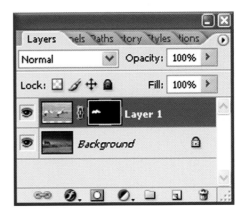

Figure 6.49: Layers palette progress check

The current state of the image is seen in Figure 6.50. At this point, you have a sepia horse and background, and bright bluish-white feathery wings protruding from the back of the sepia horse. Its current state is not very realistic, even for a mythical photograph. Some adjustment will need to be made. Duplicate the Background layer (see Figure 6.51). Can you guess where I'm going next?

That's right, you guessed it. Match Color is going to help you match the color of the horse layer to those of the wings. You can do it the other way around if you so choose, matching the wings to the ambient light of the horse layer, but in the beginning of this tutorial I mentioned seeing the Pegasus in a field in winter. Click on the horse layer in the Layers palette.

Figure 6.52 shows my Match Color settings. The thing to keep in mind in this instance is the source. You want the horse layer to match the color of the swan layer, so by sending

*Figure 6.50:
Wings in place,
but the ambient
colors don't yet
match.*

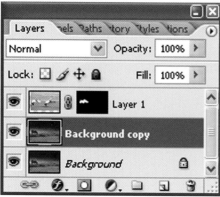

*Figure 6.51: Set the Layers palette up for a
color change.*

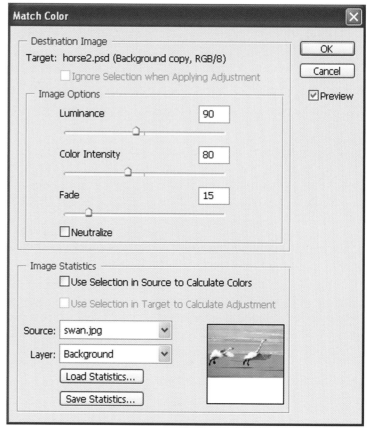

Figure 6.52: Match color between images.

Figure 6.53: I took a walk on a winter morn, and strange things did I see...

the Source in Match Color to the swan photo, the horse layer will take on those color characteristics. You may also adjust the Luminance, Color Intensity, and Fade settings to taste until you get a good blend. Keep an eye on your image while making these adjustments until you are happy with the result. My final shot of a Pegasus grazing in a midwinter field is seen in Figure 6.53.

I hope you have enjoyed this chapter on creature manipulations. As always, the creatures you make or the art you create is limited only by your understanding of the tools, their application, and your imagination. Let your imagination soar and see what materializes on the screen.

seven

CHAPTER

Digital Alterations
and Manipulations

When I was younger, *everything art-related fell into two general categories: Cool or Dumb. I didn't understand the spirit behind the art. I'd see a broken cup glued to a wall and, rather than appreciate anything the artist may have been trying to convey, I'd chuck it into the latter category (I'm still not sure about that piece). Anything by Boris Vallejo—airbrushed, seminude women with giant winged reptiles— was Good Art, and anything else was decidedly Lame, Dumb, so on and so forth.*

*I still love Boris (**www.borisjulie.com**) but now also appreciate other forms of artistic expression. I never used to understand stationary objects or common household items taking prominence in photographic art, but now can see that they play a vital role in advertising (yes, even advertising can be considered an art form), illustrating retro styles and making simple statements about our lives in the new millennium. Displaying a product to render it appealing isn't an easy process; an artist needs that right-brain imagination.*

This chapter delves into three interesting areas: advertising, object photos used as artistic renderings, and even a simple object enhanced, using its own characteristics as a form of expression. There are a couple of pretty standard takes, and a couple that are possible only because Photoshop is in the darkroom. Let's get into it, shall we?

Digital Woman

As I mentioned, advertising is an art form—or at least artistic elements are used in the advertising medium. It is called *graphic arts,* after all. To reflect that point, this tutorial will show one way to build an ad from an idea, by using Photoshop, your own gray matter, and a whole lot of imagination.

The premise is fairly direct: create a unique advertising piece reflecting people and the digital world. This image should use a logo prominently. To ensure that the logo sticks out, you can use it repetitively (or in more than one instance). The ad should not only display the logo but should also encapsulate the company slogan.

To realize this technique, you will require a logo and a face. You will capture a photo by using a converted text layer and combinations of masks, blending mode changes, and colorizing techniques to complete the final image.

To start the ad, you will first create a digital image. I can hear it already…"Wait a minute, Al, aren't we already working with digital images?" Sure we are, but that isn't really what I have in mind. How about if the main character consisted of ones and zeros, literally? It's worth a try.

Open the image **glasses.jpg** (see Figure 7.1). This photo has elements that I think will fit nicely in the final image, in particular the reflections on the large lenses. You'll soon see what I have in mind, but first let's really make this woman digital.

Now that the primary image is open, it is time again to set up the Layers palette. Create a new layer just above the Background and fill it with black. Next, duplicate the Background layer and place it above the black layer. Rename the new copy of the woman **Glasses-1,** and move the layer to the left about one-third the width of the image. This will give some space on the right for additional ad copy after the primary image is complete (see Figure 7.2).

You need a layer consisting of ones and zeros to use in the image conversion, so select the Vertical Type tool. In the options bar, set the font to Arial Black, Regular, 12 pts, Top

Figure 7.1:
Reflective with
reflections?

Justify, and set the font color to white. Starting in the upper-right corner of the face layer (you need not cover the black portion of the image), make four columns of ones and zeros, typed randomly (see Figure 7.3). Rasterize and duplicate the Type layer, move the new layer to the left to create four more columns, and merge those layers to create an eight-column layer. Repeat the process until the entire face is covered (see Figure 7.4). Rename the final merged-character layer **Numbers**.

⌘/Ctrl+click the Numbers layer to select all of the type. Select the Glasses-1 layer and copy it (⌘/Ctrl+C). Paste the pixel information into a new layer; then name the layer **Face-Numbers**. Duplicate the layer and set the blending mode for the new layer to Overlay (see Figure 7.5).

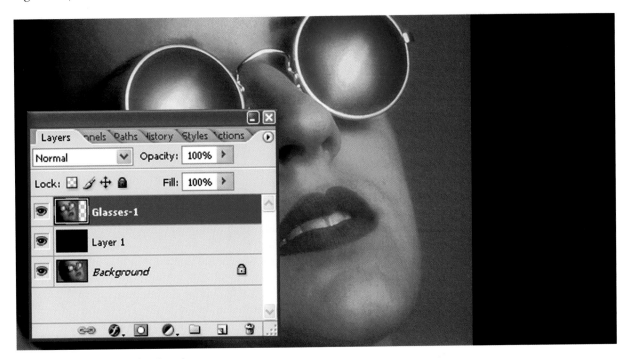

Figure 7.2: Leave space for the ad text.

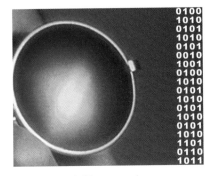

Figure 7.3: Add ones and zeros.

Figure 7.4: Digitized

Figure 7.5: Numbers construct the face.

Return to the Glasses-1 layer. My thought was to use the reflections on the glasses to display a glowing logo, which is the primary reason this photo was so appealing to me. To do that, the lenses need to be visible in their entirety while the rest of the face remains digitized. You guessed it: a mask is about to come into play.

Create a layer mask for the Glasses-1 layer and fill it with black. Set white as the foreground color and, using the Paintbrush tool, paint over the lens areas in the mask.

The process just applied needs to be reversed for the Face-Numbers layers. In other words, the numbers need to be hidden from the lenses, but revealed on the face so that the numeric construct is still visible. Create a mask for each Face-Numbers layer and fill the mask with white. Paint over the lenses with black in the masks, and also reveal the wire frame around the lenses, as seen in Figure 7.6.

The numbers bordering the faces aren't needed either, so continue to paint in the Face-Numbers layers' masks and hide the characters that do not compose the face. You may also opt to recolor the lenses of the glasses: use the Color blending mode technique seen in Chapter 2, "Techniques for Embellishing Portraits." Figure 7.7 shows the result.

Now for the logo. In considering the theme of this exercise, I worked in reverse: I knew the technique that I wanted to demonstrate before I had the product in mind. The image/effect you're creating here suggests something digital and somewhat futuristic, so a computer company would be a perfect fit. So what sort of logo would work for a computer company? What would be unique but easily associated with computers? After a bit of thought, I decided on the nearly universal On button icon. Most PCs and Macs have it embedded in the face of the button.

In the real world, of course, you'd be working with an established company, and they would usually supply their logo and product information for your design.

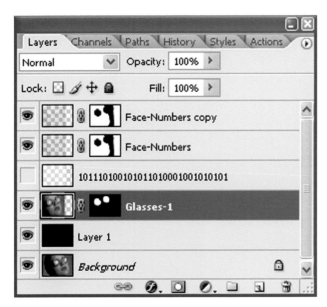

Figure 7.6: Hide the numbers in the logo area.

Figure 7.7: Mask away the excess digits.

Let's get to the logo placement. Open the image **on button.jpg** (see Figure 7.8). The logo needs to be transferred to the face image. Here's the process:

1. Use the Elliptical Marquee tool to select the glowing logo and glowing circle around the On button.
2. Copy the logo to the clipboard (⌘/Ctrl+C).
3. Paste the logo into the digital face image at the top of the layer stack.
4. With the Transform tools, conform the logo to one of the lenses.
5. Duplicate the Logo layer and move this instance of the logo to the other lens.
6. Merge the two Logo layers.

After all those steps, the logos should appear on the digital face image, as seen in Figure 7.9.

Create a mask for the Logo layer. The idea is to reveal some of the reflection seen on the original lenses but to still retain the logo. Select a median gray foreground color and paint in the mask over the center of the lenses.

If you retained the glowing ring around the button when it was copied to the face image, you followed the instructions correctly. However, it might look cooler if the glowing ring were turned to metal to appear to be new frames for the lenses. How do you accomplish that?

It isn't as hard as it may sound, really. The reflections are already present in the lights; take the

Figure 7.8: A PC On button

Figure 7.9: The glowing logo is reflected on the glasses.

color away and you should have a nice metallic frame. Create a new layer at the top of the layer stack and set the blending mode for the new layer to Color. You should already have gray set as the foreground color, so reduce the size of the paintbrush to compensate for the width of the frame. Then just paint away the color on the frame.

To enhance the reflections, simply select the Dodge tool and apply it to taste on the lower-right and upper-left quadrants of the logo rings. You may also need to do this to the actual Logo layer to enhance the effect, as seen in Figure 7.10.

In the final image, I've simply added another instance of the logo, a company slogan, and information (see Figure 7.11). Something to think about when creating ad pieces (as I've tried to reflect here) is how to tie the text to the image or vice versa—for instance, the wistful look on the digital woman paired with the "Wishful Thinking" statement in the text.

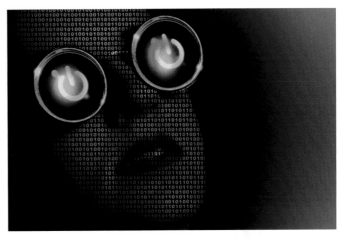

Figure 7.10: Create metallic highlights.

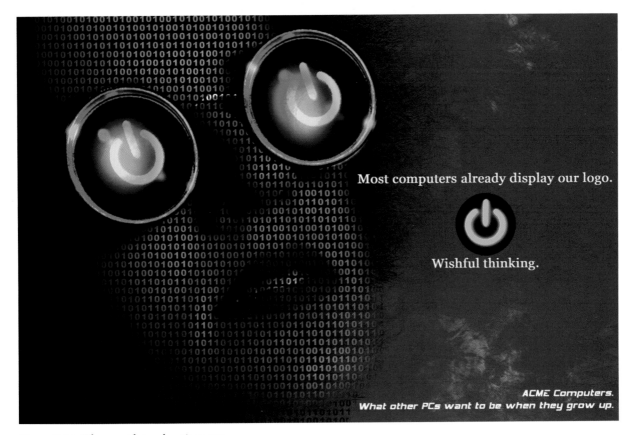

Figure 7.11: The complete advertisement

Enticement: Reverse Advertising

Something that has always baffled me is the use of personal vices to sell products in advertising. I understand why advertisers take this approach, but why in the world would the consumer connect, say, beer with sports? If a quarterback shows up for a game drunk, he certainly isn't going to perform very well. Yet alcohol advertisements and sports are intricately woven together in the minds of the public.

Some of these ads have evolved to the point of being ridiculous, but they have also bred and fed another advertising art form: the public service message. Many of these commercials initially seem to be promoting a product, but as the ad ends, some tragic result ensues because of overindulgence and negligence. That is the point of this technique.

Alcohol was a problem for me for years, so here is what I envision: an ad using some enticing image of alcohol combined with a situation where consumption could prove not only dangerous but deadly. To get this message across, you'll use some standard Photoshop techniques, extracting part of one image and placing it in another image. This technique will also show you one way of extracting the reflections from glass: a very cool trick to have in your arsenal.

Open the image **construction.jpg** (see Figure 7.12). At first glance, the hard-working blue-collar guy appears to be taking a break from his duties, but what if he were adding a little spice to his break? Taking a breather is one thing, but adding alcohol to a dangerous job is something else entirely.

The secondary image reflects the vice. Open the image **scotch.jpg** (see Figure 7.13). The glass needs to be extracted from this photo and placed in the other one.

Choose Filter → Extract, and outline the glass as you would for any other extraction (see Figure 7.14). This extraction is slightly different, however, because the glass is meant to be transparent. That means a little extra thinking is required when selecting

Figure 7.12: A hard day's work

Figure 7.13: What could it hurt?

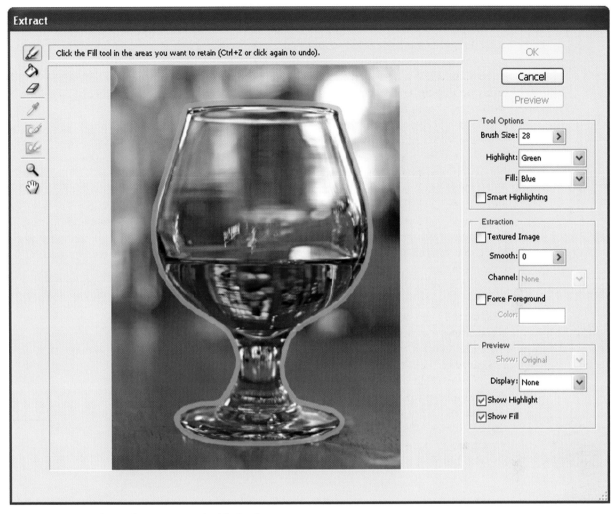

Figure 7.14: Initial area for extraction highlighted

areas to extract. You certainly do not want the room in the background to carry through to the other image, yet you still need the reflections to show that this is indeed glass. Take a look at Figure 7.15. Within the boundary of the original highlighted area, highlight around areas that you want to omit, leaving the reflections intact but removing the room seen through the glass. Leave the liquid alone—that will be needed in the final image also. Fill the highlighted area with the Paintbucket and click Preview.

The extraction will probably be a bit rough, so some edge cleanup will be needed (see Figure 7.16).

After you have the glass fairly well cleaned up, copy and paste it into the construction image. Use the Transform tools to resize the glass to fit the image, and move the glass to the left side so that part of it is lost beyond the image. Also, move the glass down so that the base is partially obscured. This will create a little less work in cleaning up the glass, yet still get the message across (see Figure 7.17).

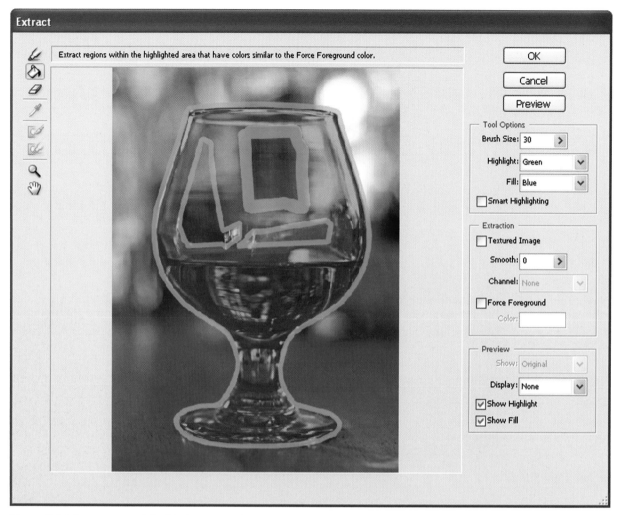

Figure 7.15: Room omitted, highlights retained

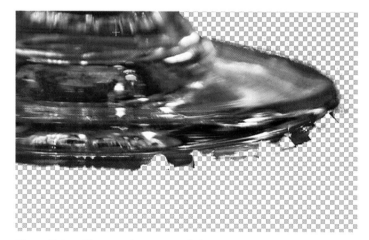

Figure 7.16: Clean up the extracted object.

Create a mask for the glass layer and hide any offending pixels by painting over their corresponding area in the mask (see Figure 7.18). Work within the boundaries of the glass also, hiding any jagged edges along the reflections carried over during the extraction.

If you look at the liquid, you will notice a couple of red areas that were retained from the room in the original glass image. There isn't any red in the construction scene, so this needs to go. You can clean this up quickly by selecting the Clone Stamp tool, sampling areas where the liquid has the proper golden tone, and stamping the sample over the red areas.

Figure 7.17: Place the glass in the original document.

Figure 7.18: Mask the jagged pixels.

Now that the reflections are cleaned up and the glass, for the most part, appears to belong in the construction photo, one more item needs to be addressed to make the glass truly look at home. Curved glass has a lens effect on objects seen through it, so the power lines behind the glass need a bit of tweaking. To do this, use the Magic Wand tool and select the area outside of the glass in that layer. Choose Select → Inverse and click the Background layer. Copy the selection and paste it into a new layer beneath the glass (see Figure 7.19).

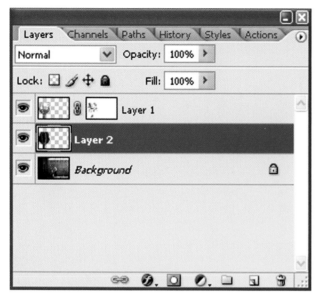

Activate the selection (⌘/Ctrl+click the new layer). Now choose Filter → Distort → Spherize. Set the Mode to Horizontal Only and the Amount to 100% and click OK. Open the Spherize filter one more time, set the Mode to Normal and the Amount to 100%, and click OK again. The background behind the glass will appear warped, as though seen through a lens or, go figure, a glass! Now simply add your message and hope that someone, somewhere, will pay attention (see Figure 7.20).

Figure 7.19: Create a background for the glass.

Figure 7.20: Public awareness message

Common Images in Art

Most photographic art does not use or require a lot of digital manipulation to inspire, to evoke, or to appeal. For this piece, you will simply apply two similar images to a background to reflect a theme.

I was a thespian in my high school days (an actor, to those unfamiliar with the term). The Comedy and Tragedy masks were commonplace on the stage and in posters we created to advertise upcoming plays. In this section, you will create such an image by placing the masks of Comedy and Tragedy on a simple background. The process for realizing this will be a piece of cake, and with some help from Photoshop you can complete a professional-looking poster in very little time.

To start, open the image **roughBG.jpg** (see Figure 7.21) to serve as the background.

The background looks pretty good as it sits, but some shadow could be added to imply a border and take the emphasis away from the background in the final image. This is done easily with a quick layer style. Duplicate the Background layer and open the Layer Style dialog box, selecting Inner Glow. Enter the following settings for the glow:

Blend Mode	Multiply
Blend Color	Dark Brown
Opacity	75%
Noise	25%
Technique	Softer
Source	Edge
Choke	0%
Size	220%

Don't worry about any of the other settings; just click OK. This will darken the border of the background gradually, as seen in Figure 7.22.

Figure 7.22: Darken the border.

Figure 7.21: Background for the poster

Open the image **tragedy.jpg** (see Figure 7.23). For this project, you can omit the extensive extraction described for previous exercises, because the background is a solid color and the mask is clearly defined. Use the Magic Wand to select the areas of white (press the Add To Selection button in the options bar), select Inverse, choose Select → Contract → 2 px, and copy and paste the mask into the background image. Use the Transform tools to reduce the size of the mask if you need to, and then move it to the right side of the background until only half of the face is showing (see Figure 7.24).

Make the mask appear to float above the background by applying a drop shadow. Use the following settings for the shadow:

Blend Mode	Multiply
Opacity	50%
Angle	50 degrees (with Global Light turned *off*)
Distance	385 px
Spread	0
Size	100 px

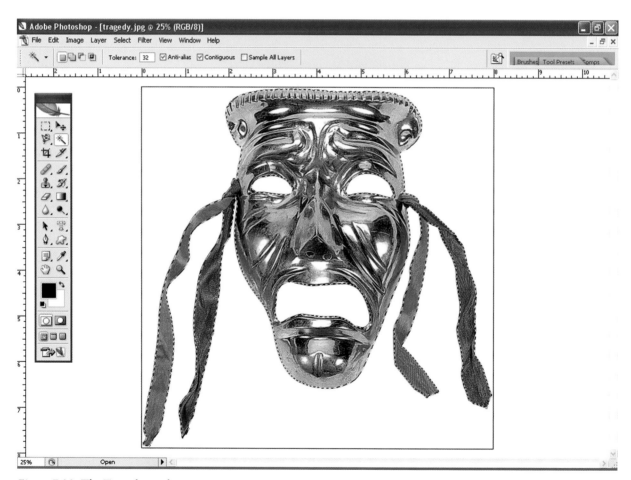

Figure 7.23: The Tragedy mask

The edges of the mask could be darkened as well, just as the Background was. With the Layer Style dialog box still open, select Inner Glow from the left side and apply the same settings as with the Background. After the settings are entered, click OK.

To enhance the mask in both tone and reflection, create two new copies of the mask and change the blending mode for both to Soft Light. Delete the applied styles for these two layers.

The mask appears a bit grainy, but you don't really want to blur the primary Mask layer. Instead, a blur applied to the Soft Light layers will help clean up the graininess. ⌘/Ctrl+click a Mask layer and run a Gaussian blur on both Soft Light layers (see Figure 7.25).

Figure 7.24: The mask finds a new home.

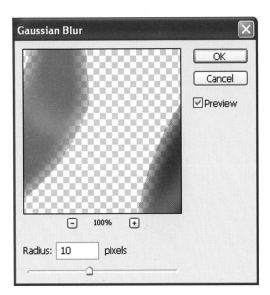

Figure 7.25: Blurring the grain

Figure 7.26: New mask in place; effects reapplied

 Now open the image **comedy.jpg**, which is the Comedy mask image. Repeat the entire process done to the other mask, with the exception of the placement on the Background. Instead, angle this mask as seen in Figure 7.26; repeat all other processes done to the Tragedy mask to this mask also.

To finalize the image, you really only need to darken the shadows a bit and lighten the highlights. A quick combination of two adjustment layers will work in this case. First, create a Curves adjustment layer; use the settings seen in Figure 7.27.

Figure 7.28 shows the final image. The process was painless and short, yet the result looks professional.

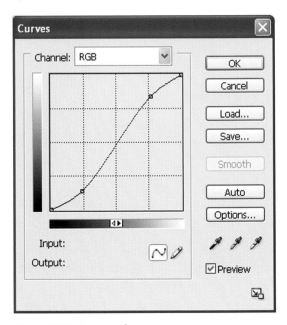

Figure 7.27: Curves adjustment

Figure 7.28: Comedy and Tragedy poster

Enhanced Close-up: Macro Art

Macro art or *macro photography* uses high-definition close-ups, showing us details that require extreme magnification to be revealed. Generally these shots require high-resolution equipment and a very steady hand. (The latter is something I've never had.) As you have seen in previous chapters, Photoshop has the tools to help generate high-definition images from pretty standard photographs. This project will bring out the richly patterned structure of a delicate flower. Open the image **flowers.jpg** (see Figure 7.29).

First, enhance the image with the High Pass filter found in various places throughout the book. As a reminder, here's the process I use:

Duplicate the Background layer twice.

Change the blending mode for the top layer to Overlay (see Figure 7.30).

Figure 7.29:
Delicate petals

Figure 7.30:
Duplicate the
Background
layer twice; set
the blending
mode to Overlay.

Choose Filter → Other → High Pass. Set the Radius for the filter to 15 pixels (see Figure 7.31).

Note that the actual veins in the petals begin to appear as you adjust the slider. When you have a good contrast, click OK. To further enhance the effect, duplicate the High Pass layer and set the blending mode to Soft Light (see Figure 7.32). The enhanced image can be seen in Figure 7.33.

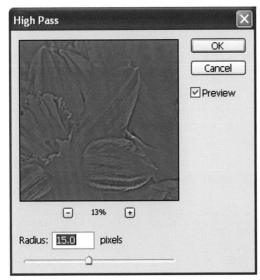

Figure 7.31: Apply the High Pass filter trick.

Figure 7.32: Further enhance the image by duplicating the High Pass layer and setting the blending mode to Soft Light.

Figure 7.33: A well-defined floral arrangement

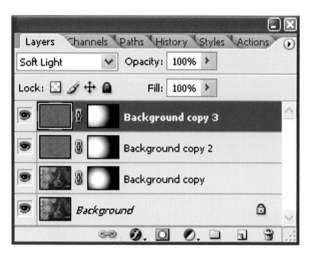

Figure 7.34: Layer masks in place

I'm not going to play with this much, other than to add masks to all layers except the background. In photos such as this, the focus is usually on a single flower, while the rest of the arrangement and the background is softened. Creating a layer mask for each of the top three layers and drawing a white-to-black radial gradient in each with the primary flower as the center of the gradient will allow it to retain its definition while the rest of the image slowly blurs. Figure 7.34 demonstrates what the Layers palette should look like when all three masks are securely in place. Figure 7.35 shows the enhanced photo.

In the first edition of *Photoshop for Right-Brainers*, I demonstrated how this effect can be

Figure 7.35: From distinct focus to soft focus

Figure 7.36: Get ready, get set…

applied to a close-up of a rusty wrench to make the rust appear as though it were growing out of the paper. For that technique I concentrated on a macro-style photo, but the applications of this technique are limited only by your imagination and your needs. For instance, Figure 7.36 shows a seagull about to take flight. The photo appears to have been taken on a somewhat gloomy day, softening the sharpness of the image.

In Figure 7.37, I've followed all the steps from the technique demonstrated on the flowers, using the neck/head of the gull as the focal point and drawing the gradients through the masks accordingly.

Figure 7.38 shows the enhanced photo. This effect brightened the area I want to focus on (that is, the head and neck) while adding definition to the feathers along the under part of the wing. The effect

Figure 7.37: All layers and masks in place

gradually fades toward the wing tip and leaves the house in the blurry distance.

The sharpening technique still works wonders on metal as well. Figures 7.39 and 7.40 show the effect on a piece of hand-tooled metal. Keep in mind that to make the effect a bit more subtle, changing the blending mode for the High Pass layers from Overlay to Soft Light and/or reducing the opacities of those layers will allow you to control the amount of sharpening on the object or subject. In these two examples, I have not included the layer masks.

Figure 7.38: A gull in focus

Figure 7.39: Soft, hand-tooled metal

Figure 7.40: Drastically enhanced

I'm including the following two figures as a reminder that not all sharpening is good sharpening! Figure 7.41 shows a pair of already grumpy eyes. Bad day at work, perhaps? Figure 7.42 is the result after having applied this sharpening technique. The pores, the stray hairs, the blemishes, the freckles—everything a person generally wants to correct in their photos is brought forth with less than flattering results!

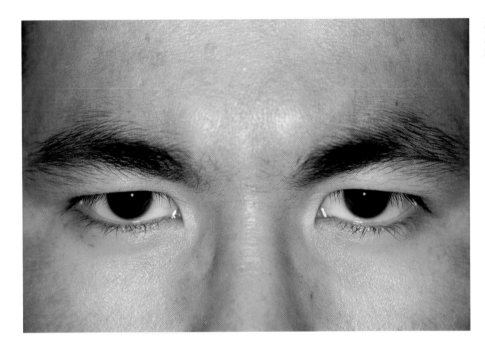

Figure 7.41:
Having a
bad day

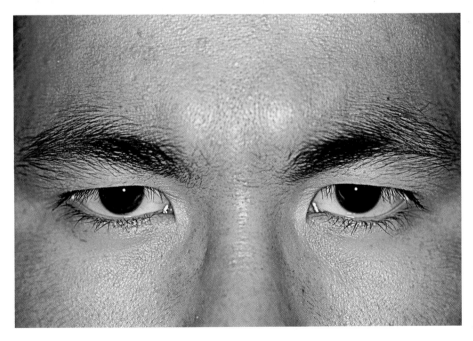

Figure 7.42:
What are you
looking at?

eight

Going Beyond Canned Filters

Filters are one of the first features that a new Photoshop user typically starts with. They spark interest in the software, providing instant gratification with just a few clicks. You don't need to know the theory behind a filter in order to apply it to an image. The drawback to using filters is that no matter how cool an image may look after a particular filter is applied, other Photoshop users will notice the "canned" filter in an instant. Many is the time I've been asked to critique someone's "masterpiece," only to see that they applied one or two filters and sent it out to the digital world to stun the masses. The masses, especially those who use Photoshop, are usually left unstunned.

The key to using filters is to know when and where to apply one (and which one to apply) to an image that incorporates other features and tools in the program. Filters are spices; they are not the meal. Use them sparingly. This chapter shows several ways to make your photos appear aged, drawn, painted, and vectorized, without using the Filters menu exclusively. I think you will find that the end results not only have a greater realism but are far more satisfying.

Retro Photo: Aging

Photoshop is not only a photo correction tool, but as you have seen in previous chapters, it is also a great program for manipulation. The concept for this section is to take a perfectly good photograph that could have been taken yesterday and age it 60 years, complete with damage to the paper.

Open the image **thoughtful.jpg** (see Figure 8.1). This photo is clearly intended to look like a period capture; the clothing and hat are certainly not something you would expect to see in these so-called modern times. One can almost imagine that the woman was caught waiting at a train station decades ago, perhaps waiting for her sweetheart to return home from the war. Will he be on the train? Will he remember the one he left behind?

In the Layers palette, duplicate the Background layer. Rename the new layer **Aged**. Create a duplicate for this layer also, but shut off the layer (Aged Copy). You will return to it soon, but a few things need be done to the Aged layer first. Shut off the Background layer. With the Aged layer selected, choose Image → Adjustments → Desaturate and remove all the color from the Aged layer (see Figure 8.2).

Figure 8.1: Waiting for a lost love

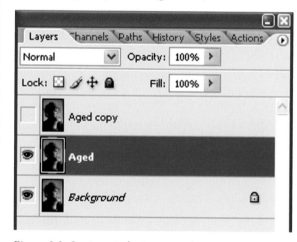

Figure 8.2: Setting up the Layers palette

This layer will provide the foundation for the aging process. Create a Brightness/Contrast adjustment layer just above the Aged layer, but beneath the Aged Copy layer. Leave the Brightness slider alone, but increase the contrast to 25 and click OK.

One problem with a lot of old photographs is the quality of the camera or film available at the time. Graininess was a definite problem, so adding some will increase the aged look of this piece. Select the Aged layer and choose Filter → Noise → Add Noise. In the Add Noise dialog box, set the Amount to 8% and the Distribution to Gaussian, and select Monochromatic at the bottom (see Figure 8.3). Click OK.

Figure 8.3: Add Noise filter in action

If you apply the Add Noise filter with Monochromatic unchecked, the filter will change the color of some pixels. With Monochromatic checked, the filter affects only the tonal elements of the image or layer, leaving the colors alone.

Create a new Hue/Saturation adjustment layer above the Brightness/Contrast adjustment layer. This layer will give the black-and-white layer beneath it a sepia tone. Most aged photo techniques stop there, but this technique will allow some original color to be retained.

With the Hue/Saturation dialog box open, move the sliders (or type in the settings manually) as follows:

Colorize (lower-right corner)	Checked
Hue	30
Saturation	20
Lightness	0

Click OK to apply the settings. The Layers palette at this point will look like Figure 8.4.

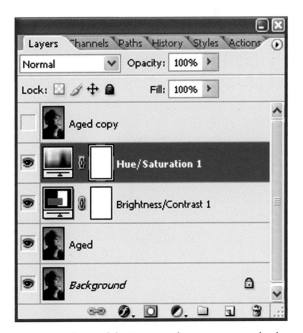

Figure 8.4: State of the Layers palette—progress check

I mentioned that some of the original color will be retained, and the Aged Copy layer will be the medium used for that color. Some manipulation of the pixels needs to take place to combine the color of this layer with the sepia from the layers beneath. You may think that a simple blending mode change or opacity reduction will give the desired effect, but this technique is a bit more involved than that.

Select the Aged Copy layer. Change the blending mode to Overlay and reduce the opacity to 50%. Many old photos were originally black-and-white or sepia toned, and later colored by hand. You are going to use this layer to give the photo that hand-colored effect, while retaining the original sepia in other areas of the picture.

Choose Select → Color Range. The default selection (indicated by white in the viewer window) should grab the shadowed areas of the image. If not, use the Eyedropper to sample the dark areas, and move the Fuzziness slider to 200. Click OK.

With the selection active, press the Delete key. If you hold down the Option/Alt key and click the eye icon next to the layer, all other layers will become invisible and you can see the state of the current layer (see Figure 8.5). The dark areas have been wiped away, leaving only faint colored pixels in the areas of sky, skin, and clothing. Option/Alt+click the eye icon again to turn all the layers back on.

Figure 8.5: Layer after shadow deletion

Figure 8.6: Remove a few more pixels.

There still seems to be a bit too much color in the overall image, so choose Select →
Color Range again. This time, select Midtones from the Select menu at the top of the Color
Range dialog box and click OK. Again, press the Delete key to wipe away the selected
pixels from the layer. Figure 8.6 shows the image thus far. The overall tonal effect is sepia,
with just a hint of color left in the sky and on the woman's face. Trust me, it is there. If you
would like a bit more color, just increase the opacity of the layer.

With the image appropriately colored for age, you may now simulate damage to the
photo produced by years in a box. Normal wear and tear produces scratching; moisture can
bubble or blemish the photo as well as produce mold and age spots. Photoshop can do this
too, or at least give the illusion of such.

Create a new layer above the Aged Copy layer; name the new layer **Clouds**. Press the D
key to reset the swatches to Black (foreground) and White (background); then choose
Filter → Render → Clouds. The new layer will be filled with a random pattern of blacks,
whites, and grays merging in a cotton candy pattern of gradual fluffiness. OK, how else
would you describe it?

Choose Filter → Brush Strokes → Sprayed Strokes. Set the Stroke Length to 0, Spray
Radius to 25, and Stroke Direction to Left Diagonal. Click OK. Now choose Image →
Adjustments → Brightness/Contrast. Set the Brightness to 75 and the Contrast to 100. Click
OK. Change the blending mode of the Clouds layer to Multiply.

This layer can also be used to add color to the photo. Choose Image → Adjustments →
Hue/Saturation and set the options as follows. When you're done, click OK (see Figure 8.7).

Hue	25
Saturation	25
Lightness	−20

Duplicate the Clouds layer and change
the blending mode to Screen, the opacity to
20%. This will lighten the image somewhat.

It may be a good idea to save your work
thus far. You can either save the image as a
.psd file to retain the layers, or simply open
the History palette and create a new snapshot.
You can return to this state of the image at
any time by selecting the snapshot in the History palette. Your image should look like Figure 8.8 at this point.

I had you save a snapshot at this point
because you're going to merge all the layers
with the exception of the original background. Link all the layers in the Layers
palette (except the Background). Open the
Layer menu, and near the bottom of the
menu, select Merge Linked (⌘/Ctrl+E). Duplicate this layer and name the copies **Aged-1**
and **Aged-2** (see Figure 8.9).

A few more blemishes can be added in
the form of cracking or peeling. To do this,
create a new layer named **Cracks** and run the

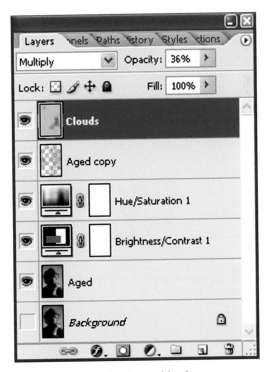

Figure 8.7: Using clouds to add color

Figure 8.9: Merged new layers

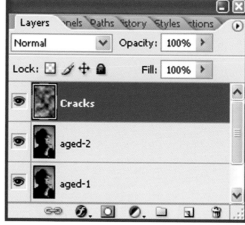

Figure 8.10: Working with clouds

Clouds filter on this layer also (Filter → Render → Clouds). Figure 8.10 shows the Layers palette.

The Clouds filter generates patterns by using soft variations between the foreground and background colors. To generate a more emphasized cloud pattern, hold down Option/Alt as you choose Filter → Render → Clouds. When you apply the Clouds filter, the image data on the active layer is replaced. (Pixels are added on layers that have no image data.)

Open the Filters menu again, this time choosing Texture → Craquelure. This filter reproduces the effect of cracks on a plaster surface. Apply the following settings in the Craquelure dialog box:

Crack Spacing   90
Crack Depth   8
Crack Brightness   8

Click OK. Choose Image → Adjustments → Brightness/Contrast and increase the Brightness of the layer to +75 and the Contrast to +100. Click OK.

The whites and blacks of this layer need to be swapped (the cracks will be darker than the photo), so press ⌘/Ctrl+I to invert the colors. You will not need the white in the image, so choose Select → Color Range, and select the white portions of the layer with the Eyedropper (see Figure 8.11). Click OK, and press the Delete key to wipe away the white pixels. Deselect.

The image is nearly done; a couple of quick styles will top it off nicely. Open the Layer Style dialog box for this layer and select Bevel And Emboss. This setting will allow for depth in the cracks. Adjust the Bevel/Emboss options as follows:

Figure 8.11: Select white to delete.

Style	Inner Bevel
Technique	Chisel Soft
Depth	1%
Direction	Down
Size	1px
Soften	0px
Use Global Light	Unchecked
Angle	120°
Altitude	10°
Gloss Contour	Default
Highlight Mode	Screen
Highlight Color	White
Highlight Opacity	28–30%
Shadow Mode	Multiply
Shadow Color	Black
Shadow Opacity	35–40%

Before closing the Layer Style dialog box, select Color Overlay from the left-hand menu. Set the color to a tan-gray, the blending mode to Color Burn, and the opacity to 20%. Click OK to accept the style.

You aren't quite done with styles just yet. Select the Aged-2 layer. By manipulating an inner glow, you can add a studio-style shadow around the perimeter of the image. Open the layer styles for the Aged-2 layer and select Inner Glow. Tweak the settings for the style as follows:

Blend Mode	Multiply
Opacity	100%
Noise	0%
Color	Tan/Gray
Technique	Softer
Source	Edge
Choke	0%
Size	200%

The default settings will work for the remainder. Click OK. Figure 8.12 shows the final aged photograph.

Figure 8.12: Final shot—aged and scratched

Photo to Line Art: Sketching

This section is a bit complicated for me as a teacher. Not that creating drawings from photographs is difficult; quite the contrary. It is an easy process, no matter which approach you take. Therein lies my problem; there are so many ways to generate line art and pencil drawings, which do I demonstrate? The variations on line-art effects could take up a book or two themselves.

For this section I've selected just two methods to give you a general idea of how to approach your sketches. The first retains shading from the original to create pencil effects; the second converts edges into lines for the effect of a pen-and-ink sketch.

Pencil Drawings

Start the first technique by opening a photo of a watch and map. The image used here is **watch.jpg** (see Figure 8.13).

First, convert the mode of the image to Grayscale (Image → Mode → Grayscale). Duplicate the Background layer and choose Image → Adjustments → Invert. Set the blending mode for the new layer to Color Dodge (see Figure 8.14).

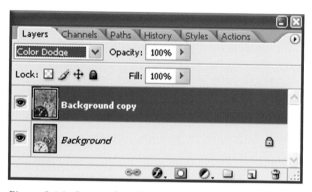

Figure 8.14: Grayscale → Invert → Color Dodge

Figure 8.13: A time and a place

The image now appears nearly entirely white, with a few spots of gray. The watch can barely be seen (if at all) as a result of creating and inverting the Color Dodge layer and interacting with the Background layer.

The Color Dodge blending mode samples the color information in each channel and brightens the base color to reflect the blend color. This is done by decreasing the contrast.

Figure 8.15: Gaussian blur for sketching

The trick for creating a drawing is only one step away. With the Background Copy layer selected, choose Filter → Blur → Gaussian Blur. Set the radius of the blur to 4.5 pixels (see Figure 8.15) and take a look at the image (don't click OK just yet). The watch and map now appear drawn, with thin pencil lines outlining the contours and edges (see Figure 8.16).

Increase the Gaussian blur to 8. The more you increase the blur, the more the layer beneath is revealed, making the lines in the drawing appear thicker and the shading more pronounced (see Figure 8.17).

Let's go through the process once more, only this time you will not convert the image to grayscale. Open the image **younggirl.jpg** (see Figure 8.18). By running

Figure 8.16: A light pencil sketch

Figure 8.17: Deeper, bolder lines

Figure 8.18: Time for a nap

Figure 8.19: Pencil art colorized

through the same steps as given previously, only without the grayscale conversion, you will create a colorized line-art drawing (see Figure 8.19). The amount of blur again dictates the amount of color and sketching revealed.

Pen-and-Ink Art

The second trick I want to show you for generating line art has a completely different approach, but it is excellent if you want clearly defined lines.

 The image **OK.jpg** (see Figure 8.20) is well suited for this because it has plenty of contrast that you can turn into linear detail.

Duplicate the Background layer and choose Image → Adjustments → Desaturate. Press ⌘/Ctrl+I to invert the colors of the gray layer. Now choose Filter → Blur →

Figure 8.20: O.K.!

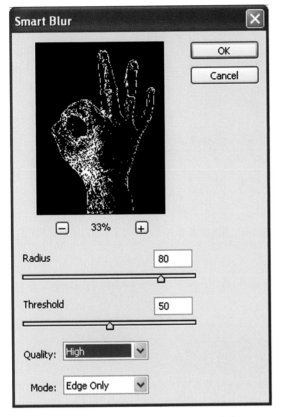

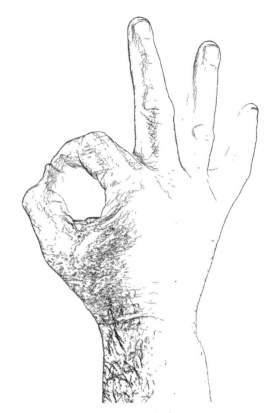

Figure 8.21: Radius and Threshold control the intensity of the drawing.

Figure 8.22: Inverting black and white

Smart Blur and select Edge Only from the Mode list at the bottom of the Smart Blur dialog box. Take a look at the viewer; the image appears to be made of white lines on a black background. When you move the Radius and Threshold sliders, more lines are added or more are removed, depending on the Radius and Threshold values (see Figure 8.21). Click OK. Press ⌘/Ctrl+I again if you want to invert the black and white (see Figure 8.22).

For added effect, duplicate the Background layer again, placing the new layer just above the original background. Choose Filter → Artistic → Cutout. This filter is cool for making photos appear vectorized. Set the Number Of Levels to 5, Edge Simplicity to 3, and Edge Fidelity to 2 (see Figure 8.23). Click OK. Figure 8.24 shows the new image, combining vector-style color and line-art sketching.

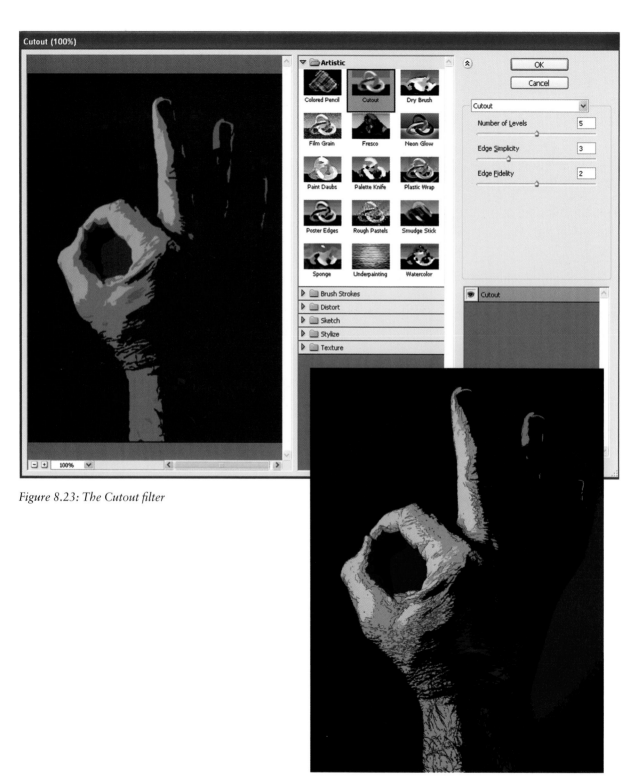

Figure 8.23: The Cutout filter

Figure 8.24: Etched and colored

Portrait to Painting: Artistic

There are dozens of ways to achieve paint effects in Photoshop, so as with sketch-style effects, deciding which paint effects to demonstrate is a tough choice. Many of the techniques forget one vital element: a realistic portrayal of what they are supposed to reflect. Realism is the focus of this project; the fine details will turn the photo into a realistic oil-on-canvas painting.

I want to take a photograph and have it appear to have been painted on a textured background sometime in the distant past. Photoshop has several tools to help you realize a painting. The trick is to know what else is required from the toolbox to make the technique work. Sometimes all a car needs to turn over is a spark plug and an oil change. You have the parts and the tools; the trick is getting the pieces under the hood in the right way, saving a bundle on a mechanic.

To begin, open the image **Oldportrait.jpg** (see Figure 8.25). I've chosen this photo due to its obvious age; I just think the effect will be best demonstrated as an old painting. Don't let that deter you from trying this on newer images!

Duplicate the Background layer twice. Name the first copy **Untouched**; this will remain as named (for the time being, anyway). Name the second layer **Paint-1**; this is where you will

Figure 8.26: Setting up the layers/canvas

Figure 8.25: Portrait of great-great-grandpa as a young man

start applying the effects. Set the blending mode for the Paint-1 layer to Overlay (see Figure 8.26).

The first layer of paint is actually an application of the Median filter to the Paint-1 layer. Choose Filter → Noise → Median, set the Radius to 8 pixels, and click OK (see Figure 8.27).

That softened the layer somewhat; now you can add some defining lines within which the paint will fall. This process is nearly a reverse of the actual painting process, but the results will be almost the same as the real thing.

Choose Filter → Stylize → Find Edges. Now invert the layer (⌘/Ctrl+I). See how the image (see Figure 8.28) is taking on a painted quality?

Now duplicate the Paint-1 layer; rename the new layer **Paint-2**. Set the blending mode for the layer to Soft Light and drop the opacity to 50%. This will lighten the painting back up a bit, counteracting some of the darkness imposed by the Paint-1 layer.

By adjusting the Hue/Saturation for this layer, you can tweak the base paint strokes to appear as if they were laid with the same color. Trust me, it works. Choose Image → Adjustments → Hue/Saturation, enter the following settings, and click OK.

Colorize	Checked
Hue	360
Saturation	25
Lightness	0

Create another instance of the Background layer, placing it at the top of the layer stack, and name it **Paint-3**. I couldn't go through a painting tutorial without using one of the paint filters, could I? Sure I could, but I'm not going to.

Set the blending mode for the new layer to Soft Light. Choose Filter → Artistic → Paint Daubs. Set both the Brush Size and Sharpness to 15, set the Brush Type to Simple, and click OK (see Figure 8.29).

Figure 8.27: The Median Noise filter acts almost like a blur.

Figure 8.28: Some paint-like qualities appear.

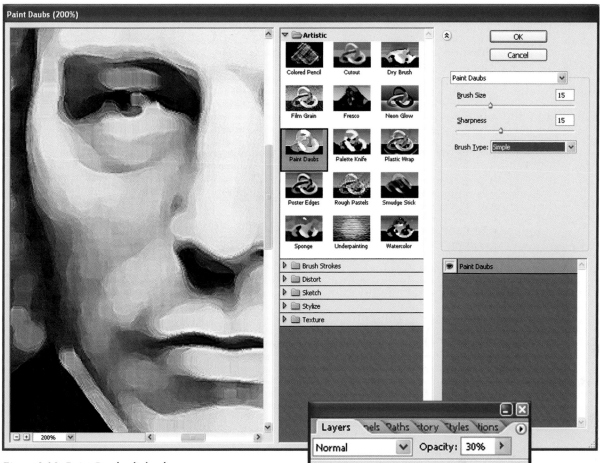

Figure 8.29: Paint Daubs dialog box

Duplicate the Untouched layer and set the opacity to 30%. Run the Paint Daubs filter once more on this layer. Rename the layer **Base Paint** (see Figure 8.30).

That's a pretty fair painting, but thus far the canvas being painted on has no texture. As I said, this is actually being painted nearly in reverse. The pixels needed to be in place prior to manipulating them into a canvas.

Select the Untouched layer. I just can't leave it untouched; something has to be done. This will provide the foundation for the canvas. Choose Select → Color Range. Select an area in the face (see Figure 8.31). Quite a bit will come up in the selection, but no worries. It needs to be that way (see Figure 8.32).

Figure 8.30: Rename the working layer to Base Paint.

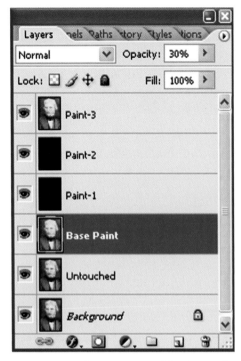

Figure 8.31: Select a portion of the face in the Color Range dialog box.

Figure 8.32: The active selection

Figure 8.33: A rough canvas surface is applied to the new painting.

With the selection active, open the Channels palette and create a new Alpha channel. Select the RGB channel and run the Paint Daubs filter again, this time setting the Brush Size to 5 and Sharpness to 10. Stay with the Simple Brush and click OK.

Select the Alpha channel and choose Filter → Texture → Texturizer. Select Canvas for the texture, and set the Scaling to 100% and Relief to 5. Click OK.

Deselect, and click the RGB channel. Run the Texturizer one more time with the same settings as before. The image now appears to have a rough surface similar to those used in standard oil paintings (see Figure 8.33).

It almost looks good enough to frame, don't you think?

Anime Woman: Vector Art

Sometimes a photo will lend itself to the imagination, stirring up ideas for art inspired by the image. In the first edition of *Photoshop for Right-Brainers*, I turned a photo of an action model into a reasonable facsimile of a Japanese cartoon character. It is a fun effect, to be sure, but can it be taken a step further? You bet it can!

My thoughts for this next piece stem from the same vein—anime style art. It occurs to me that, with Photoshop, you can experiment and see what such a person might look like in real life. Anime style has a few

Figure 8.34: Some images inspire the art.

characteristics that run fairly consistently through the genre, in particular for women. The eyes are usually exceptionally large and innocent, with glossy, wet reflections. Other facial features are greatly reduced: the mouth and nose are generally small, and pointed chins are prevalent. Hair color and skin color are other features that rarely follow normal, lifelike conventions. Hey, in cartoons anything is possible. In Photoshop, you can also bring those characters and their wild characteristics into our dimension.

Open the image **flowerchild.jpg** (see Figure 8.34).

Duplicate the Background layer. You will find that this technique is very similar to that performed on the puppy in Chapter 6, "Animals," and as such the Liquify filter will be the starting tool of choice. Choose Filter → Liquify and begin by applying the Bloat tool to the eyes. The effect you are looking for is seen in Figure 8.35.

Figure 8.35: All the better to see you with…

Figure 8.36: Reduce the size of the nose and mouth.

When the eyes are about the size of silver dollars, switch to the Pinch tool and narrow the nose and reduce the size of the mouth. This takes some finesse, so be careful and work slowly, reducing the size of the brush (or increasing) as needed (see Figure 8.36). Do not click OK just yet—you have more to do.

Next, carefully run the Pinch tool along the jaw (both sides) and the cheek. Not too high on the cheeks, mind you. The cheekbones need to remain emphasized while the chin is brought to a point. If there is a little distortion in the color around the mouth (see Figure 8.37), don't worry. That can be corrected soon. Right now focus on the shape rather than the texture.

After you are happy with the shape, click OK. The next step is to clear up any distortions in color where the tools were applied or skin was moved around. The Clone Stamp tool will work well in this instance (see Figure 8.38). Use the Clone Stamp to

Figure 8.37: A well-defined chin

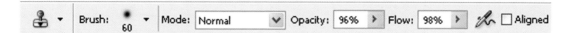

Figure 8.38: Clone Stamp for cleanup work

sample unblemished areas close to the distortions and then apply the stamp over the blemishes and stretched pixel marks. Figure 8.39 shows the model at this stage of the game.

For now I think you've toyed with her face enough: it's time to move on to color. This, of course, can be done in a number of ways. This time you are going to color the model in a manner not used in this book yet: color-filled paths. This keeps in theme with the vector-style art, yet with a raster-style twist.

In the following steps you will separate certain areas that belong together and create filled paths for those areas. Select the Elliptical Marquee tool and make a selection around the flower in the model's hair (see Figure 8.40).

When the selection is active, create a new blank layer and switch to the Paths palette. At the bottom of the palette, click the icon labeled Create Path From Selection; a new path in the shape of the flower selection will be made. Double-click the name of the path and change it to **Flower** (see Figure 8.41).

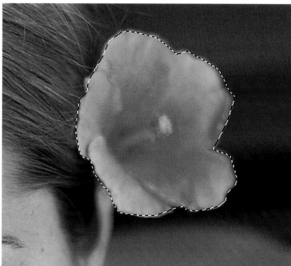

Figure 8.40: Generate a selection around the flower.

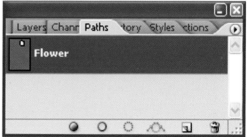

Figure 8.39: The model's new face-lift

Figure 8.41: Rename the path.

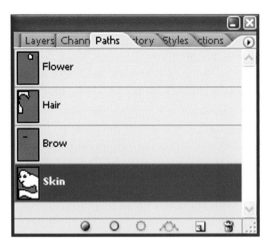

Figure 8.42: Fill the path with the foreground color.

Figure 8.43: The model's regions separated into color-filled paths

Figure 8.44: Keep it or change it.

Figure 8.45: I prefer this color combination.

Set the foreground color to something festive: I've set mine to bright yellow. Right-click on the path (or open the Paths menu). Choose Fill Path from the list. This allows you to fill the path with a color such as the foreground color (see Figure 8.42).

Repeat the Selection → New Layer → Named Path → Fill Path process on all the major areas of the model. In Figures 8.43 and 8.44, I've separated the hair, the eyebrows, and the skin into their own filled paths: separating the face and filling it with a brighter hue than the skin is another possibility. Also, manipulating the colors on the layers can be done at this point to find a combination you like (see Figure 8.45).

After you are satisfied with the colors, it is time to apply them to the skin. This can be done simply by changing the blending mode of each colored layer to Soft Light. To remove the jagged color transitions, a simple Gaussian blur applied to each color layer works wonders (see Figure 8.46).

Figure 8.47 shows the model up to this point.

Remember the pooch in Chapter 6? The eyes are everything in that shot, and they are equally important for this effect (see Figure 8.48).

Using the same techniques in the "Comical Critter Alteration" section of Chapter 6, work with the Dodge tool (lighten irises), Burn tool (darken pupils) and a paint layer set to Color blending mode to enhance the eyes. If you are unhappy with the color, simply adjust the Hue/Saturation of the paint layer (see Figure 8.49).

Figure 8.46: A blur removes the hard color transitions.

Figure 8.48: Focus on the eyes

Figure 8.47: A cartoon no more

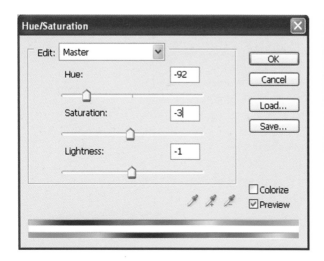

Figure 8.49: *Change to a more suitable hue if you like.*

Figure 8.51: *A line-drawn version*

Figure 8.50 shows my anime woman, residing in relative comfort in the real world.

You can, of course, return her to the hand-drawn-art world in short order, again by using techniques found in Chapter 6. Applying the Cutout and Posterize filters will give you a line-enhanced version of the model, as seen in Figure 8.51.

I'll leave you with one more variation: this enhancement will probably put your brain in color-overload, but some people enjoy that sort of visual jolt. You can select the model layer beneath all the colored layers and choose Image → Adjustments → Posterize. This works similarly to the Posterize filter, although it gives you control over only the number of posterization levels.

Adding a Hue/Saturation adjustment layer after applying Posterize with the Saturation increased to

Figure 8.50: *The Eyes Have It*

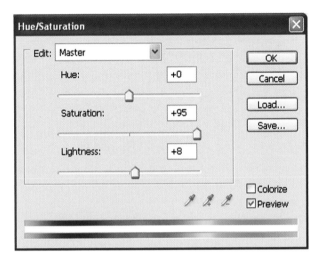

Figure 8.52: Increase the Saturation of color with a
Hue/Saturation adjustment layer.

between +90 and +100 (Figure 8.52) will bring tones
out of the image you didn't know existed. Figure 8.53
shows the result.

    I included these last steps, again, simply to
demonstrate that in Photoshop you are always only a
couple of quick steps from something radically different. You placed an Anime Woman in the real world,
and quickly used that final shot to create what could
be a poster for suntan lotion or a travel agency; the
choice is up to the artist.

Figure 8.53: Aloha

nine

People as Art: Digital Manipulation

It seems you can *barely trust your eyes anymore, and computers serve to compound the problem. Not that I'd give up computers (yet), but it seems everything you see on TV, in movies, or online is suspect. For instance, this evening I sat down to watch our local news. During one feature, the newsperson is seen every night standing in front of a wall of monitors and a huge logo positioned above them. Tonight, however, some dude working in the wings forgot to turn on the effect, leaving her standing in front of a blue wall. My wife and I were stunned; we had been duped for months thinking they actually had this big wall of digital news somewhere in their studio.*

I've made no pretense of being an artist of any vein outside of computers. Photoshop is a tool that releases the inner artist in those who, like me, have brains that are creative to a fault but lose it when attempting to re-create the visions with a pencil or paintbrush. Photoshop has given digital artists new media in which to work; media that real-world artists would never think to use. Some artists use the human body as a canvas; a digital artist can use it as their clay. We can shape it, mold it, color it, add appendages or remove them, with no harm to the model. (If the model sees the art, some harm may come to the artist, but I digress.)

This chapter is specifically about using the human form as a medium for artistic molding and manipulation. You will color it, texture it, melt it,

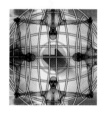

and mold it. Of any chapter in this book, this is the one closest to my heart because the manipulations in this chapter are from my imagination working with the medium I love. In this chapter you get to open my head and see the right side of my brain, and in the process I hope you will pick up some ideas on how to apply what you see to your own work. Grab your magnifying glass, screw off the top of my skull, brush away the cobwebs, and see what makes me tick.

Chex-Girl: Impressionist

I categorize this piece as impressionist, but the art being formed varies from the original definition. Impressionism took shape in France in the 1870s. The focus was the initial visual impression of a work, with the primary elements of the style being unmixed primary colors and small strokes that simulated reflected light.

This piece may better be categorized as digital impressionism. Stark primary colors come into play, and lighting is of the essence; the medium is photography and how these elements work together in a photo intended to generate instant reactions.

What I see in my mind's eye is a woman whose body paint mimics the pattern on the wall behind her. I think of those people who endure hours of having their bodies painted for Mardi Gras. Like the whole tattoo issue, I just gotta ask: *Why in the world…?* At the same time, the body paint idea offers inspiration for this technique, but you get the effect without having to spend hours having your body painted.

To realize this effect, only two images are needed: the subject and the background that the subject will attempt to blend with. Photoshop and you will do the rest.

Open the images **wallpose.jpg** and **checkers.jpg** (see Figures 9.1 and 9.2).

Following the well-practiced extraction techniques, extract the model from her background. You may either copy her and paste her into the checkerboard image, or you may place the checkerboard image in her document. Either way, ensure that she appears above the background, as seen in Figure 9.3.

Turn off the checkered layer and create the displacement map of the woman's body (see Figure 9.4). Duplicate the checkered layer and move it to the top of the layer stack. Name this layer **CheckerOverlay**, as seen in Figure 9.5. Use the Displace filter (see Figure 9.6) in conjunction with the displacement map just created and saved to distort the new CheckerOverlay layer. When done this layer should look close to the example in Figure 9.7.

Click on the CheckerOverlay layer and change the blending mode to Hue (see Figure 9.8). This will cause the color in the woman's layer to become a series of gray and light gray checkers. I would like to retain some color, and once again Blend If is going to help. Open the layer styles for the CheckerOverlay layer and, with Blend If: Gray selected, move the Black slider for This Layer to 60 (see Figure 9.9). Click OK.

This adjustment wipes away the color where the white checkers overlay the skin, but the color is retained where the black overlays the skin, as seen in Figure 9.10.

Figure 9.1: Bahamas vacation

Figure 9.3: Extract the model and replace the background.

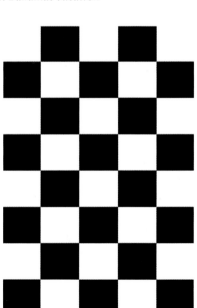

Figure 9.2: Checkers, anyone?

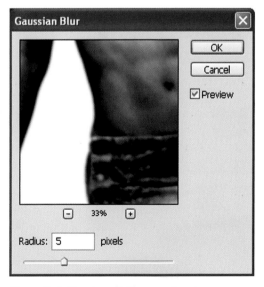

Figure 9.4: Create a displacement map.

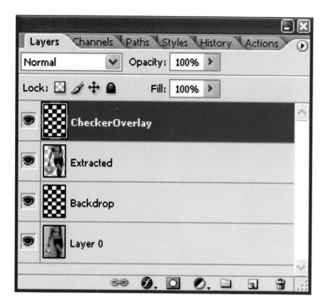

Figure 9.5: Duplicate the checkered layer.

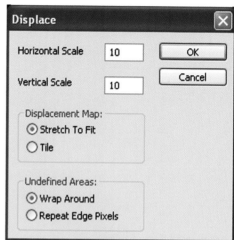

Figure 9.6: Displace the new layer with the woman's displacement map.

Figure 9.7: The texture will distort based on the lights and darks in the map.

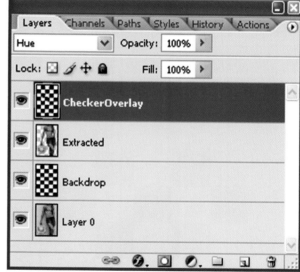

Figure 9.8: Blending mode change

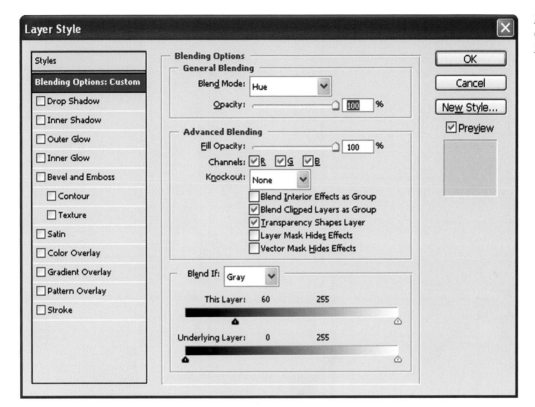

*Figure 9.9:
Our old friend,
Blend If*

*Figure 9.10: The
white overlay
removes color;
black retains it.*

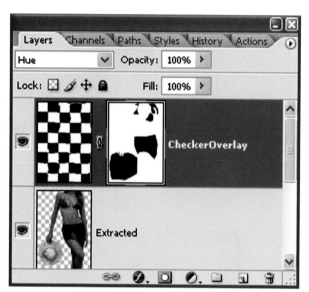

Figure 9.11: Return of the mask

Figure 9.12: The clothing and hair appear untouched.

My interest in this piece is to have only the skin affected by the checkered layer above. You can do this by attaching a layer mask to the checkered layer with black painted over the woman's clothing and hair (see Figure 9.11). This leaves only the skin changed as a result of the Hue blending mode of the CheckerOverlay layer above (see Figure 9.12).

Another variant that you can quickly achieve is to make the checkered pattern appear as tan lines on the woman's body. For instance, changing the blending mode of the CheckerOverlay layer to Overlay (see Figure 9.13) and applying a Gaussian blur of 30 pixels or so (see Figure 9.14) alters the result to make it appear as though the woman slept beneath a hole-filled awning on the beach, creating quite a unique tan. Figure 9.15 shows the result.

Blend If can add to the mix, generating an entirely different result but maintaining the checkered pattern theme. If you select the Extracted woman layer (see Figure 9.16) and adjust that layer's Blend If settings (see Figure 9.17), only those areas of white checkers will be displayed on the woman's layer, leaving the black areas black. Figure 9.18 displays the outcome.

Figure 9.13: Change the top layer's blending mode to Overlay.

Figure 9.14: Blur the top layer.

Figure 9.15: A unique tan

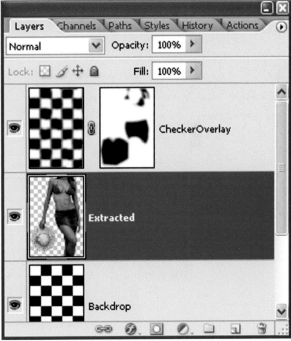

Figure 9.16: Get ready to adjust the Extracted layer.

*Figure 9.17:
Make a quick
Blend If
adjustment.*

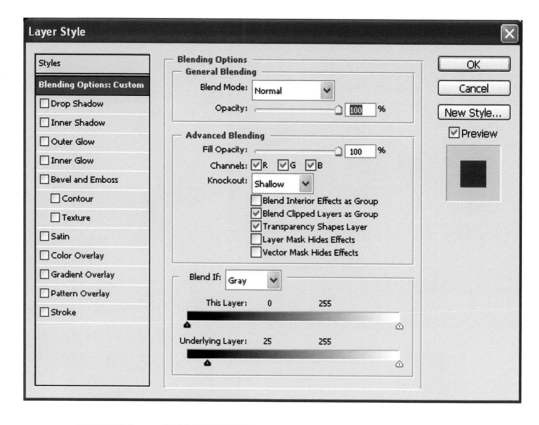

*Figure 9.18: The
woman is visible
only in the white
squares.*

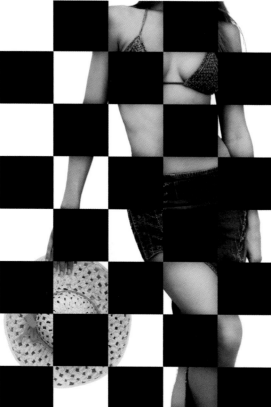

In turn, if you alter the Blend If settings by decreasing the White slider of the Underlying Layer for the Gray channel to 240 or so (see Figure 9.19), the reverse is true: the woman will be visible only in the black squares, and invisible in the white (see Figure 9.20).

Techniques where you can get multiple variations from simple setting changes are what I live for, and this series of techniques exemplifies the power of Photoshop when in the hands of an imaginative right-brainer. See how many variations you can come up with.

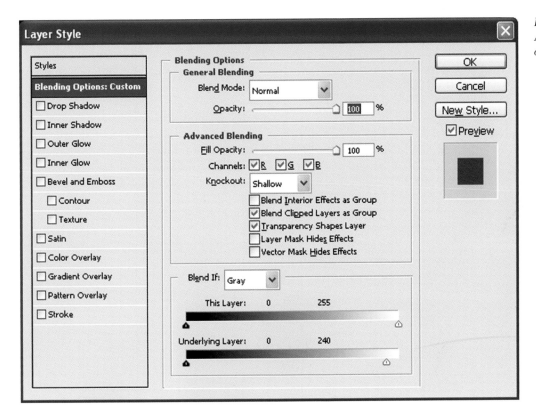

Figure 9.19:
Another tweak
of Blend If

Figure 9.20: She's
back in black.

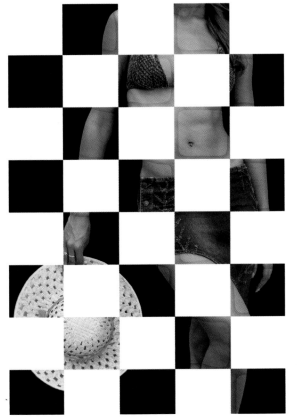

Zebra-Woman: Adventures in Advertising

This next technique is similar to the previous one. This time, however, the texture being applied is a pattern out of nature rather than geometric textiles created by man.

The concept is this: merge a pattern taken from nature and blend it with a human face. The convergence of two elements from the natural world will help to put forth the feeling of intelligence combined with a wild element. Unlike the last piece, this project I see as a facial close-up. The primary subject will have a smart yet feral appearance. I also see a lot of color in natural tones to help the end effect. Following the same idea (if not the same process) as the Chex-girl tutorial, this will be a piece of cake to realize. One hopes, anyway!

To begin, open the images **really.jpg** and **zebra.jpg** (see Figures 9.21 and 9.22). Copy the zebra and paste it into a new layer over the woman. Resize the zebra layer with the Transform tools so that the fur pattern covers the woman's skin, as seen in Figure 9.23.

The following steps will come fast and furious, as you should be an old hand at them by now! Shut off the zebra layer. Create a displacement map of the woman's face and save it to your hard disk (see Figures 9.24 and 9.25). Turn the zebra layer on again and displace it by using the newly created displacement map (see Figure 9.26).

Figure 9.21: You are going to turn me into what?

Figure 9.22: Borrowing a pattern from nature

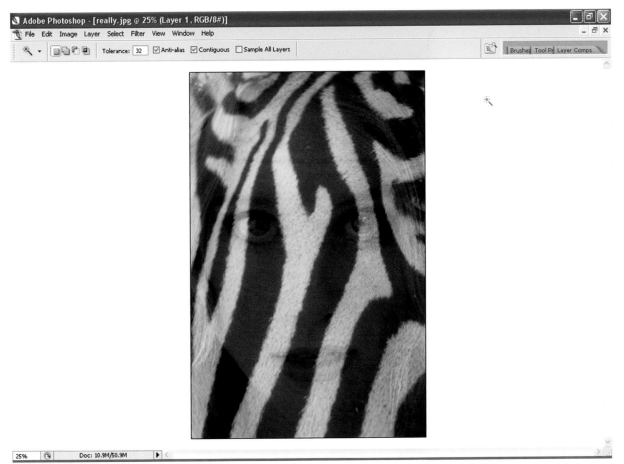

Figure 9.23: Conform the zebra pattern to the face image by using the Transform tools.

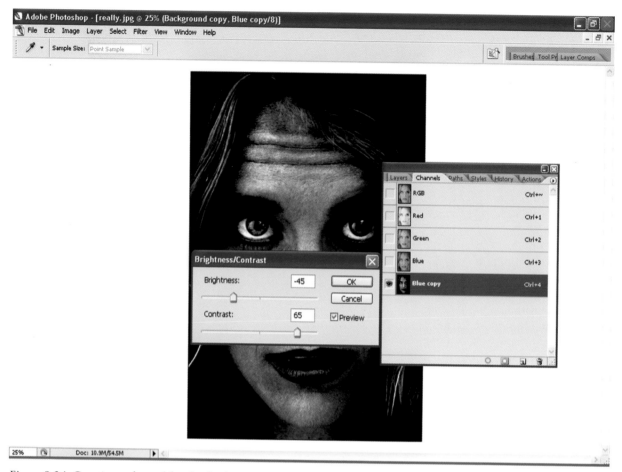

Figure 9.24: Creating a channel for the displacement map

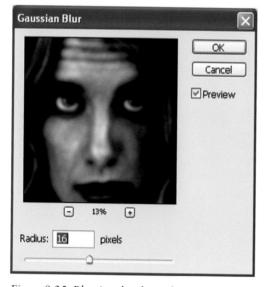

Figure 9.25: Blurring the channel

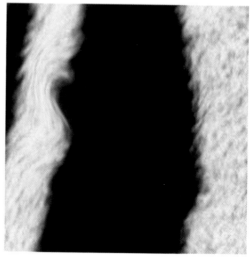

Figure 9.26: Displacing the fur

In order for the skin of the woman's face to appear as though the zebra pattern belongs there naturally, the color beneath the stripes needs to be removed or altered in some way. A Hue/Saturation layer with a mask that displays only the black stripes (in other words the black stripes in the pattern are visible, or colored white, in the mask) with the Saturation slider moved all the way to the left moved color from that area of the woman's face in the layer below. Create the Hue/Saturation adjustment layer between the Background Copy layer and the zebra pattern layer, or Layer 1. See Figure 9.27.

In the next step, create a mask for the zebra pattern layer, or Layer 1 in this case. With a feathered brush, paint with black in the mask over the areas where the woman's hair is seen. This will reveal her natural hair from the Background Copy layer, while leaving the zebra pattern on her face. Next, select a smaller brush without much feather to the edges and paint over the eyes and lips in the mask. Again, this will reveal the natural eyes and lips.

Change the blending mode for the zebra pattern layer to Soft Light. Duplicate this layer twice, and apply a slight Gaussian blur to one of the pattern layers. You may also increase the contrast between the whites and blacks by creating a Levels adjustment layer and manipulating the sliders for greater contrast. You will want to ensure that only the white areas of the pattern are manipulated by the Levels adjustment. In the Levels adjustment layer's mask, paint over the hair, eyes, lips, and black stripes with black. Then make your Levels adjustment. When all these steps are completed, the Layers palette should look something like Figure 9.28. The image should bear a reasonable facsimile to Figure 9.29.

You have just a short way to go. Click on the Background Copy layer and set the blending mode to Overlay (see Figure 9.30). This will help bring the color out in the overall piece. Next, create a new layer at the top of the layer stack and set the blending mode to Color. Set the foreground color to a nice earth tone and paint over the irises with a small brush, taking away the blue and replacing it with a wilder, more feral hue (see Figure 9.31). You may also opt to set the foreground color to red and paint over the woman's lips in the same layer. Figure 9.32 shows my final image.

Figure 9.27: A Hue/Saturation layer is used to remove the woman's face color beneath the black stripes.

Figure 9.28: Stacking layers for maximum effect in the Layers palette

Figure 9.29: The Zebra-Woman thus far

Figure 9.30: A blending change deepens the color of the overall image.

Figure 9.31: Giving her eyes a wilder tone

Figure 9.32:
Zebra-Woman
realized

You didn't really use any new tricks to realize this final image beyond what you've seen in the rest of the book. This is key: more often than not the techniques to achieve different effects are the same—only the way they are applied changes. Again, this is where imagination and learning curve meet.

Cyborg: Digital Distortions

A few years ago, I coauthored a book with my good friend Colin Smith called *Photoshop Most Wanted*, in which I demonstrated one way to turn a person into a cyborg. In that tutorial, I used the Borg from *Star Trek* as the foundation for the technique.

In this section I want to revisit the cyborg, but this time with an entirely different approach. In the aforementioned book, I was looking for photo-realism in my cyborg. With this approach, I want to stay close to the types of effects you've already seen in this title. Perhaps a better description of the following effect would be "Create a Digital Man"—I will allow you to decide. There are a couple of cool things I'm going to show you in this technique that I have not approached elsewhere. I hope you enjoy this trek into my imagination.

Begin by opening the image **contemplate.jpg** (see Figure 9.33). As you can already tell, I am a fan of head shots; the personality and structure of the face and head of my subjects lend themselves to the creative process and often serve as inspiration for the final piece. In this instance, I took one look at this man's head and thought, "Wouldn't it be cool if the top of his skull were made of metal?" Granted, this is probably not something that would pop into everybody's head, probably not even into a fraction of people's heads. Some days it's fun to be me!

Once again you start by duplicating the Background layer (see Figure 9.34). I want to pull the top of this man's head off, so the first part of this process is to create a thin dark line around the man's head. The Burn tool with an

Figure 9.33: A contemplative stare

Figure 9.34: Duplicate the Background layer.

8-pixel Round slightly feathered brush with the range set to Midtones and Exposure to 50% will work perfectly in this instance. Draw a line around the man's head by using the Burn tool.

Right now the Burn line probably just looks like someone took an eyeliner pencil and drew a ring around the skull. The Pucker tool in the Liquify filter dialog box will help pinch the line together, making it appear more like a scar or seam rather than a drawn line. With a narrow brush, use the Liquify filter to tighten the line around the man's head. Where the line meets the background, use the Pucker tool to draw in the side, making it appear as though the side of his head were dented. This helps add to the illusion. See Figure 9.35.

I've not touched on much photo-realism in this book, in particular making metal out of nothing as I have done in other books. I can't let this slip by; metals are some of my favorite effects. Let's create rivets to bolt the two pieces of the man's skull together.

Create a new layer and rename it **Rivets** (see Figure 9.36). Using the Elliptical Marquee tool, draw oval/round selections, and fill them with a gray to dark gray radial gradient. On the side of the head, the rivets will be oval as you are looking at them from an angled perspective. As you create rivets on the front of the forehead, they will be round (see Figure 9.37).

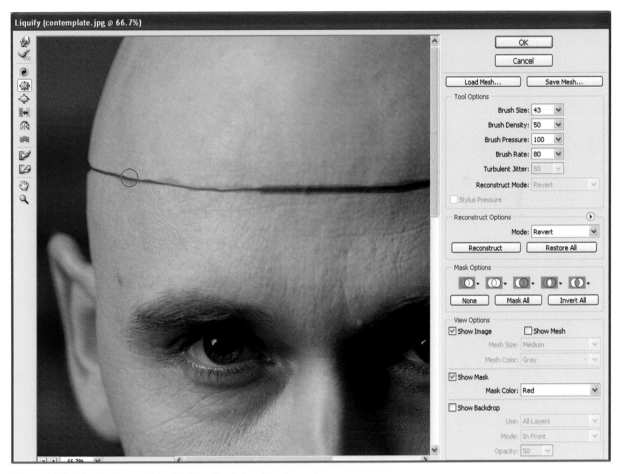

Figure 9.35: The Pucker tool in the Liquify dialog box is used to create a seam or scar.

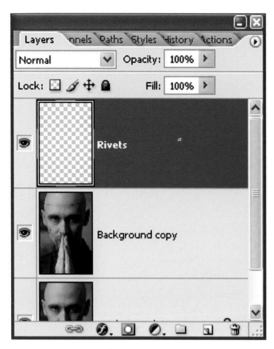

Figure 9.36: Rivets layer

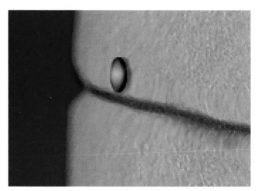

Figure 9.37: A radial gradient serves as the foundation for the rivets.

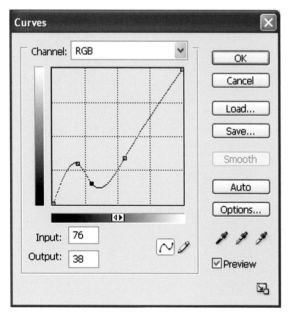

Figure 9.38: Metal curve

For a tighter rivet effect, adjust the Curves for the Rivet layer. Use Figure 9.38 as a guide for the Curves adjustment and click OK. This will give you a greater separation between the light in the black, making the radial gradients appear more closely as rivets. See Figure 9.39.

To turn the top portion of the skull into metal, that portion needs to be separated from the rest of the man's head. Using the Polygonal Lasso tool with zero feather, select the top portion of the man's head along the seam and separate it from the background. Choose Layer → New → Layer Via Cut. Name the new layer **SkullCap**. It should be located beneath the Rivets layer in the Layers palette (see Figure 9.40).

The color needs to be removed from that SkullCap layer in order for the metal effect to work. Adjust the Hue/Saturation of the SkullCap layer, decreasing the Saturation to −100. Click OK. Adjust the Curves for this layer as well, using Figure 9.41 as a guide, and click OK. The result should be close to that seen in Figure 9.42. The top of the man's head should appear as though a metal plate is bolted or riveted to it.

Figure 9.39: Skullcap fastened firmly in place

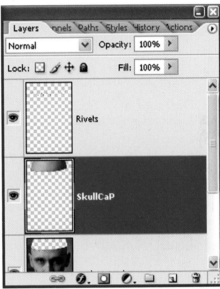

Figure 9.40: Separate the skullcap from the head.

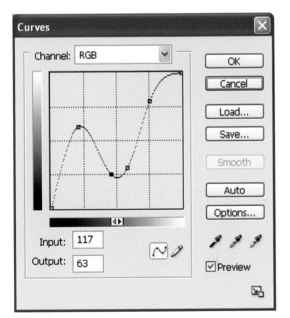

Figure 9.41: Metal Curves adjustment

Figure 9.42:
Skin and bone
is replaced by
stainless steel.

If anyone ever tells you that human flesh cannot be turned into metal, now you have proof to the contrary! Photoshop makes a lot of things possible that were previously unheard of.

The creation of the scar, the removal of the head, and the conversion of the skin to metal were the primary techniques I wanted to demonstrate in this tutorial. The following steps have been repeated a couple of times (in some cases many times) throughout the book so I won't spend additional space explaining what's going on; you have seen and performed

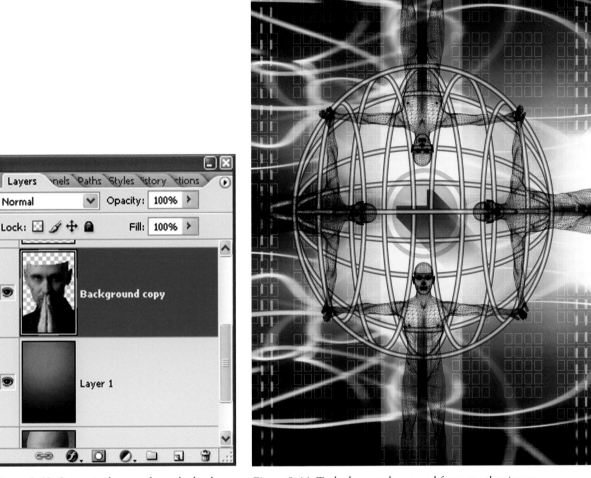

Figure 9.43: Separate the man from the back-ground and replace the red with a green-to-black radial gradient.

Figure 9.44: Tech elements borrowed from another image

it before. I do, however, want to dress up this image a bit and complete the Digital Man, so please try to follow along visually.

The next action you're going to perform is to extract the man from his background and create a new background by using a green-to-black radial gradient (see Figure 9.43). With a Hue/Saturation adjustment layer at the top of the layer stack, remove some of the saturation from the man's face and body, and tweak the color a bit for a slightly less natural tone, perhaps +9 for Hue and −55 for Saturation.

You are now going to borrow another image and use it to dress up portions of the Digital Man image. Open **techrings.jpg** (see Figure 9.44). Copy the entire image and paste it below the extracted man layer. Set the blending mode to Overlay.

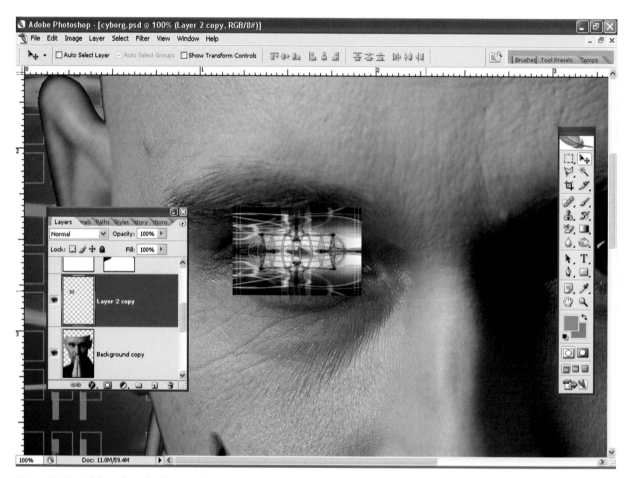

Figure 9.45: Adding digital effects to the eye

Duplicate this layer and drag that copy above the extracted man layer. With the Transform tools, reduce the size of this layer and position it so that it resides above the man's left eye (see Figure 9.45). Trim away the edges so that only the eye is covered. The Eraser tool will work in this instance, or the Marquee tools: it's your call. Set the blending mode for this layer to Linear Light. See Figure 9.46.

The image **circuit.jpg** will also assist in digitizing this person. Open it now (see Figure 9.47). Copy and paste it into a new layer in the man image at the top of the layer stack. ⌘/Ctrl+click the extracted man layer and select Inverse. Delete the circuits from the background, leaving them to cover only the man. Expose the left eye by creating a mask and painting over the eye in the mask with black. Change the blending mode for the circuits layer to Overlay (see Figure 9.48).

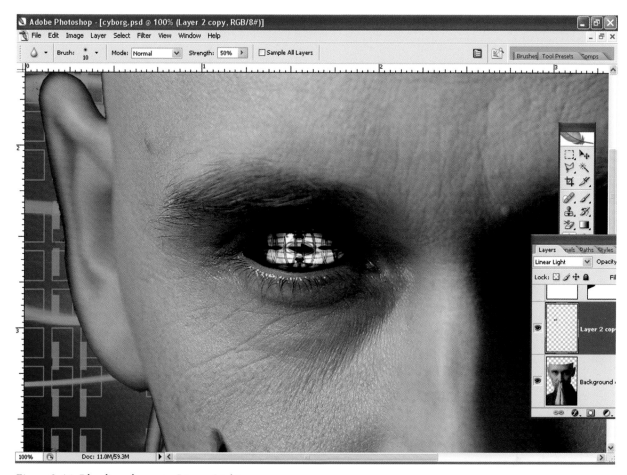

Figure 9.46: Blending change to Linear Light

A quick Levels adjustment will help you adjust the contrast. Move the center slider to the right and the White, or right-hand, slider to the left, stopping where that color information begins in the Levels dialog box (Figure 9.49). Selecting the man's shirt and hands with the Marquee tools, you can further increase contrast and make those parts darker by using Levels (see Figure 9.50).

After a bit of doctoring—for instance, by using the Dodge tool on the man's left eye to brighten the pupil and by creating a displacement map of the man's face and applying that Displace filter to the circuits layer—the result thus far is seen in Figure 9.51.

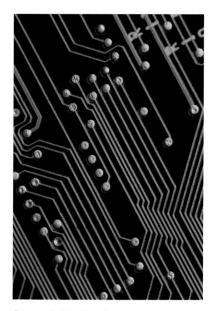

Figure 9.47: Circuits

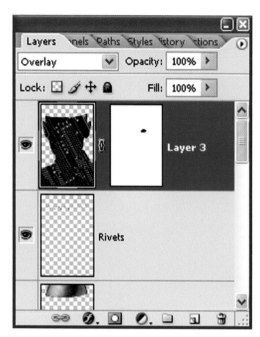

Figure 9.48: Circuits cover the man, not the eye or the background.

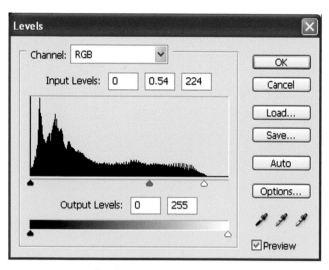

Figure 9.49: Levels adjustment

Figure 9.50: Darkening the shirt and hands

Figure 9.51: The image thus far after some additional tweaking

To finish this off, let's apply two more quick adjustment layers to change this from a manipulated photograph into a painted or artistic rendering. First, apply a Gradient Map adjustment layer by using the Metals gradient (see Figure 9.52). Changing the blending mode of the Gradient Map adjustment layer to Linear Burn will aid in this regard (see Figure 9.53).

A final tweak of the Levels adjustment layer will complete the painted version of the Digital Man (see Figure 9.54). Figure 9.55 shows the final image.

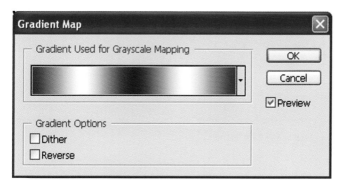

Figure 9.52: Gradient map with the Metals gradient

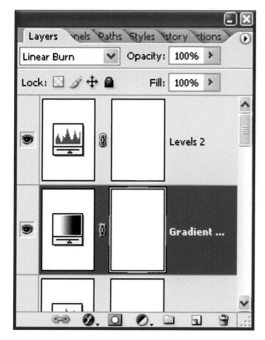

Figure 9.53: Linear Burn the gradient map

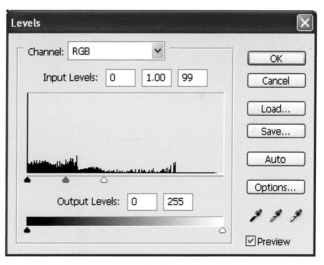

Figure 9.54: One more Levels adjustment

Figure 9.55: The Digital Man

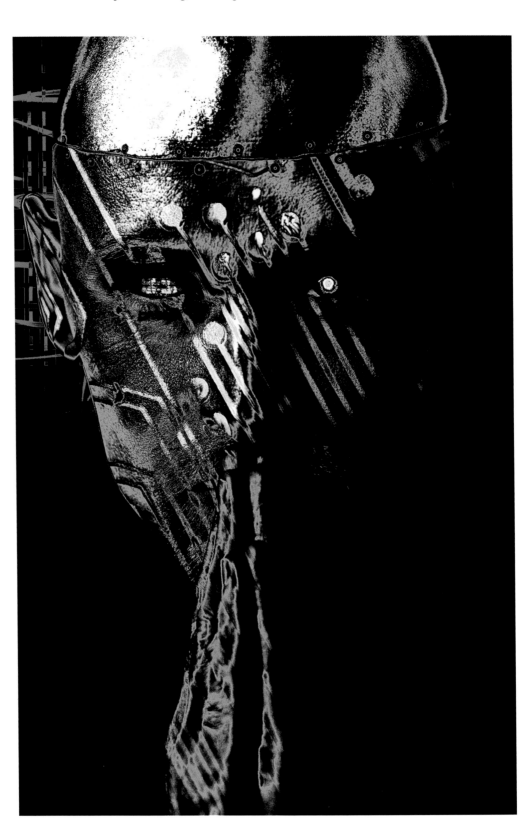

Flesh to Stone

As my mind visualizes this piece, I see a gradual transition of flesh to marble. Recalling a bit of mythology as well as a few old movies, a vision of a Medusa turning her victims to stone with her gaze comes to mind. What if that Medusa had fallen in love with her victim? Realizing too late that his fate had been sealed by her adoring stare, she opts to share his fate, embracing his statuesque form and then casting her spell upon herself. Okay, this may seem like a scene from a bad romance novel, but it will serve well for this particular project.

First, open the image **hug.jpg** (see Figure 9.56). This photo lends itself well to the effect I envision, because skin dominates the majority of the photo. Something that just came to mind is that the end result would be more effective if a portion of the "statue" were removed as though broken. A finger should work nicely.

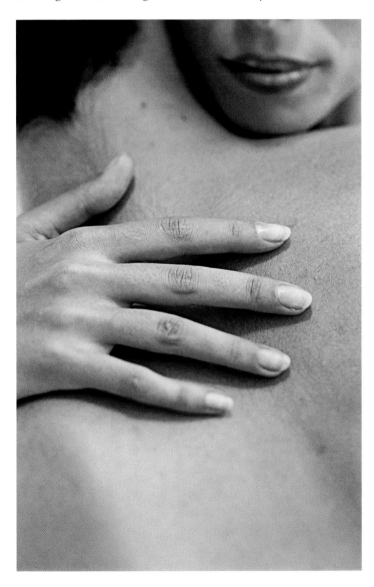

Figure 9.56: Her gentle yet deadly embrace

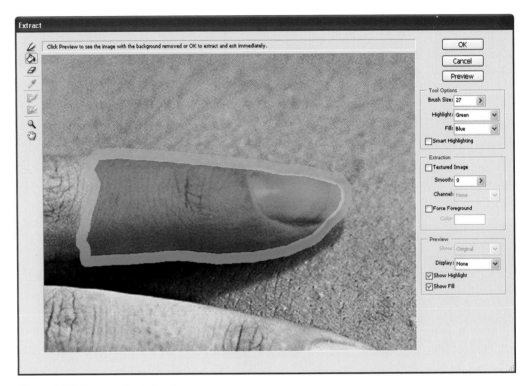

Figure 9.57: Extract the index finger.

Duplicate the Background layer and rename it **Couple**. Duplicate the Couple layer. Use Extract to highlight a portion of the index finger and fill it with the fill color. Make the selection at the breaking point of the jagged edge, as seen in Figure 9.57.

Click the Preview button prior to accepting the extraction and clean up the edges with the tools found on the left-hand side of the dialog box. Accept the change to remove the finger from the surrounding skin (see Figure 9.58).

Figure 9.58: The extracted finger

⌘/Ctrl+click the layer with the extracted finger to generate the selection, render that layer invisible in the Layers palette, and select the Couple layer (see Figure 9.59). With the selection active, press the Delete key. Deselect. As an aid to better see the area you are working on, create a new layer beneath the Couple layer and fill it with black. Return to the Couple layer. Choose Select → Reselect. Figure 9.60 shows what the image will look like.

Click the Clone tool and begin sampling and filling the empty area where the finger was with the skin from the man's back (see Figure 9.61). Be sure to clone over the shadow at an angle down to the other finger so that the lighting appears correct. Adjust the hardness setting of the brush (see Figure 9.62), increasing it as you move closer to the finger so that no soft edges will be seen at the breaking point (see Figure 9.63).

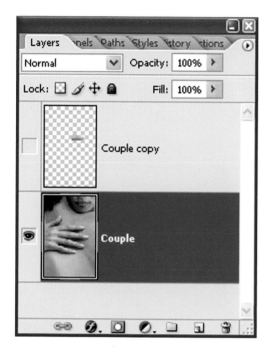

Figure 9.59: Working on the Couple layer

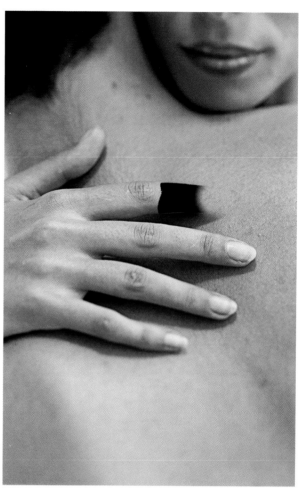

Figure 9.61: Clone over the removed finger area.

Figure 9.60: Remove the finger.

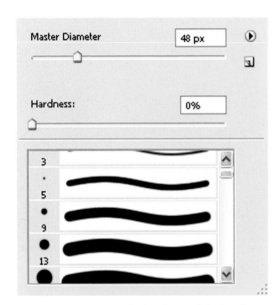

Figure 9.62: Increase the hardness of the brush.

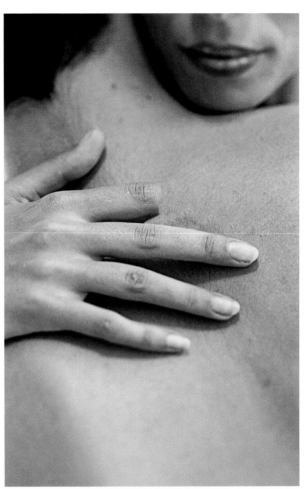

Figure 9.63: The finger remove

Figure 9.64: Generate a selection at the finger breaking point.

Take a look at Figure 9.64. Using the Lasso tool, make a similar selection, because you will make it appear as though excess stone can be seen at the breakaway point. To do this, choose Image → Adjustments → Brightness/Contrast and decrease the brightness to −50 and increase the contrast a few points to +50. Click OK to accept the adjustment.

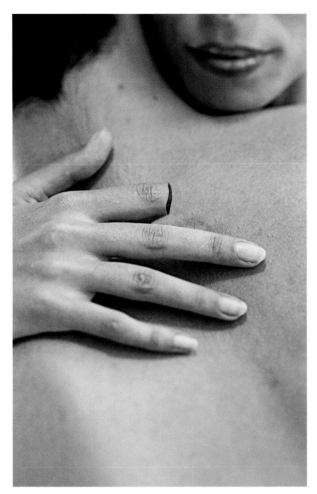

Figure 9.65: Broken finger

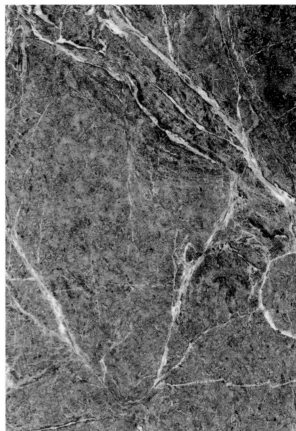

Figure 9.66: Marble photo

As it stands, the breaking point appears to be burnt flesh. With an adjustment to the Hue/Saturation of the selection, the breaking point of the finger can be made to look a bit more like stone. Choose Image → Adjustments → Hue/Saturation and decrease the Saturation to about −60. You may want to increase the Lightness a bit also, to about +8.

Now select the Burn tool and with the range set to Midtones, burn along the edges of the selection with a small brush (see Figure 9.65).

Now open the image **veined_marble.jpg** (see Figure 9.66). Because you will be using Apply Image to apply this image to the couple, both images need to be the same dimensions. Resize the marble image to match the exact dimensions of the couple, as seen in Figure 9.67.

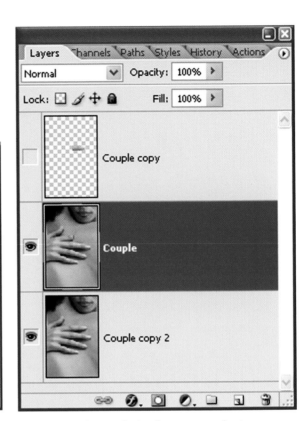

Figure 9.67: Resize the marble photo.

Figure 9.68: Get ready for the metamorphosis…

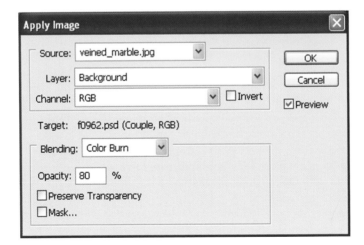

Figure 9.69: Apply Image settings

Select the Couple layer (see Figure 9.68) and choose Image → Apply Image (see Figure 9.69). Note that you will need to select **veined_marble.jpg** as the source image. Set the rest of the Apply Image attributes as seen in the figure.

Figure 9.70 shows the result of applying the marble texture to the couple. I find this interesting because the veins in the stone maintain the same pattern on both individuals.

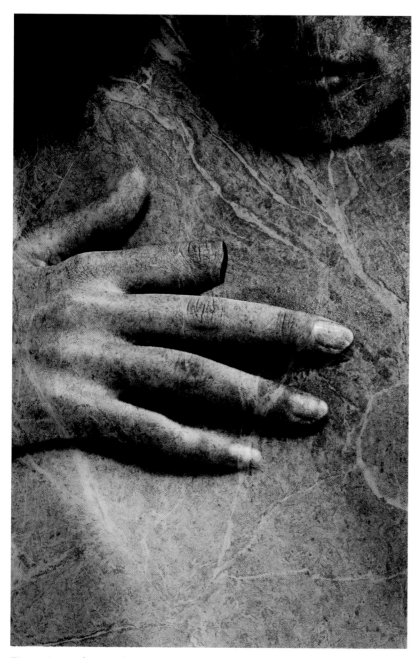

Figure 9.70: The couple in stone

Now create a mask for the Couple layer. There should be a point in the image where the flesh appears to be gradually changing to stone to remain true to the original concept/vision. A mask will work great here, because another unedited version of the Couple layer already resides beneath the one merged with stone. With the mask selected, set your foreground color to black (see Figure 9.71) and paint over the back of the woman's hand,

Figure 9.72: Transition from flesh to rock

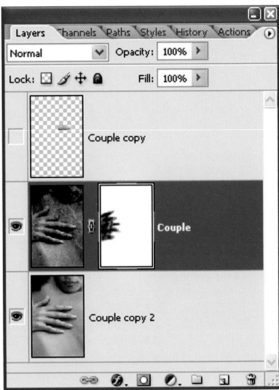

Figure 9.71: Masking away some of the rock

extending up the fingers a short way but not to the point where the finger is broken. The result should look like Figure 9.72.

Just a couple of finishing touches and you are all set. First, choose Image → Adjustments → Hue/Saturation and decrease the Saturation of the Couple layer to −86. You may also adjust the color of the rock at this point with the Hue adjustment slider, but try to reach a nice granite hue, perhaps +6 for Hue and +2 for Lightness.

Next, you can burn a few cracks into the stone with the Burn tool set to Shadows (with a Brush Size of 19 and Exposure set to 50%) and applied to darker portions or veins in the marble.

You may duplicate the Couple layer and change the blending mode to Overlay, tweaking the opacity to taste until you get a result you like, or similar to the one seen in Figure 9.73.

Figure 9.73: A sweet yet sorrowful goodbye

ten

CHAPTER

Digital Intensive:
Crash-Course Projects

You've covered a lot *of material in the first nine chapters, learning quite a bit of information regarding techniques, processes, and their application in Photoshop to create desired results. Up to this point I've approached each technique with a specific result in mind, demonstrating the techniques, filters, and so forth I would use to achieve that final effect.*

This chapter is certainly similar in that regard. Where this chapter differs from the rest is that it omits much of the explanation walking you through the techniques. Instead, I show a version of the final image and then show you step-by-step how it might be achieved. This is not a comprehensive "everything you learned in one basket" chapter, but rather three quick projects to test your creative chops.

As you begin this final series of projects, I ask you to do one thing first: look at the final image and, before starting the project, see if you can figure out what processes I used to get the end effect. Call it a mini-quiz, but an open-book quiz to be sure.

Project 1: Contrast Woman

Many advertisements, especially those for trendy, hip products, combine multiple photos with stark color combinations, especially those residing on opposite sides of the color spectrum, to draw attention to the product. Often the ad has nothing to do with the item being sold; it is more about the image the company is trying to convey.

You can see the final shot for this project in Figure 10.1. The images used to get there are in Figures 10.2 (**bluelips.jpg**) and 10.3 (**bluesky.jpg**). Before you begin going through the technique, see if you can pinpoint what steps or processes were used to get to the final shot. At the end, gauge how close you were.

Figure 10.1: A study in contrast and color

Figure 10.2: The model

Figure 10.3: The backdrop

Again, I won't be explaining every detail this time, so if you have trouble you may want to review those areas in previous chapters where the techniques were examined in greater detail. Let's begin.

Start by having both photos open. Switch to the image **bluelips.jpg**.

Choose Filter → Extract (see Figure 10.4). When the Extract dialog box opens, use the green Highlighter tool to outline the model. Increase the brush size as needed to get any stray hair strands you may want to capture. After the model has been separated from the background with the Highlighter, fill the area to extract with the Paintbucket (see Figure 10.5).

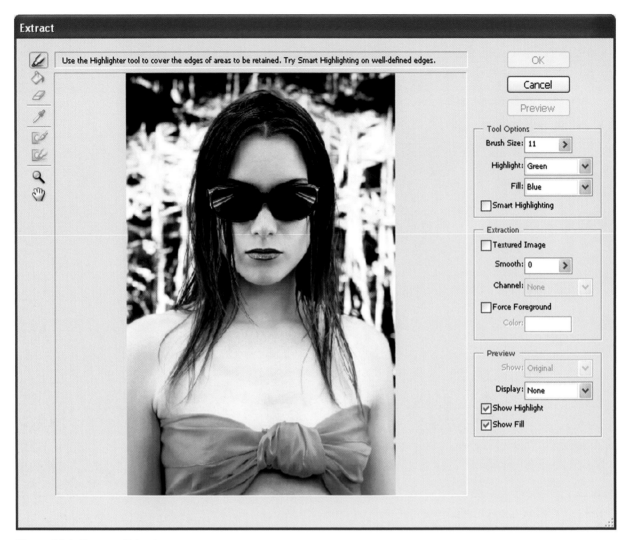

Figure 10.4: Extract dialog box

The model will have some stray background pixels hovering around her (see Figure 10.6). Clean these up with the Eraser tool. Also, any stray, flyaway hairs that did not make it through the extraction process intact can be wiped away. They will not be required for the final shot.

It's time to move the model to her new background. Select the entire layer (⌘/Ctrl+S, or Select → All), copy it to the clipboard (⌘/Ctrl+C, or Edit → Copy), and switch to the **bluesky.jpg** photo. Then place the model in a new layer, above the blue sky background (⌘/Ctrl+V, or Edit → Paste). Figure 10.7 shows the image at this point.

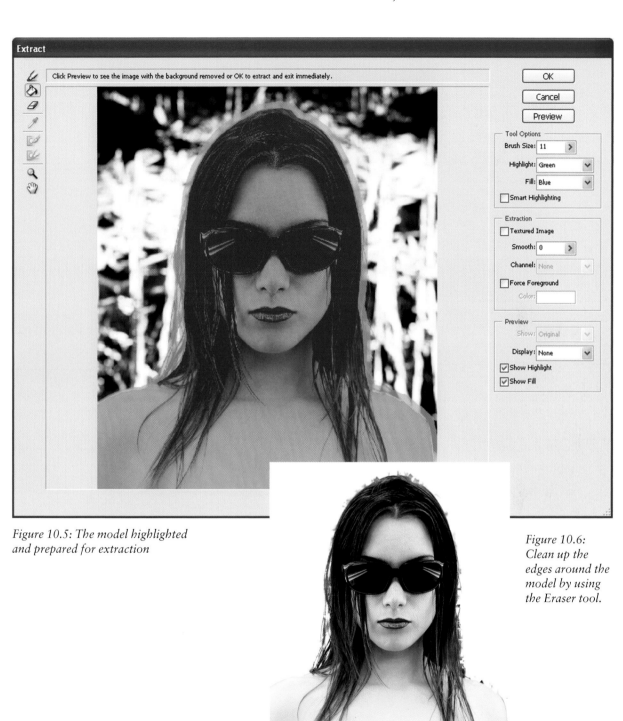

Figure 10.5: The model highlighted and prepared for extraction

Figure 10.6: Clean up the edges around the model by using the Eraser tool.

Figure 10.7: Paste the model into the blue sky background.

Figure 10.8: Carefully color the lips orange with the Paintbrush tool.

Let's play with the color a bit. If you look at the final image, the background has taken on the orange cast, and the woman the blue rather than the other way around. First let's adjust her makeup—her lipstick in particular.

Select the Eyedropper tool and take a sample of the bright orange somewhere on her top. Select the Paintbrush tool and change its Blend Mode to Color. Paint over the woman's lips with a small feathered round brush, changing the hue to orange/gold (see Figure 10.8). Be careful not to erase the area where the lipstick is applied.

The next step is a piece of cake. You will turn the model a stylish shade of blue. Create a Hue/Saturation layer at the top of the layer stack. Select the Colorize check box in the dialog box and set the Hue to 245 and Saturation to 50 (see Figure 10.9).

You should manipulate the background separately, and the lips and glasses do not have the blue hue in the final shot you looked at in the beginning. Using Black, paint in the Hue/Saturation layer's mask to cover these areas so only the skin, hair, and top are changed (see Figure 10.10). The image is almost done, as seen in Figure 10.11.

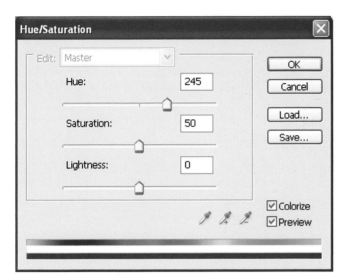

Figure 10.9: Make a Hue/Saturation adjustment to alter the woman's color cast.

Figure 10.10: Use the mask to hide the blue hue from the sky, lenses, and lips.

Figure 10.11: Almost there…

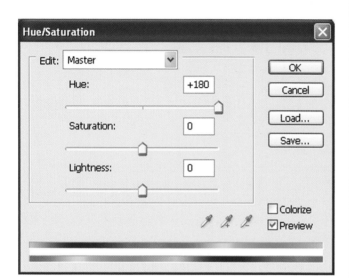

Figure 10.12: One more adjustment layer

Figure 10.13: The final state of the Layers palette

The final step to create the finished image is simply to alter the background color. Again, a Hue/Saturation layer will work wonders. Create a Hue/Saturation layer just above the Background. Set the Hue to 180 and click OK (see Figure 10.12). This time you don't need to alter the mask. The Layers palette will now look like Figure 10.13. The final piece is realized in Figure 10.14.

So how did you do? This was a fairly straightforward exercise in colorizing, with an extraction thrown in for good measure. Still, it is a frequently used technique and is good to have in your bag o' tricks.

Project 2: Portrait Collage

This project will try your hand at creating a portrait collage, such as you may find in any yearbook. This final image is seen in Figure 10.15.

There are two reasons I'm including this in the book. First, this is a real-world project you may face as a portrait photographer. Second, this technique is one of the most attempted yet is seldom satisfying. In particular, the area where the two photos blend is often blended poorly. With Photoshop there is no need for this, so let's get to work.

The photos for this project are **serious.jpg** and **smiling.jpg** (see Figures 10.16 and 10.17).

Begin by copying **smiling.jpg** and pasting it into a new layer in the **serious.jpg** document (see Figure 10.18).

Figure 10.15: What to strive for in Project 2

Figure 10.16: Serious pose

Figure 10.17: Smiling candid shot

Figure 10.18: *The foundation for the merge*

Figure 10.19: *Select the black area in the Background layer.*

Figure 10.20: *Use a mask to wipe away the top layer's offending overlap pixels.*

Figure 10.21: *Getting there slowly but surely*

To blend the two images together seamlessly, some of the top layer needs be removed so the model in the Background layer is not covered by the second photo. Using the Magic Wand tool, create a selection of the black background in the Background layer (see Figure 10.19).

Select Layer 1 in the Layers palette and add a layer mask. When the new mask is created, the overlap between the photos will be removed, although the line between the two will be stark and jagged (see Figures 10.20 and 10.21).

Here's where the soft merge comes in. Select the mask for the top layer and choose Filter → Gaussian Blur. Set the blur for the mask to 250 pixels, the highest setting (see Figure 10.22). Click OK. Take a look at the image now. The two layers blend together nicely, with soft, subtle blending between the two, yet both remain clearly visible (see Figure 10.23).

With the blend accounted for, you may now work to enhance the color and contrast of the image. Both photos appear a bit light or washed out, so this step will work to enhance the overall tone and give the model a nice, healthy glow.

Figure 10.22:
Blur the mask.

Figure 10.23: Both images blend nicely in the same document.

Figure 10.24: Duplicate the Background and change the blending mode to Overlay.

Figure 10.25: Getting there slowly but surely

Duplicate the Background layer and set the blending mode to Multiply (see Figure 10.24).

The last step will enrich the color a bit. Another thing to consider is that, especially in this style of image collage, the foreground image is usually the one that warrants the most attention, while the second image is subdued a bit. Select the masked layer and reduce the opacity to 75% (see Figure 10.25).

A Curves adjustment layer will help bring out the highlights while increasing the shadows somewhat, causing still more contrast between the two photos. Create a Curves adjustment layer and use Figure 10.26 as your guide to darkening/lightening the overall image. This adjustment layer needs to go at the top of the layer stack.

Add a Hue/Saturation layer above the Curves layer to enrich the color a bit more. This adjustment need not be too drastic: a setting of +20 for Saturation will do (see Figure 10.27). The image thus far is seen in Figure 10.28.

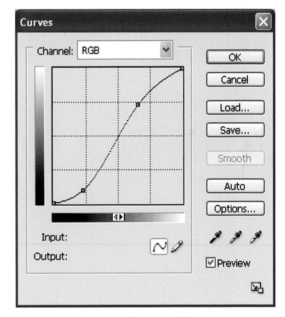

Figure 10.26: Curves adjustment for increasing contrast

With these adjustments, the color has been brought out but so have the lines and pores in the skin. That is rarely, if ever, an appealing touch, so let's correct that. Duplicate the

Figure 10.27: A relatively small Hue/Saturation adjustment

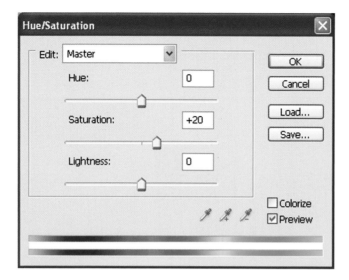

Figure 10.28: Progress check

Background layer again and place the new copy just below the adjustment layers. Leave the blending mode at Normal but reduce the Opacity to 35% (see Figure 10.29). Choose Filter → Blur → Gaussian Blur and set the Radius to 20 pixels (see Figure 10.30).

The blur will have removed some of the detail in the eyes and lips, so use a mask to clean up these areas (see Figure 10.31). You may also want to reduce the amount of adjustment caused by the adjustment layers: you can reduce these in specific areas by painting over them in the appropriate masks with gray. In Figure 10.32, the Curves adjustment over the woman's face has been reduced slightly by using this technique.

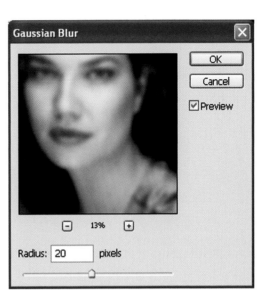

Figure 10.29: A new layer will help clear up a few enhanced characteristics that may not be desired.

Figure 10.30: Blur the new layer.

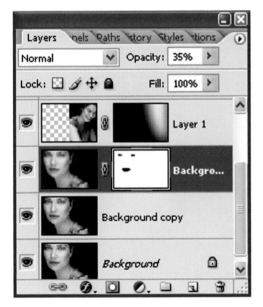

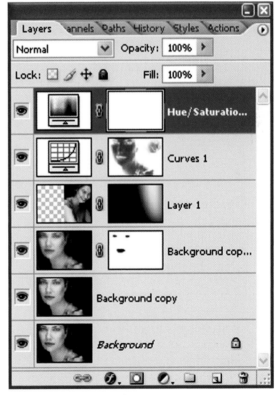

Figure 10.31: Remove the blur from the eyes and lips.

Figure 10.32: Paint with gray in the masks to reduce, not remove, the effect of adjustment layers on the photo.

Figure 10.33: The final collaged photo

Figure 10.33 shows the final image again in all its glory.

That was a bit more involved than the previous technique, but I'm sure you did just fine!

Project 3: From Photo to Graffiti

For this final project, let's revisit one of my favorite techniques: converting a photo and text to a contoured wall painting. If you have trouble with the process, please review the more detailed version in Chapter 1, "Tools for Building Your Masterpiece."

Figure 10.34 shows the final shot, which appears to be paint on the side of an old building.

The images to be used in this project are **wallwindow.jpg** and **neon-3.jpg** (see Figures 10.35 and 10.36).

Quick review: what Photoshop technique or setting or dialog box will turn the neon into paint? If you said a combination of a displacement map and Blend If, you are exactly right! If you didn't say that—well, you came close I'm sure.

Select the **wallwindow.jpg** photo and duplicate the Background layer. Set the blending mode to Overlay.

You are well versed at making displacement maps by now, so create a displacement map of the wall and save it to your hard disk (see Figure 10.37).

Figure 10.34:
Someone has
been playing
with the spray
paints again.

Figure 10.35: An
aged wall

Figure 10.36:
Flashy neon

Figure 10.37: Create the displacement map.

Figure 10.38: Place the sign on the rock.

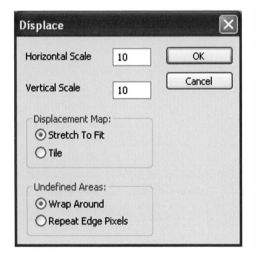

Figure 10.39: Displacement settings

Figure 10.40: Not very pretty…yet

Okay, let's get painting. Go to the **neon-3.jpg** image and copy it. Paste it into a new layer in the wall image. Move the sign so that it is off the window area; then use the Transform tools to reduce the size so it fits over the bricks to the left of the wall. Reduce the opacity so you may see the wall behind while placing the sign (see Figure 10.38).

Increase the opacity of the sign layer back to 100%. Choose Filter → Displace and enter Horizontal and Vertical Scale settings of 10 each (see Figure 10.39). Click OK, select the map you saved, and apply it to the layer (see Figure 10.40).

This effect is finalized with our old friend Blend If. Open the Layer Styles menu for the sign layer and select Blending Options. When the Layer Style dialog box appears, hold down the Option/Alt key and move the sliders in the Blend If: Gray section as seen in Figure 10.41. Change Blend If to Red and move the sliders as seen in Figure 10.42.

To enhance the color a bit, duplicate the sign layer. There will be a bit of the dark background that bleeds over onto the wall, so use the Eraser tool to wipe away some of the black from the topmost layer. Set the blending mode to Multiply and Opacity to 50% (see Figure 10.43).

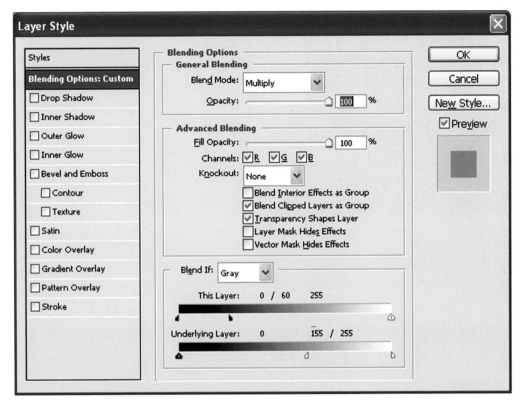

Figure 10.41:
Blend If, Part 1

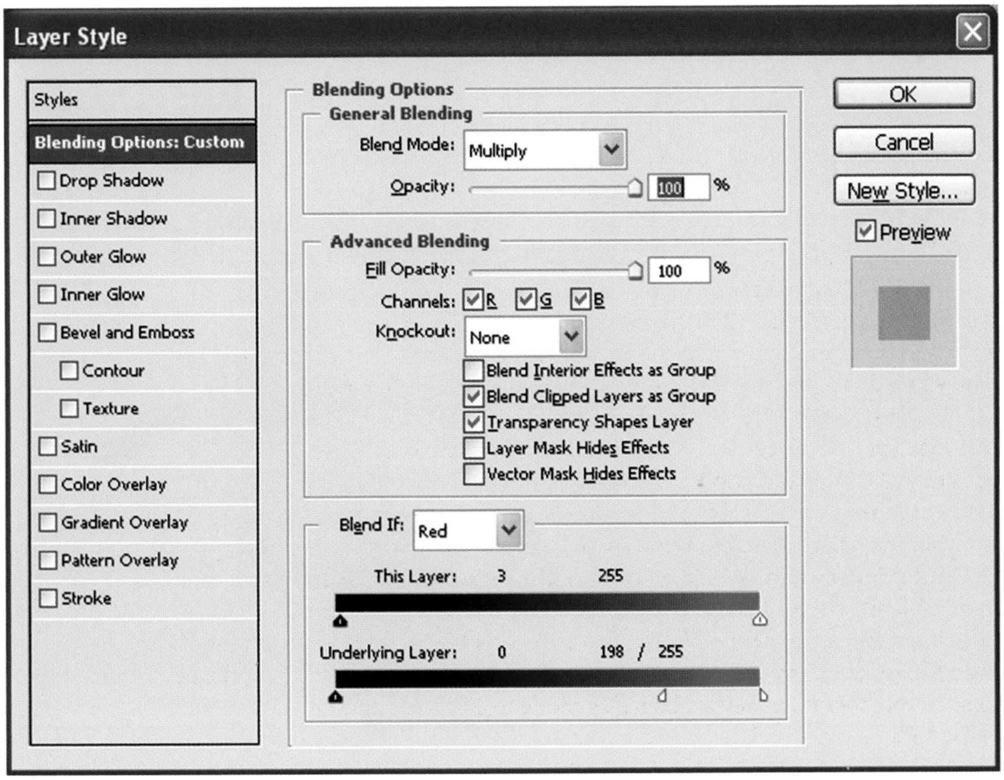

Figure 10.42:
Blend If, Part 2

Figure 10.43:
Enhance the
color of the paint.

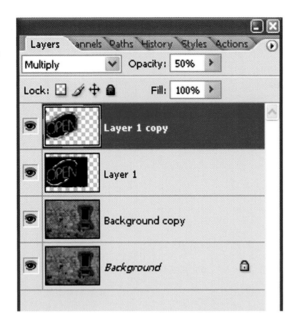

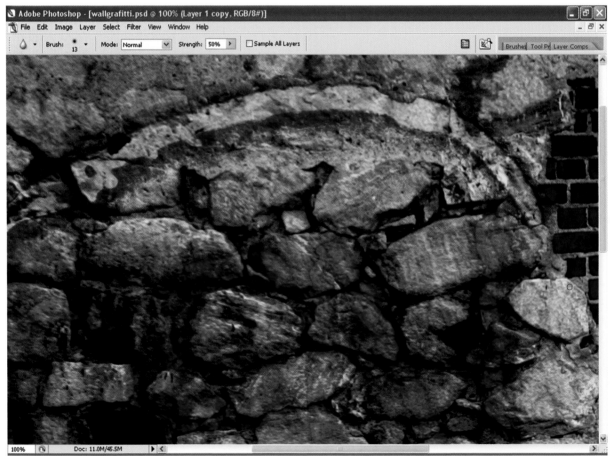

Figure 10.44: Paint on the pixels.

Figure 10.45: Poor man's neon

The technique is done at this point. To clearly see the paint as it affects the wall, zoom in to 100% as I've done in Figure 10.44. Zoom back out, and your final shot will look like Figure 10.45.

That is it for the projects. How did you do? I hope that by approaching the end result with an idea first, even with a visual aid, you were able to see the process in your mind's eye and then understand what needed to be done to realize that vision. If you can get to that stage in your knowledge of how Photoshop works as a tool, your imagination can run wild and you will soon find yourself realizing digitally what you envisioned mentally.

APPENDIX

Managing and Displaying
Your Work

Whether you're just starting a project or have finished several, you need to find the way that works for you to organize your work. In this appendix, I offer a few solutions to some common image management and display issues.

Using the Bridge

Photoshop users who have used versions of the software prior to CS2 will note that their beloved File Browser no longer exists. Photoshop CS2 has included a substitute designed to operate not only within Photoshop but to interact with other programs in the CS2 suite.

Called Adobe Bridge, its name indicates what it is intended to do—bridge the ability to manage files between CS2 suite programs. As it relates to Photoshop, it is a capable replacement for the File Browser, allowing you to view your files, navigate folders, batch process, and view/edit image data. The Bridge keeps native **.psd**, **.ai**, **.indd**, and Adobe **.pdf** files along with other Adobe and non-Adobe files available and easily accessible. You can drag these items into your layouts, preview them, and add metadata information to them. Bridge is available from within Adobe Photoshop, Adobe Illustrator, Adobe InDesign, and Adobe GoLive, or you may access it independently.

In Photoshop CS, the File Browser was accessed from the Windows menu. CS2 places Bridge access under File → Browse, or with the shortcut of Alt+⌘/Ctrl+O. When the Bridge opens, it looks similar to the File Browser (see Figure A.1).

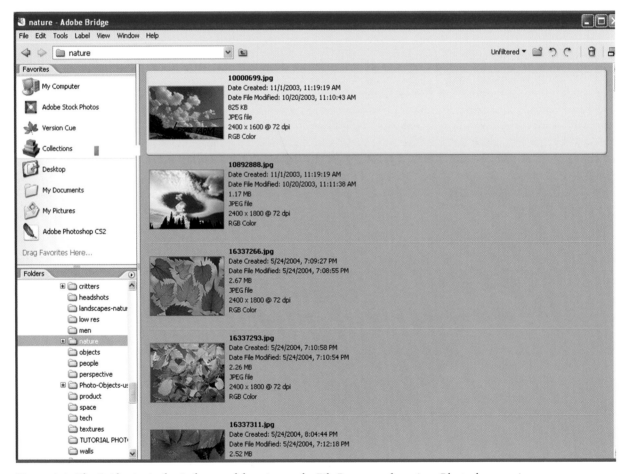

Figure A.1: The Bridge is similar in form and function to the File Browser of previous Photoshop versions.

I'm not going to go into great detail concerning the Bridge, but I would like to point out how to access the standard Photoshop commands that users were used to finding in the File Browser. When the Bridge and Photoshop are open, Batch Rename and other Photoshop-related commands are found under the Tools menu. For instance, to Batch Rename a folder, you would (from within the Bridge) choose Tools → Batch Rename. For other Photoshop tools, such as batch processing entire folders with an action, you would choose Tools → Photoshop → Batch. You may then set up the batch normally as you would have in Photoshop 7's or CS's File Browser.

Displaying Your Work

Now that you have several masterpieces on your hard disk, what to do with them? The same software that allows for the creation of digital art also supplies several options for displaying your hard work. This section will take a look at some of these options, one by one: Web Photo Gallery, PDF Presentation, Contact Sheet, Picture Package, and Photomerge. The odd-ball in the mix is Photomerge. This one isn't so much about displaying pictures, but in tying successive images together. Still, Adobe groups this function with the display group, so it will be covered in this section also.

Web Photo Gallery

The Web Photo Gallery allows you to generate web pages complete with navigation, thumbnails and image information, and any additional information about the photo or photographer that you care to display. The pages are generated automatically with minimal input from you. Adobe even ships several templates to choose from, or web-savvy artists can create their own pages in their WYSIWYG web page creation software and import them into Photoshop. You need to know a bit about cascading style sheets to generate one from scratch, but changing the images in an existing template and then saving it as a new template is relatively simple.

You access the Web Photo Gallery from the File menu in Photoshop CS2, or in the Bridge under Tools → Photoshop → Web Photo Gallery. With the File menu open, select Automate; Web Photo Gallery can be found near the bottom of the listed menu that appears (see Figure A.2).

When you open the dialog box attached to this feature, you'll note first that it is extremely large. Unlike the Layer Style dialog, the size here won't affect you much. The Layer Style dialog box is so large that it is hard to see the effect on the image you are working on. In this case, you are setting the dialog box to work on folders, or categories of images saved to the hard disk.

Take a look at the dialog box in question in Figure A.3. It doesn't look too daunting—easy to navigate with a nifty little viewing window on the right-hand side. Let's walk through the process of creating a page and see whether it is as easy as it seems, shall we?

The first drop-down list at the top of the dialog box lists the styles resident in the Photoshop CS2 folder. Here you

Figure A.2: *Finding the Web Photo Gallery option*

Figure A.3:
The Web
Photo Gallery
dialog box

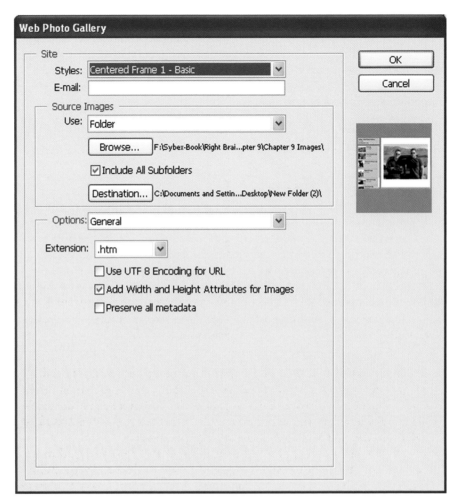

have 11 selections to choose from (at least at this writing). The styles here have changed a bit from those included with Photoshop 7; actually the CS WPG styles seem a bit simpler and, quite frankly, don't look quite as hot as the ones in Photoshop 7. If you have Photoshop 7, however, you can add those Web Photo Gallery Styles to CS2:

- Go into the Adobe Photoshop 7 folder on your hard drive and open the **Presets** folder.
- Open the folder called **WebContactSheet**. The folders here are the Web contact sheet styles.
- Select them all and copy them to the clipboard.
- Go to the Photoshop CS2 → Presets folder.
- Open the folder called **Web Photo Gallery**.
- Paste the Photoshop 7 Web Photo Gallery style folders into Photoshop CS2.

You will be asked whether you want to overwrite the folder called **Simple**; I recommend you not do this. Simply say no, and the rest will find a new home in Photoshop CS2. This gives you a broader choice when creating your gallery, and a broader range of choices is (almost) always a good thing.

Figure A.6: Select or create the destination folder for the gallery.

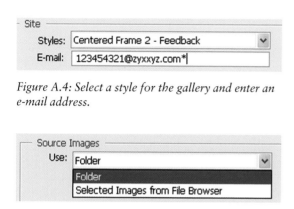

Figure A.4: Select a style for the gallery and enter an e-mail address.

Figure A.5: You may select a folder of images or flagged images in the File Browser.

To create a Web Photo Gallery, you must first have two folders set up on your computer: a folder full of source photos that you would like to display, and a destination folder that resides outside of the folder that your source images are in. You cannot have the destination folder inside the folder where the source files reside or this function will not work. If you have not created a folder, you may do so while setting up the gallery.

The best way to demonstrate setting up and creating a gallery is to simply go through the process. Have a folder full of images ready for the gallery; any will do at this point. In Photoshop, open the File menu and then choose Automate → Web Photo Gallery to open the Web Photo Gallery dialog box.

In the Styles drop-down list at the very top of the dialog box, select Centered Frame 2 - Feedback as the style for the page. You can see the example thumbnail layout on the right side of the dialog box. Enter an e-mail address in the field below (see Figure A.4).

The next section allows you to select the source images and a destination where the completed HTML pages will be deposited. In the Use drop-down list you have two options: selecting a folder (the option to be used here) or using selected images flagged in the file browser (see Figure A.5).

The next item you will see is the Browse button, which is available only if Folder is chosen as the source. Clicking the Browse button sends you to another dialog box, where you can choose which folder contains the files you want to use in your gallery.

Next you are given the choice to include subfolders. In this instance I'll choose none so it is left unchecked, but if you had additional images to include in the gallery that were in subfolders, you could select the folder for inclusion here. The last option in the Source Images area is to select a Destination folder where the WPG will be placed (see Figure A.6).

You can use a folder already created, or create one from the dialog box by clicking the Make New Folder button. A hierarchy of folders will actually be created after the gallery has been processed; this hierarchy categorizes where the images, their HTML, and thumbnails will be kept.

The Options area is where most of the customization for your Web Photo Gallery takes place. These options fall into six categories, seen in the Options drop-down list:

- General
- Banner
- Large Images
- Thumbnails
- Custom Colors
- Security

When you select one of these options from the list, the attributes specific to that option appear below. For example, with General selected in the Options drop-down list, you are given the opportunity to set the extension of the pages created (**.htm** or **.html**). You are also given the following choices: Using UTF 8 Encoding For URL, Adding Width And Height Attributes For Images, and Preserve All Metadata (see Figure A.7).

> What is UTF 8 encoding? This is probably more than the average photographer would ever want to know, but because the Web Photo Gallery makes pages that are compatible with it, a brief explanation is warranted. At its most basic, UTF 8 is a Unicode system that allows for more characters to be displayed on a web page, in programming, and so forth. Because I am not a programmer, this may be a bit simplistic; if you want to know more about what UTF 8 entails (left-brainers may find this intriguing), then I suggest reading online definitions such as the one found at dict.die.net/utf-8/.

Adding width and height attributes for images is pretty self-explanatory, but the Preserve All Metadata option might need a bit of explanation. Metadata is any additional information attached to an image, such as copyright status, origin, history of documents, and contents. These can be added via the Metadata palette. A brief walk-through on adding metadata can be seen directly following this tutorial.

The second item in the Options drop-down list is Banner. This allows you to set attributes for the banner of the page, such as Site Name, Photographer, Contact Info, and Date. Go ahead and enter the information for your images at this time.

Select Large Images from the Options list. This area lets you customize how the large versions of your photos and art will be displayed on the web page. It is strongly recommended that you have Resize Images selected, or who knows how big the web page will be! This is especially true if you have many high-resolution shots. Photoshop will adjust the sizes and resolution for best viewing online, so the defaults should work well here (see Figure A.8).

Next on the list is Thumbnails. Again, the default settings should be just fine.

Figure A.7: Web Photo Gallery general options and settings

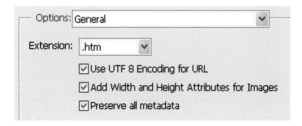

The next selection, Custom Colors, gives you the option of changing the color of various elements in the web page: Background, Banner, Text, and the links. Some pages do not allow for the text and links to be altered.

The last selection available in the Options list is Security. This embeds a watermark on the images to be displayed so that they are not easily stolen online for use by the viewers. When you set the attributes here, you are telling Photoshop the font to use, the attributes of the font (size, color), and the location where the watermark will be placed on the image.

After all the Options have been set and changed according to your tastes, you can click OK. Photoshop will then create the HTML pages for your new Web Photo Gallery. When the pages are complete, your web browser will open the website for your inspection (see Figure A.9).

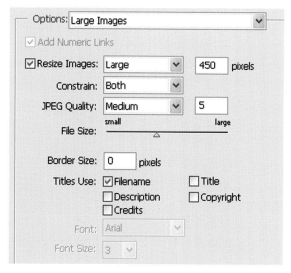

Figure A.8: Options for large images

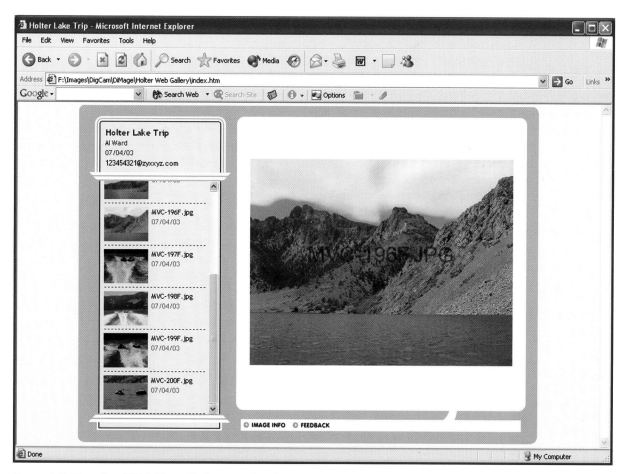

Figure A.9: Completed Web Photo Gallery seen in a browser

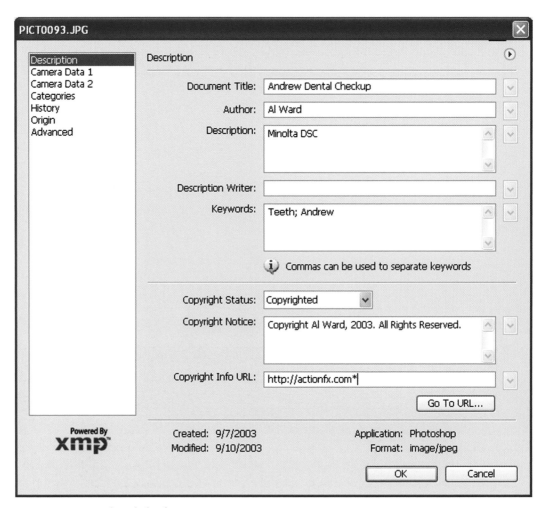

Figure A.10: Metadata dialog box

Adding Metadata to an Image

Photoshop has the fantastic ability to embed information into an image document, and these settings can be saved as a template to be applied to other images.

To attach metadata to an image, open a photograph from your hard disk. Select File Info from the File menu, or use the shortcut keys (⌘+Option+I for Mac, Ctrl+Alt+I for Windows). This opens the Metadata dialog box. From here you may enter descriptions, camera data, categories, history, origin, and advanced properties (see Figure A.10).

After you enter all your information, select the Advanced option from the left side of the dialog box and save the settings as an **.xmp** file. To apply these settings to another image, open the photo, select Advanced, and select either Replace or Append from the buttons at the bottom of the dialog box. You may then select your saved settings and apply them to the new image.

Figure A.11: Items added to the PDF Presentation

PDF Presentation

PDF, or Portable Document Format, has become a standard for file distribution across the Web and over networks. PDF stands out in that image and text data, search components, links, and navigation can all be embedded in the document and preserved, allowing anyone with Adobe Reader to view documents created half a world away. PDF allows for encryption and securities, supports 16-bit per channel images, and allows for minor editing of the images in the documents.

PDF Presentation allows you to create a multipage document or slideshow presentation in PDF format. You can specify the images to be used in the presentation, select transitions between the images, and save and distribute them quickly and easily.

The PDF Presentation option is found under File → Automate → PDF Presentation. When you open the PDF Presentation dialog box, it looks a bit sparse if you have no images open. If you have some open, you are given the option of adding them to the presentation. To add files, simply click the Browse button, which gives you access to your hard disk. Track down the images you would like in the presentation and add them to the list; they will appear in dialog box in the order added (see Figure A.11).

Figure A.12:
Additional
options

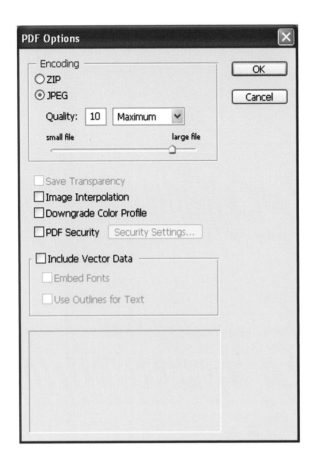

Below the Source Files area you will find Output Options. This area gives you two choices for outputting the PDF: either as a Multi-Page document (similar to a standard series of text documents) or as a Presentation. The latter operates much as a slide show, displaying each image for a few seconds and then transitioning to the next.

If you save as a Multi-Page document, Photoshop will then ask you to fill in a few options for the new PDF file (see Figure A.12).

If you select PDF Security, another dialog box opens that allows you to set passwords for viewers and editors of the document. You can also establish just what the document is compatible with (that is, which versions of Reader). You may also set restrictions on printing, changes to the document, content copying, or changes to comments and form fields (see Figure A.13). For sensitive file transfers, security may be added so that only those in the know have access to the files. If you just want to send a cool slide show to Grandma, you can probably bypass this feature.

If you select to view the file after it is created, you will see one more dialog box when it opens in Adobe Reader. This simply tells the viewer of special features attached to the document (see Figure A.14).

When you select to save your PDF as a Presentation, you are given different options. You can set the time an image will be displayed before transitioning to the next, you can tell the document to continue looping the images or stop after one pass, and you can select a

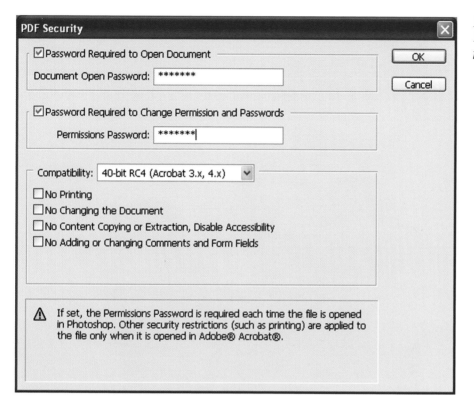

Figure A.13:
Restrictions and
passwords

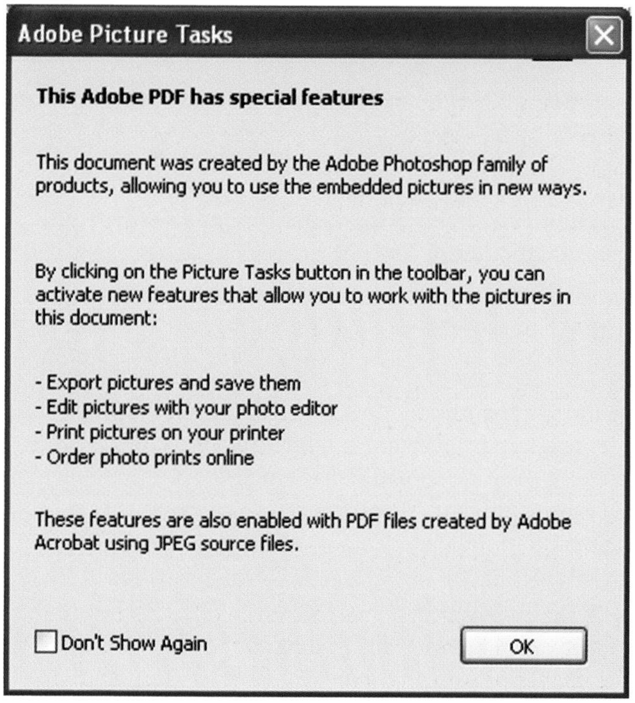

Figure A.14:
Adobe Reader
special features
dialog box

Figure A.15: New PDF document viewed in Adobe Reader

variety of transitions such as cool little shutters, screen swipes, dissolves, and so forth. Or, you may simply return to Reader in normal mode and view the images by selecting their thumbnails under the Pages tab (see Figure A.15).

Contact Sheet II

Contact sheets can be invaluable to photographers and artists alike, in that they allow you to create pages of thumbnail-sized images that can be placed in a binder for cataloging, review, and easy locating of specific files. Generally they are created on a standard 8.5-by-11-inch page, complete with filename beneath each thumbnail. You can create a contact sheet via the File menu, or from files in the File Browser.

When you open the Contact Sheet II dialog box in Photoshop CS2, choose the location of your source images at the top, set the document size in the center, choose thumbnail attributes and layout toward the bottom third of the box, and allow (or not) for the use of the filename as a caption for the thumbnails. You even have a couple of selections for fonts. And you can set the size. The display on the right side of the dialog box shows how the layout for the

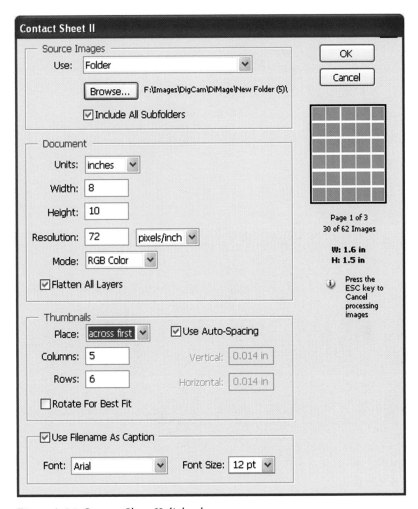

Figure A.16: Contact Sheet II dialog box

images you have selected will be displayed, the number of pages required, and the total number of images to be thumbnailed (see Figure A.16).

When you click the Browse button to select some files and click OK, Photoshop CS2 will take every image in the folder (or those flagged in the File Browser) and generate thumbnails of each. If you select the naming option, a title will appear below each image (see Figure A.17).

Although I don't have a lot to say about this feature, there is one extremely cool thing besides the ability to quickly categorize and print sheets of examples. This may be of particular interest to web designers: Photoshop places the images in a layered **.psd** document named for the first image in the series (see Figure A.18). What makes that so cool? Simply put, it generates tons of thumbnails for you, with very little loss of resolution. You can then put them on your website as buttons, icons, examples, and so forth, which is useful if you plan to create web pages for photographs without using the Web Photo Gallery option.

*Figure A.17:
Newly generated
contact sheet*

*Figure A.18:
Contact sheet
saved as layered
.psd file*

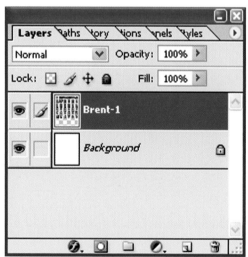

Picture Package II

Picture Package II is basically the same as your typical student-picture sheets. You select the images you would like to have printed, their sizes, and how they will appear on the sheet, and generate a document that has your photos ready for printing.

Figure A.19 shows a basic Picture Package II dialog box with a single photo selected. In the Document area, the page size is set to 8 inches by 10 inches; this accounts for margins of 0.5 and 1 inch on the sides and top, respectively. By selecting (2)5×7 for the layout, the viewer shows that two photos will be placed on the resulting page sideways. Opening the Layout drop-down list shows a vast assortment of possible sheet styles (see Figure A.20).

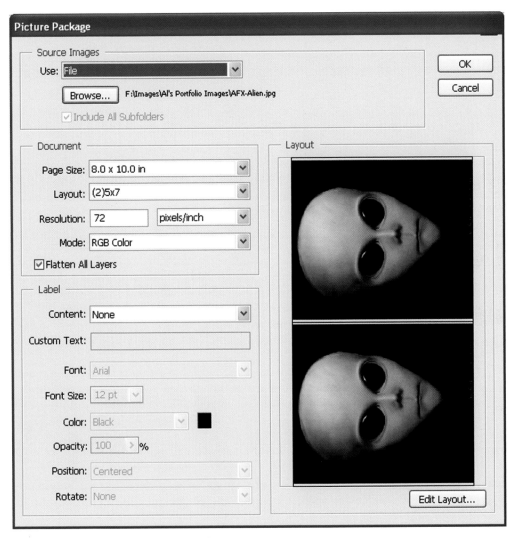

Figure A.19: Picture Package II dialog box

You can set your other page attributes from this box, including custom text to be placed on each image, its font, the location where it is to be placed, and so forth. If you are unhappy with the layouts provided by Photoshop, you may create your own by clicking Edit Layout and creating your own image dimensions and the number of times an image is repeated.

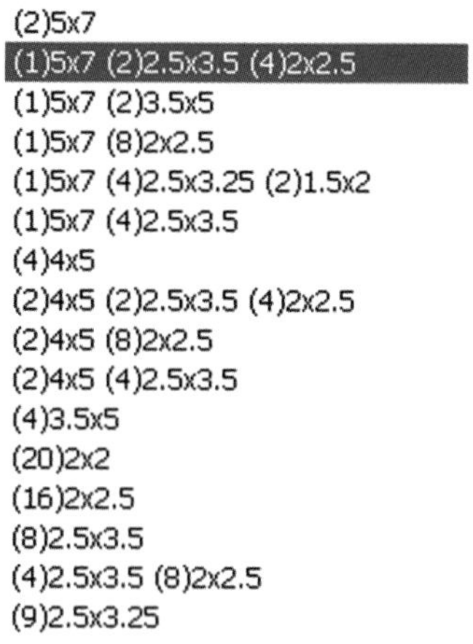

Photomerge

Living in western Montana, my family and I are deluged daily with beauty that is difficult to describe. Many have tried, but only a few authors and painters have been successful at scratching the surface. Charles M. Russell drove cattle on the plains where I grew up long before he gained fame trying to capture the land and sky on canvas. Teddy Roosevelt spent much time in the valley where I now live as a respite from the duties of the presidency.

```
(2)5x7
(1)5x7 (2)2.5x3.5 (4)2x2.5
(1)5x7 (2)3.5x5
(1)5x7 (8)2x2.5
(1)5x7 (4)2.5x3.25 (2)1.5x2
(1)5x7 (4)2.5x3.5
(4)4x5
(2)4x5 (2)2.5x3.5 (4)2x2.5
(2)4x5 (8)2x2.5
(2)4x5 (4)2.5x3.5
(4)3.5x5
(20)2x2
(16)2x2.5
(8)2.5x3.5
(4)2.5x3.5 (8)2x2.5
(9)2.5x3.25
```

Figure A.20: Multiple layouts to choose from

While writing this book, my family moved into a home that is several miles from anything that resembles a city. Lewis and Clark wintered just north of here, and though the valley has filled with homes and small ranches, the wilderness surrounding us has remained largely unchanged since their famous trek. Lewis and Clark were sent with the charge to catalog and describe in detail what they encountered; their task would have been much easier with a digital camera and Photoshop at their disposal.

Photomerge works, or is intended to work, just like it sounds. It allows you to take sequential photographs spanning an area and seamlessly merge them into one panoramic image. This was tricky and difficult in prior versions of the software, and still may take a bit of work on your part to pull off with successful results. The point to note is that it can have excellent results with a bit of forethought and some additional adjustments.

The Photomerge function is accessed, like the previous functions in this chapter, from the File → Automate menu. If you want to try this technique, I've provided two images of the western view from my deck. Open the images **PICT0008.tif** and **PICT0009.tif** (see Figure A.21).

In previous chapters you have seen me use Match Color in a variety of situations, but this is actually one of those instances where it is used as intended by the Adobe programmers. You may find that, even with shots taken immediately after one another, variations in lighting and tone occur between your images. Even slight variations can hinder the merge, so running Match Color before attempting the merge could save a lot of frustration.

Select **PICT0009.tif**. Open the Match Color dialog box (Image → Adjustments → Match Color) and take a look at Figure A.22. The variation between the two images is faint at best, so the default settings need not be changed. Just change the Source at the bottom of the dialog box to **PICT0008.TIF** and click OK.

The color cast and lightness in the two images should be extremely close at this point, so you may attempt the merge. Choose File → Automate → Photomerge. Set the Use option to Open Files, and make sure both images are listed in the viewer window (see Figure A.23). Click OK.

Figure A.21: Two photos taken from my front deck

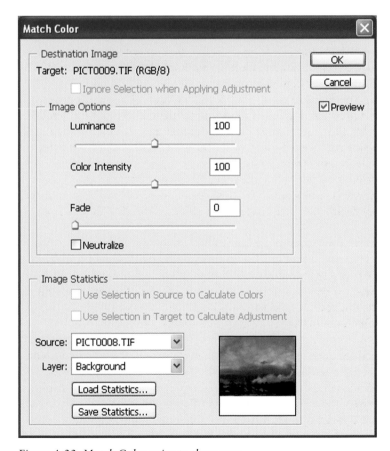

Figure A.22: Match Color prior to the merge

Figure A.23:
Selecting files to
link together

Photomerge

Source Files

Choose two or more files to create a panorama composition, or click the "Open Composition" button to view an existing composition.

Use [Open files ▾]

PICT0008.TIF
PICT0009.TIF

[Browse...]

[Remove]

[Open Composition...]

☑ Attempt to Automatically Arrange Source Images

[OK]

[Cancel]

Figure A.24:
Two photos
imperfectly
joined

Photoshop is going to take a look at the scenes and try to find where the two should be linked. When you ran the merge, your image may have turned out to look something like the one in Figure A.24. The merge is close, but not perfect, as elements such as the deck overhang on the right side of the photo have caused the merge to be a bit off. Also, changes in the clouds, perspective between the photos, and so forth have caused a faint diagonal seam to appear where the photos come together. This can be fixed within the Photomerge dialog box, so don't close it just yet.

Zoom in and take a closer look. When you get in close, you can really tell where the two images did not merge correctly. The land is a bit off also, and there is definite variation in the clouds. That is one problem with clouds; they change so quickly that it is hard to

Figure A.25: Clouds are a difficult merge.

Figure A.26: The land in the foreground is askew also.

create a quality merge right out of the shoot, even if the photos were taken moments apart (see Figures A.25 and A.26).

In the Photomerge dialog box, you have the freedom to select and reposition the photos. Select the Move tool at the top left, and click directly on the image to the right. The opacity of the photo is lowered to reveal the other photo beneath, and you can then move the photo on the right so that the landmarks (tree, house, ridgeline) match in the two photographs (see Figure A.27). When you are done matching the landmarks, the two photographs (in this case, at least) will be even more askew as far as placement, but you will trim that later in the project (see Figure A.28).

Figure A.27: You can line up the landmarks from within the Photomerge dialog box.

After the landmarks in the images are straightened out and match properly, you can click out of the Photomerge dialog box. Photomerge is rarely, if ever, a cure-all function; you will still need to do a bit of standard image correction after the merge.

Take, for example, the seam in the clouds, which is still very apparent. You've had a lot of practice over the course of these pages to use the Healing Brush, and it will serve well here. Select the Healing Brush and, in the options bar, select a 100- to 150-pixel Round Feathered brush. Set the Mode to Normal and the Source to Sampled.

Now simply sample clouds on one side of the seam (as close to the seam as possible without the feather of the brush interfering) and heal the disjointed areas in the sky. You may want to take a few samples, reduce the brush size, and so forth, but the cleanup should not

Figure A.28: The land is joined, but the photos are farther off center.

Figure A.29: Healing the clouds

Figure A.30: Removing the seams in the field

take too long (see Figure A.29). Repeat the process where the land in the foreground appears to have a seam (see Figure A.30).

When the seams are sufficiently hidden, select the Crop tool and trim away the edges of the image so that it no longer appears to be two photos overlaying one another, but rather one panoramic shot (see Figure A.31).

Ah, the problem with digital shots. This image, though seamlessly joined, still requires some simple image correction. It is far too dark and too blue to properly show what I see from my front yard. First, duplicate the merge photo layer (the Background layer). Then run through the standard practice of adjusting the Levels, one channel at a time. The blue channel Levels adjustment is seen in Figure A.32.

The photo should now appear brighter and with more contrast, but an additional Curves adjustment can help bring out the details in the mid range even more. Open the Curves dialog box and set an anchor point on the dark side, halfway through the first square, and an anchor point on the light end, at the inner corner of the top-right grid square. This allows

Figure A.31: Crop away the edges of the merged photos.

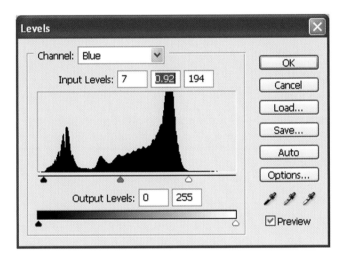

Figure A.32: Standard Levels adjustments

you to make adjustments between the two points without adjusting the very light or very dark areas. Add another point and increase the brightness of the Midtones slightly.

In the photo I'm working on, the mountains peeking through the clouds are extremely bright, to the point where the trees are not well defined. Create a Brightness/Contrast adjustment layer, and decrease the Brightness to −30 to −35, and increase the Contrast to +45 to +50.

The Brightness and Contrast did not need to be adjusted to the entire image; just to the peaks really. With all you have learned about masks, the answer to this should be an easy one: select the Paintbrush tool, set Black as the Foreground color, and paint in the Brightness/Contrast's layer mask to hide and therefore remove adjustment from the areas that don't require altering (the lower portion of the image, areas of the clouds, and so on).

When all is said and done, you should have an excellent view of the Bitterroot Range—something I'm blessed to wake up to every day (see Figure A.33).

Figure A.33: Montana truly is the last best place.

Accessing Additional Resources

It's been said that no matter how much you know about Photoshop, you never stop learning more. To help guide your further explorations of the software, here are some of the most valuable online resources.

The Manufacturer's Site

Adobe Online (www.adobe.com): For all the latest in Adobe's software releases and technology, check out the source of it all.

Information and Discussion Sites

Action Fx Photoshop Resources (www.actionfx.com): The author's website. A vast resource for Photoshop training and custom add-ons for the software, including actions, layer styles, brushes, and so on. A large Free area and a huge Members area give access to thousands of custom-made Photoshop goodies and to training information.

   Photoshop Café (www.photoshopcafe.com): A website run by award-winning author and trainer Colin Smith. Tutorials, reviews, and more. Also one of the best Photoshop forums online. Stop in and say hello; I'll be lurking somewhere.

   PS6.com (www.ps6.com, also accessible via www.photoshopcs.com or www .photoshopx.com): Fellow Sybex author Richard Lynch's excellent website. Not only is Richard a qualified expert in Photoshop, but his talents have helped to unlock incredible features for Elements users also.

   Digital Mastery (www.digitalmastery.com): If I had to recommend one person on this planet above all the other Photoshop gurus out there for in-depth training and understanding of the program, Ben Willmore would instantly come to mind. Ben is one of the most sought-after teachers in the field, and I highly recommend checking out his website and getting on his mailing list. You definitely will not regret it. 'Nuf said. Note that this site does not offer free services.

Photoshop Groups and Organizations

National Association of Photoshop Professionals (NAPP) (www.photoshopuser.com): The premier organization for Photoshop users around the globe, founded by Scott Kelby, renowned author and editor-in-chief of *Photoshop User* and *Layers* magazines. Although NAPP charges an annual membership fee, it is well worth the price for any serious Photoshop professional. I write for the website, so drop me a line when you visit.

Planet Photoshop (www.planetphotoshop.com): Also operated by the team at NAPP, Planet Photoshop is a free resource for Photoshop users everywhere. Tutorials (many by yours truly), discounts, and resources abound; come check it out!

Adobe Photoshop Tutorials Online

Photoshop Workshop (psworkshop.net): When people ask me how to create a specific effect or where to find tutorials on a technique, this is the website I recommend. As of this writing, there are more than 1,700 tutorials linked to this site—definitely one for the books.

Team Photoshop (www.teamphotoshop.com): Tutorials, forum, actions, resources galore—by people who love what they do and do what they love. Thanks for an excellent website!

Sue Chastain's About.com Photoshop Pages (graphicssoft.about.com/cs/photoshop): Sue Chastain has been helping people master Adobe Photoshop for years, and her section at About.com is one of the best "how to" places that I know of online. Tell her I said howdy.

Designs By Mark (www.designsbymark.com): You like effects? This guy knows effects! Mark Monciardini has been around longer than I have in this biz, and he remains at the top of his game in the Photoshop world. His website is ultra cool, and be sure to check out his new training videos. Mark is a designer's designer, is innovative in his tutorials, and has the unique ability to teach others and make learning fun as well as informative.

Stock Images

Stock photography websites, while not free, are great resources for designers who are seeking to increase the professional level of their work. Many of these resources offer complete access to low-, medium-, and high-resolution versions of their photos, taken by professional photographers.

Some of those websites listed here allow members to download the images online, others offer their photos on CD, and a couple give you both options. If you have a high-speed Internet connection, membership is probably more appealing because you do not have to wait for your photos; those of you with slow Internet connections may want to save on download time and opt for the CDs.

So why pay for a service when there are so many free resources online for photographs? When you pay for a service, chances are you can get the resolution and professionalism that will make your work shine. Free resources, while they have their place, simply don't hold up to the quality that the paid sites offer. Free resources are generally operated by people who, while they have a passion for the photography, are not generating income for their website and must keep the image files small to save on bandwidth. Paid sites are set up so that bandwidth is not usually a concern, and they offer great service for those who choose their products.

Photos.com (www.photos.com): One of many excellent resources operated by Jupiter-Images, this site has a vast amount of stock photography available for download to their members. Most of the images in this book are from this great resource.

PhotoSpin (www.photospin.com): This website offers to members over 100,000 images to download at the time of this writing. Another excellent online repository for high-quality photography.

Clipart.com (www.clipart.com): Also run by JupiterImages, this website offers over 6 million downloadable images (clip art, photography, animations, and so on) to subscribers.

Getty Images (www.gettyimages.com): A vast resource for professional photographs, including Time & Life Pictures and National Geographic. Categories include creative, editorial, film, custom imaging, and media management.

Comstock Images (www.comstock.com): Specializes in commercial stock photography for advertising, graphic design, corporate marketing, publishing/desktop publishing, and web design. Offers royalty-free images that may be purchased individually or grouped on a CD.

PictureQuest (www.picturequest.com): Offers hundreds of thousands of images, free low-resolution comps, and high-resolution downloads. As of this writing, PictureQuest has nearly 500,000 images available.

Wetzel & Company (www.wetzelandcompany.com): Offers background, pattern, and photographic texture images on CD.

AbleStock.com (www.ablestock.com): Over 100,000 royalty-free digital images in three file sizes available to members for download.

iStockPhoto (www.istockphoto.com): Offers over 83,000 royalty-free files for members.

Index

Note to the Reader: Throughout this index **boldfaced** page numbers indicate primary discussions of a topic. *Italicized* page numbers indicate illustrations.